Egypt & Nasser

Volume 3

1967-72

Egypt & Nasser

Volume 3

1967-72

Edited by Dan Hofstadter

FACTS ON FILE, INC.   NEW YORK, N.Y.

Egypt
&
Nasser
Volume 3

1967-72

Library of Congress Catalog Card No. 74-154632
ISBN 0-87196-205-5

9 8 7 6 5 4 3 2 1
PRINTED IN
THE UNITED STATES OF AMERICA

CONTENTS

i

INTRODUCTION

THIS 3D VOLUME OF THE FACTS ON FILE RECORD of *Egypt & Nasser* chronicles the period from Jan. 1967 to Aug. 1972. In much of this volume the title United Arab Republic (or UAR) is used almost interchangeably with Egypt to identify the country then ruled by Gamal Abdel Nasser. This title survived from the Egypto-Syrian union of 1958–61. It resumed more significance in Aug. 1972, when Egypt and Libya agreed to establish, by Sept. 1, 1973, a "unified political leadership" and to form what was to be the largest state in Africa. Meanwhile, the UAR in 1971 had begun to style itself the Arab Republic of Egypt.

Egypt, occupying the northeast corner of Africa, is largely desert. The Nile River provides virtually all of the country's irrigation. In this valley, only 3½% of the nation's area, about 32 million people dwelt in 1969. More than 92% of the population is Sunni Moslem; about 7% is Coptic Christian. Arabic is the universal language. Almost 35% of the population was illiterate as the decade of the 1970s opened.

Egypt was ruled by foreigners from the time of Alexander the Great (4th century BC) until recently. Egypt became independent in 1922, but the last foreign rulers, the British, retained paramount influence until the end of World War II. A clandestine junta of military officers (the "Free Officers") seized power July 26, 1952 and overthrew the last monarch, King Farouk. By early 1954 their leader, Lt. Col. Gamal Abdel Nasser, established himself as virtual dictator of Egypt.

Volume 1 of the FACTS ON FILE series on Nasser's Egypt tells of the strongman's overthrow of King Farouk; of Nasser's elimination of his major domestic enemies; of his negotiation of the withdrawal of British troops from Egyp-

1

tian soil; of his unsuccessful bid for U.S. credits to finance a
new Nile dam at Aswan and of his subsequent break with the
U.S.; of his nationalization of the Suez Canal, which led to
the Suez Canal crisis of 1956, and of the aftermath of this
crisis, including certain events of 1957.

Volume 2 continues the story of Egypt and Nasser from
Jan. 1957 until Dec. 1966. This period was one of unprecedented domestic peace, economic development and expanded
foreign prestige for Egypt. It was also, however, the era of 2
major Egyptian fiascos in the Arab world—the ill-fated union
with Syria (1958–61) and the disastrous military involvement
in the Yemeni Civil War (1961–7). The details of both of
these foreign adventures are related in Volume 2.

This 3d volume deals with the period Jan. 1967–Aug.
1972, *i.e.*, from the rapid deterioration of the Mideastern
political scene preceding the June war of 1967 through the
death of Gamal Abdel Nasser Oct. 1, 1970 and Pres. Anwar
el-Sadat's explusion of most Soviet military advisers in July
and Aug. 1972. The INTERIM HISTORY book *Israel & the Arabs:
The June 1967 War* fully covers the 1967 Egypto-Israeli conflict; the present volume touches mainly on Egypt's reaction
to its crushing defeat in this short war. Scanting the details
of the military confrontation and its international repercussions, it concentrates instead on Egypt's domestic plight and
its attempted recovery. Thus, for example, Volume 3 of
Egypt & Nasser presents detailed information about the
mutiny and trials of Egyptian army officers, about Marshal
Abdel Hakim Amer's suicide, about the drastic cutbacks in
Egypt's postwar budget and about Egypt's USSR-sponsored
military reorganization.

The period covered by this volume was the final phase of
Gamal Abdel Nasser's presidency and the opening phase of
Anwar el-Sadat's. The information presented includes facts
on Egypt's adjustment to defeat, its relations with the USSR,
its war of attrition with Israel and eventual cease-fire on the
Suez Canal, the death of Nasser and the succession of Anwar

el-Sadat, Sadat's thwarting of an attempted *putsch* by Aly Sabry and the Egypto-Libyan move toward political union.

Israel's occupation of 2 areas previously governed by Egypt presented a special problem. A large block of territory, the Sinai Peninsula, rich in oil and of strategic importance to the entire world, is internationally recognized as falling *de jure* under Egyptian sovereignty. But as the Sinai Peninsula has been administered *de facto* by the Jerusalem government since June 1967, events occurring in this occupied territory since that date have not been chronicled herein unless directly relating to the Suez Canal confrontation.

Another parcel of land, the Gaza Strip, although never regarded as a part of territorial Egypt, had been—with one brief interruption—under Cairo's control since the Egypto-Israeli armistice agreement of 1949. This largely refugee-inhabited area was defended by an Egyptian garrison until June 1967; since then it has been militarily occupied and administered by Israel. The Jerusalem government disclosed Aug. 3, 1968 its intention of annexing the Gaza Strip. Cairo's policy, however, has been to regard Gaza as part of an eventual sovereign Palestinian Arab state, and Egypt has continued to take a lively interest in its future. Hence the present volume records the growth of a Palestinian resistance movement in Gaza with close links to Cairo. Other developments in Gaza are not treated.

USSR Replaces U.S. in Sending Wheat to Egypt

Egypt, chronically short of food, had relied on U.S. aid during much of Gamal Abdel Nasser's regime to stave off widespread starvation. Pres. Nasser, however, made it clear that he found this dependence galling, and he reacted with anger when the U.S. curtailed its supplies.

At a rally in Cairo Dec. 25, 1966, Nasser revealed that the U.S. had stopped providing wheat or other food aid. He warned the Egyptian people that this would require austerity on their part, but, he said: "No one be it king or president can bring economic pressure to bear on us. We are not prepared to accept any conditions."

The seriousness of Egypt's position was well-known. Egypt had to import 2 million metric tons of wheat a year; only 1½ million tons were produced by Egypt. Much of these imported 2 million tons came from the U.S. Public-Law-480 food-aid plan. In 1966 the U.S. had shipped almost 755,000 tons of wheat to the United Arab Republic.

According to Nasser, the U.S. had suspended some wheat shipments in 1965 for political reasons. At one point, Egypt, left with only 15 days' supply, had been saved by a Soviet diversion of food-bearing vessels from Australia, he said. The U.S. had suspended surplus food shipments to the UAR from February through June 1965 in reaction to the destruction by a Cairene mob Nov. 26, 1964 of the U.S. Information Library and to Nasser's Dec. 23, 1964 advice to the U.S. that Egyptians were prepared to forgo aid from the U.S., which could go "drink from the sea" ("jump in the lake") if it did not approve of Egyptian policies.

Nasser, accusing the U.S. of instigating a "war of starvation," declared Dec. 25, 1966: "It is not less ruthless than the war of bullets, since in both cases the result is the same: to make us surrender to pressure. I say here and now that

5

neither hunger nor armed war will overcome us." (The rally
had been held to celebrate the 10th anniversary of the evacuation of British and French troops after the 1956 Suez crisis.)

Meanwhile Cairo spokesmen disclosed that the Soviet
Union had promised wheat to the UAR. The 1966 Soviet
wheat harvest was good—but reliable informants had revealed that the Soviet Union was hesitant to undertake any
food relief role that might be interpreted as a commitment.
The Egyptian population was growing at a rate of 3% a year,
and Soviet agriculture lagged behind its American counter-
part.

It was announced in Cairo Jan. 3, 1967 that Egypt had
signed an agreement with the USSR for the shipment of
250,000 tons of Soviet wheat and that the Soviet Union had
promised to ship 400,000 more tons later. Some observers
concluded that Egypt would pay for the wheat with cotton,
textiles, alcoholic drinks and shoes. The first report appeared
in *Al-Ahram*, the semi-official daily of Cairo. *Al-Ahram* also
mentioned current UAR-USSR negotiations for an $8 million
shipment of fats, oil and sugar to Egypt. An initial Russian
shipment of 6,500 tons of wheat arrived Jan. 12 in the port
of Alexandria.

A UAR-USSR protocol was initialled Jan. 7. The USSR
agreed to supply $17 million worth of wheat in 1967. New
commodities shipments specified under the protocol were:
250,000 metric tons of wheat, 50,000 tons of sugar, 5,000
tons of vegetable oil, 5,000 tons of animal oil and 2,000 tons
of industrial oil. The payment for most items was to be made
by UAR exports to the USSR in 1967.

Similar trade protocols were also signed in Jan. 1967 with
Korea and Yugoslavia. Further protocols were signed in February with Italy and Hungary. Agreement was reached with
Italy for the supply of 2,000 railway cars for domestic wheat
distribution.

As the Cairo government was negotiating for commodities shipments from abroad, *Al-Ahram* had reported Jan. 9

the results of a 1966 all-Egypt census, the first comprehensive census of the 1960s. The census found 15,179,312 males and 14,904,107 females, a total of 30,083,419 people then living in Egypt. (The population at the end of 1960 had been 26,085,326.)   There were 27,943,707 Moslems, 2,008,075 Christians, 2,484 Jews and 3,493 adherents of other religions. Egyptians living abroad numbered 70,294 and non-Egyptians living in the UAR 90,600. It was estimated that the population had risen 30,000 since Jan. 1966, but observers called this estimate conservative.   At the same time, it was reported in Cairo that the government would accelerate the land-reclamation plan before "the world food crisis in 1970."

Nasser was disclosed Jan. 30 to have rejected all suggestions for cuts in the UAR's agriculture investment for 1967. Nasser reportedly took the view that, in the light of the relative decline in world food production, it would be unwise for Egypt to count on extensive purchases of food abroad in the future.   Nasser conjectured that the market value of such commodities might rise and that Egypt was in no position to part with its precious foreign exchange.

Nasser accused the U.S. Feb. 22 of using food aid as a means of interfering in the affairs of the UAR. According to Nasser, the USA had demanded since 1965 that American officials be allowed to inspect Egyptian rocket installations (Egypt had produced 2 types of military rockets in 1964, the el-Qahir [the Conqueror] and the el-Zafir [the Prophet]). Nasser said that his refusal to allow American inspections had led to the halt in U.S. food shipments to Egypt.

In his Feb. 22 speech, Nasser denied that Egypt was approaching serious economic hardships.   In reporting the speech Feb. 23, the London *Financial Times* said that Nasser had threatened to withhold all loan repayments to Western countries that "exert economic pressure on Egypt." "They will have to run after us for their money," he warned. (The Central Bank of Egypt in early Jan. 1967 had issued a budget report for the fiscal year 1965–6. Ahmed Zendo, the bank's governor, had supervised the report, which asserted that the Egyptian economy was healthy in many sectors.)

The Beirut newspaper *Al-Shaab* interviewed Nasser Mar. 20, and Nasser repeated his threat that Egypt would not repay foreign loans if further credit was refused. Nasser claimed that this maneuver had worked already with Britain and Italy. Nasser recommended that other "3d world" nations do the same.

Nasser asserted that in mid-March he had definitely withdrawn his request to the U.S. for $150 million worth of wheat because of "U.S. stalling." But U.S. officials contacted in Washington contradicted Nasser's statement that he had withdrawn the request. They asserted that a decision on the request was still pending but had been delayed on account of reports of Egyptian gas warfare in Yemen and of UAR support of terrorism in Aden.

Muhammad Hassanein Heykal, editor of *Al-Ahram* and a frequent spokesman for the government, had reported Mar. 17 that Nasser had withdrawn his wheat request. He said Nasser had asked retiring U.S. Amb. Lucius D. Battle to tell U.S. Pres. Lyndon B. Johnson: "When we want American wheat in the future, we will buy it at market prices. . . . We have been very patient despite all the pressure you have applied to us, but our patience has run out." (Heykal had written in *Al-Ahram* Mar. 10 that the U.S. sought to dominate the Arab world in order to safeguard its strategic and petroleum interests, to protect Israel and to support the "reactionary Arab forces.")

Nasser said at an Egyptian industrial production conference in Cairo Mar. 18 that "the challenge facing us is either to progress and be free, to progress and live, or to stand still, increasing the gap between us and those who are progressing—and then lose liberty and consequently life itself." Nasser has admitted that Egypt was suffering from a grave shortage of foreign exchange because it had assumed tasks beyond its economic capacity.

It was disclosed in March that the UAR had defaulted on a monthly payment to the International Monetary Fund due Feb. 28. Egypt had also defaulted on several previous payments. (Its debt to the IMF was said to total at $12 million.) The IMF officially warned the UAR government that it would be expelled from the Fund unless it repaid $8 million of the outstanding debts shortly.

This indicated the general state of Egypt's economy as the UAR approached its 1967 confrontation with Israel. Israel was also suffering from severe economic setbacks referred to in the semi-official Israeli newspaper *Ha-Aretz* as a *mitun* or economic recession. But the UAR's economic instability was exacerbated by Egyptian support of more than 50,000 troops in Yemen.

UAR Mobilizes in Sinai

The Mideast crisis of May 1967 resulted from many factors, one of which was the conclusion Nov. 4, 1966 between Syria and Egypt of a military agreement making the UAR responsible for the defense of Syria.

Egypt and Syria had agreed Nov. 3, 1966 to resume diplomatic relations and to establish a joint defense command. The agreement was reached by UAR Pres. Nasser and Syrian Premier Youssef Zayen during talks held in Cairo Nov. 1-7. (When Soviet Premier Aleksei N. Kosygin had visited Cairo in May, he had urged Nasser to reopen political negotiations with Syria.) The agreement on diplomatic relations, signed Nov. 3, called for an early exchange of ambassadors. Syria had not had diplomatic relations with Cairo since it broke away from the UAR union in 1961. The defense agreement, signed Nov. 4 by Zayen and UAR Premier Muhammad Sidky Soliman, committed Syria and the UAR to come to each other's assistance if either was attacked by a 3d country. Gen. Muhammad Fawzi, UAR chief of staff, was to be in command of UAR and Syrian forces in the event of joint military operations.

A communiqué issued at the conclusion of the Egypto-Syrian talks declared that the UAR and Syria would undertake preliminary measures "in the spheres of economy, culture, information and other fields" leading to a possible reunification of the 2 countries in order to "defeat the offensive being launched by reaction to cooperation with imperialism and Zionism." Citing a provision in the bilateral agreement for "the coordination of political action," the joint statement said that the UAR and Syrian defense and foreign affairs ministers would meet every 6 months or whenever conditions required.

Israeli-Syrian clashes of Apr. 1967 in the Israeli-Syrian border area east of the Sea of Galilee, followed by continued fighting in early May, built up to the crisis that erupted June 5, in all-out war between Israel and the Arab states. Troops of the UAR and Syria began to mass on the borders of Israel May 14, and ultimately Egyptian and Syrian forces there totaled 85,000 and 12,000 troops, respectively. Cairo and Damascus said that they were making these military moves because Israel was preparing to attack Syria. Other Arab states, in a display of traditional solidarity against Israel, acted immediately to aid Cairo and Damascus. Troops of Jordan, Iraq, Algeria, Saudi Arabia and Kuwait were alerted. Iraqi and Saudi troops joined Jordanian forces on the Israeli border. The UAR and Jordan signed a mutual defense pact May 30, and Iraq signed the accord June 4.

As Israel responded to the Arab show of force by deploying its own troops, the UAR increased the pressure on Israel. Cairo asked UN Secy. Gen. U Thant May 18 to withdraw UN Emergency Force (UNEF) troops that had been stationed for 10 years as a buffer between Israel and Egypt. Thant complied immediately, removing the UNEF forces along the Sinai-Negev border and also those in the Gaza Strip and at Sharm el–Sheik (sometimes transliterated Sharm ash-Shaykh), near the mouth of the strategic Gulf of Aqaba (the Gulf of Eilat to Israelis). Egypt May 23 closed the gulf to Israeli shipping and enforced the blockade by announcing the mining of the entrance to the waterway. International efforts to avert war proved unavailing. The UN Security Council met fruitlessly in emergency session May 24–June 3. The "maritime powers," led by the U.S. and Britain, deplored the blockade of the gulf and issued pronouncements upholding the gulf's international character. But they took no definitive action to support their position.

The UAR had alerted its forces May 14 and had begun moving troops to Sinai Peninsula positions bordering Israel in observance of the 1966 defense pact with Syria. A state of emergency was declared throughout Egypt May 16. A Cairo broadcast announced that all military forces were "in a complete state of preparedness for war." By May 20, the number of Egyptian troops deployed along the Israeli frontier was estimated at 58,000. A Damascus broadcast May 17 said that Syria's forces had been brought to "maximum preparedness" in view of "information about the Israeli build-up along the Syrian border and threatening statements by Israeli officials." It was reported that Syria had massed 12,000 men along Israel's border. The UAR mobilized its full 100,000-man army reserve May 21, and Cairo announced May 22 that Iraq had agreed to send army and air units to Egypt to strengthen the build-up.

The UAR-Syrian moves apparently had been coordinated at meetings held in Damascus May 14–15 by Gen. Muhammad Fawzi, UAR chief of staff, and Syria's 2 top military officials —Maj. Gen. Hafez Assad, defense minister, and Maj. Gen. Mahmoud Chakry, Iraqi defense minister was quoted May 18 as saying that Iraqi officials were in consultation with Egyptian and Syrian military leaders to coordinate "the use of military units in case of aggression." The Iraqi Defense Ministry announced that the country's forces were alerted and ready to support Syria. Kuwait also announced that its forces had been alerted and were at the disposal of the Arab League's Cairo-based Unified Command. The UAR's military

actions were supported May 20 by a resolution signed in
Cairo by ambassadors of 12 Arab League nations: The UAR,
Iraq, Saudi-Arabia, Syria, Lebanon, Jordan, Yemen, Libya,
Sudan, Morocco, Kuwait and Algeria.

Israel May 18 announced the adoption of "appropriate
measures" to cope with the UAR build-up. Israeli tanks were
reported May 20 to have moved to the Sinai frontier. Premier Levi Eshkol reported May 21 that his government had
"completed a partial mobilization of reserves [estimated at
230,000] and . . . taken political measures to preserve peace
and assure Israel's full rights." In an address to the Israeli
Knesset (parliament) May 22, Eshkol said that in the past few
days Egypt had increased its forces in the Sinai Peninsula
from 35,000 men to 85,000. Because of this threat, Eshkol
declared, Israel had been forced to mass its forces. Eshkol assured Cairo and Damascus that Israel intended no aggressive
moves against Egypt or Syria. He appealed for a mutual reduction of troop concentrations and pledged that Israel
would pull back its troops from the Sinai frontier if Cairo
also withdrew its forces. Eshkol asserted that Syrian-origi-
nated infiltration attacks on Israel, numbering more than 100,
were largely responsible for the current tensions. Eshkol
added: "On the heightening and growing effectiveness of
these sabotage activities, I found it necessary to address clear
and explicit warnings to Syria that we are not prepared to
put up with their continuation."

The UNEF halted its patrols in the Gaza Strip and at
Sharm el-Sheik at the mouth of the Gulf of Aqaba May 19.
U Thant had agreed to end the UNEF operations in compli-
ance with a cabled request May 18 from UAR Foreign Min.
Mahmoud Riad for the termination of the UN activities there.
Riad recalled that UNEF had been stationed on Egyptian
territory at the invitation of Cairo. He said its continued
presence depended on Egyptian approval. He requested that
UNEF be pulled out "as soon as possible." In his reply to
Riad, Thant agreed that the UAR had the right to insist on

UNEF's departure. But he expressed "serious misgivings" about such a withdrawal. UNEF "has been an important factor in maintaining relative quiet in the area of its deployment during the 10 years, and its withdrawal may have grave implications for peace," Thant asserted.

Ceremonies were held in Gaza May 19 to mark the formal ending of UNEF's operations. The UN flag was hauled down from UNEF headquarters, and the UN troops withdrew to their barracks to await repatriation to their countries. UNEF, at the time of its withdrawal, was made up of 3,393 troops supplied by India (978 men), Canada (800), Yugoslavia (580), Sweden (528), Brazil (432), Norway (72) and Denmark (3). The Gaza Strip, originally a part of Palestine, had been seized by Egypt in the 1948–9 Arab-Israeli war. Israel captured the 25-mile-long, 5-mile-wide area during the 1956 Suez-Sinai campaign but relinquished it under a Nov. 6, 1956 UN General Assembly resolution ordering it restored to Egyptian administration. The same resolution established UNEF and directed it to take positions in the strip and to act as a buffer between Israel and Egypt. Israel refused to allow UNEF troops to be stationed on its territory.

Thant May 19 formally stated his reasons for halting UNEF operations. In a report to the UN Security Council, Thant said:

(A) The UNEF was introduced into the territory of the UAR on the basis of an agreement reached in Cairo [in 1956] between the secretary general [the late Dag Hammarskjöld] and the president of Egypt, and it therefore seemed fully clear to me that since UAR consent was withdrawn, it was incumbent on the secretary general to give orders for the withdrawal of the force. The consent of the host country is a basic principle which has applied to all UN peace-keeping operations.

(B) In practical fact, UNEF could not remain or function without the continuing consent and cooperation of the host country.

(C) I have also been influenced by my deep concern to avoid any action which would either compromise or endanger the contingents which make up the force. The UNEF is, after all, a peace-keeping, not an enforcement operation.

(D) In the face of the request for the withdrawal of the force, there seemed to me to be no alternative course of action which could be taken by the secretary general without putting into question the sovereign authority of the government of the UAR within its own territory.

Thant also said that a series of harassing tactics by Egyptian troops against UNEF positions May 17–18 had made it "incumbent" on him to order UNEF's withdrawal. In a further report on the crisis, Thant told the UN Security Council May 20 that he would go to Cairo in an effort to ease tensions. Thant said the situation in the Middle East was "more disturbing, . . . more menacing that at any time since the fall of 1956." Thant said that the Arab raids against Israel were the major factor in increased tension in the area.

The UAR governor of the Gaza Strip, Maj. Gen. Abdel Moneim Hosny, had said May 19 that Cairo had found it neccessary to request UNEF's withdrawal to insure the safety of the UN troops and "to discharge fully its responsibilities for the defense of the sector in the face of Israeli agression." Troops of the UAR-supported Palestine Liberation Organization (PLO) occupied UNEF border posts in the Gaza Strip May 20. PLO Chairman Ahmed Shukairy declared: "We now stand face to face with our enemies. Previously there had been that international barrier between us and the enemy, and this barrier has now fallen forever." Egypt declared a state of emergency in the Gaza Strip May 20. Cairo radio reported May 21 that UNEF troops had started to evacuate Sharm el–Sheik and UAR soldiers quickly moved into the strategic post.

British Foreign Secy. George Brown May 18 had criticized UNEF's withdrawal. Speaking at a dinner of the UN Association in London, Brown said: "It really makes a mockery of the peace-keeping force of the United Nations, if, as soon as tension rises, the UN Force is told to leave. Indeed, the collapse of UNEF might well have repercussions on other UN peace-keeping forces, and the credibility of the United Nations' efforts in this field are thrown into question."

U.S. Amb.-to-UN Arthur J. Goldberg said May 20 that the U.S. shared Thant's concern over the explosive situation in the Middle East. But he added that the U.S. felt it was "vital" to maintain the UN presence in the area.

In his May 22 address to the Knesset, Israeli Premier Levi Eshkol assailed what he held was Thant's precipitate removal of UNEF. Eshkol recalled that the late Dag Hammarskjöld, as UN Secretary General, had informed the UN General Assembly Feb. 26, 1957 of his assurances to Israel that the proper way to decide on a request for UNEF's withdrawal would be to inform the UNEF Advisory Committee and permit it to decide whether the General Assembly should be consulted.

The UAR May 23 announced the closing of the Strait of Tiran, at the entrance to the Gulf of Aqaba, to Israeli shipping. A government statement May 24 said that all entrances to the gulf had been mined as of May 23 (but this statement was discovered by Israeli forces after the fall of Sharm el-Sheik to have been fictitious). The blockade, the statement said, was further enforced by Egyptian shore batteries on Sinai territory (another fiction), armed boats and air patrols. It warned that Israeli ships attempting to enter the gulf for the Israeli port of Eilat, at the head of the strategic waterway, would be fired on if they disobeyed orders to turn back. Cairo stated that other ships would be subject to search to determine whether they were carrying strategic material, including oil, to Eilat.

The Gulf of Aqaba, an arm of the Red Sea, is 100 miles long; its width varies from 10 miles to 30. It is bordered by 4 countries: Israel and Jordan, where each had a small coastline of about 6 miles and 2 major ports—Eilat (Israel) and Aqaba (Jordan); Egypt on the west (Sinai) and Saudi Arabia on the east. Entrance to the gulf is through an 800-to-1,000-yard-wide channel between the Sinai coast and 2 rocky islands—Tiran and Sanafir. The channel east of these 2 islands is impassable because of reefs and shoals. Egyptian guns could have commanded the western channel after UNEF's withdrawal from Sharm el-Sheik May 19.

Nasser announced the closing of the Gulf of Aqaba in a speech at an Egyptian air force headquarters in Sinai May 23. Justifying the gulf's closure and other Egyptian moves to counter Israel, Nasser recalled that Britain and France had supported Israel in 1956 during the Suez crisis. But, he said, the situation had become entirely different. Nasser continued:

Israel today is not backed by Britain and France as was the case in 1956. It has the United States, which supports it and supplies it with arms. . . . We are now face to face with Israel. In recent days Israel has been making threats of agression and has been boasting. On May 12 a very impertinent statement was made. . . . The statement said that the Israeli commanders have announced they would carry out military operations against Syria in order to occupy Damascus and overthrow the Syrian government. On the same day the Israeli premier, Eshkol, made a strongly threatening statement against Syria. . . . On May 13 we received accurate information that Israel was concentrating on the Syrian border huge armed forces of about 11 to 13 brigades. These forces were divided into 2 fronts, one south of Lake Tiberias [the Sea of Galilee] and the other north of the lake. The decision made by Israel at this time was to carry out an aggression against Syria as of May 17. On May 14 we took our measures, discussed the matter and contacted our Syrian brothers. Lt. Gen. [Muhammad] Fawzi left for Syria to co-ordinate matters. We told them that we had decided that if Syria was attacked, Egypt would enter the battle from the first minute. This was the situation at May 14. The forces began to move in the direction of Sinai to take up normal positions. . . .

On May 16 we requested the withdrawal of the UN Emergency Force. A worldwide campaign, led by the United States, Britain and Canada, began opposing the withdrawal of UNEF from Egypt. Thus, we felt that there were attempts to turn UNEF into a force serving neo-imperialism. It is obvious that UNEF entered Egypt with our approval and therefore cannot continue to stay in Egypt except with our approval. A campaign is also being mounted against the UN Secretary General because he made a faithful and honest decision and could not surrender to the pressure brought to bear upon him by the United States, Britain, and Canada to make UNEF an instrument for implementing imperialism's plans. . . . I say this quite frankly, that had UNEF ignored its basic mission and turned to achieving the aims of imperialism, we would have regarded it as a hostile force and forcibly disarmed it. . . . At the same time I say the UNEF has honorably and faithfully carried out its duties. The UN Secretary General refused to succumb to pressure [and] issued immediate orders to UNEF to withdraw. Consequently, we laud the UNEF, which stayed 10 years in one country, serving peace.

Our forces are now in Sinai, and we are in a state of complete mobilization in Gaza and Sinai.

We note that there is a great deal of talk about peace these days. International peace—international security—UN intervention—and so on and so forth, which appears daily in the press. Why is it that no one spoke about peace, the United Nations, and security when on May 12 the Israeli premier and the Israeli commanders made their statements that they would occupy Damascus, overthrow the Syrian regime, and occupy a part of Syrian territory? . . . If there is a true desire for peace, we say that we also work for peace. But does peace mean that we should ignore the rights of the Palestinian people because of the lapse of time? Does peace mean that we should concede our rights because of the lapse of time? They speak about a "UN presence in the region for the sake of peace." Does "UN presence in the region for peace" mean that we should close our eyes to everything? The United Nations adopted a number of resolutions in favor of the Palestinian people. Israel implemented none of these resolutions. This brought no reaction from the United States. Today U.S. Senators, members of the House of Representatives, the press, and the entire world speak in favor of Israel, of the Jews. But nothing is said in favor of the Arabs. . . . The peace talk is heard only when Israel is in danger. But when Arab rights and the rights of the Palestinian people are lost, no one speaks about peace, rights, or anything. Therefore it is clear that an alliance exists between the Western powers—chiefly represented by the United States and Britain—and Israel. There is a political alliance [which] prompts the Western powers to give military equipment to Israel. . . .

The armed forces yesterday occupied Sharm el-Sheik. It is an affirmation of our rights and our sovereignty over the Gulf of Aqaba. The gulf constitutes Egyptian territorial waters. Under no circumstances will we allow the Israel flag to pass through the Gulf of Aqaba. The Jews threatened war. We tell them: You are welcome, we are ready for war. Our armed forces and our people are ready for war, but under no circumstances will we abandon any of our rights. The water is ours. War might be an opportunity for Israel and Rabin [Maj. Gen. Itzhak Rabin, the Israeli chief of staff] to test their forces against ours and see that what they wrote about the 1956 battle and the occupation of Sinai was all a lot of nonsense.

With all this there is imperialism, Israel, and reaction. Reaction casts doubt on everything, and so does the Islamic Alliance. We all know that the Islamic Alliance is represented by 3 states—Saudi Arabia, Jordan and Iran. They are saying that the purpose of the Islamic Alliance is to unite the Moslems against Israel. I would like the Islamic Alliance to serve the Palestine question in only one way—by preventing the supply of oil to Israel. The oil which now reaches Israel through Eilat comes from one of the Islamic Alliance states. It goes to Eilat from Iran. Such is the Islamic Alliance. It is an imperialist alliance, and this means it sides with Zionism because Zionism is the main ally of imperialism. The Arab world, which is now mobilized to the highest degree, knows all this. It knows how to deal with the imperialist agents, the allies of Zionism, and the 5th column. They say they want to coordinate their plans with us. We cannot coordinate our plans in any way with Islamic Alliance members because it would mean giving our plans to the Jews and to Israel.

This is a vital battle. When we said that we were ready for the battle, we meant that we would surely fight if Syria or any other Arab state was subjected to agression. . . .

(Nasser said nearly 3 years later, in an interview conducted Feb. 7-8, 1970 with 2 U.S. newsmen—Rowland Evans of Metromedia Television News and William Touhy of the *Los Angeles Times*—that "we [Egypt] asked the secretary general . . . [only] about the withdrawal of the United Nations Emergency Force between Rafa and Eilat, and we asked him to keep those forces in Sharm el-Sheik and Gaza. These were our intentions. There were no intentions by that time to close Sharm el-Sheik because we hadn't asked the withdrawal of the [force] from Sharm el-Sheik. Well, but the answer came back that either we keep the force as it is or move it completely.")

Israeli Premier Levi Eshkol warned May 23 that an Egyptian blockade of the Gulf of Aqaba would constitute "an act of agression against Israel." Speaking in the Knesset, Eshkol said: "Any interference with freedom of shipping in the gulf and the strait [of Tiran]" would also be "a gross violation of international law, a blow at the sovereign rights of other nations. . . . If a criminal attempt is made to impose a blockade on the shipping of a member state of the United Nations, it will be a dangerous precedent that will have grave effects on international relations and the freedom of the seas."

U.S. Pres. Lyndon B. Johnson May 23 expressed opposition to Egypt's closing of the gulf to Israeli shipping. He described it as an "illegal" act that had "brought a new and grave dimension to the crisis" in the Middle East. The President also deplored the general deterioration of the political situation in the area. Johnson said:

. . . The government of the United States is deeply concerned, in particular with 3 potentially explosive aspects of the present confrontation. First, we regret that the general armistice agreements have failed to prevent warlike acts from the territory of one against another government, or against civilians, or territory, under control of another government. 2d, we are dismayed at the hurried withdrawal of the UN Emergency Force from Gaza and Sinai after more than 10 years of steadfast and effective service in keeping the peace, without action by either the General Assembly or the Security Council. . . . 3d we deplore the recent build-up of military forces and believe it a matter of urgent importance to reduce the troop concentrations. . . .

The United States considers the Gulf to be an international waterway and feels that a blockade of Israeli shipping is illegal and potentially disastrous to the cause of peace. The right of free, innocent passage of the international waterway is a vital interest of the international comunity. . . . We have urged Secy. Gen. Thant to recognize the sensitivity of the Aqaba question and to give it the highest priority in his discussions in Cairo.

To the leaders of all the nations of the Near East, I wish to say what 3 Presidents have said before—that the United States is firmly committed to the support of the political independence and territorial integrity of all the nations of the area. The United States strongly opposes aggression by anyone in the area, in any form, overt or clandestine. This has been the policy of the United States led by 4 Presidents— Pres. Truman, Pres. Eisenhower, Pres. Kennedy and myself—as well as the policy of both of our political parties. . . . We have always opposed—and we oppose in other parts of the world at this moment—the efforts of other nations to resolve their problems with their neighbors by aggression. We shall continue to do so. And we appeal to all other peace-loving nations to do likewise.

We call upon all concerned to observe in a spirit of restraint their solemn responsibilities under the UN Charter and the general armistice agreements. These provide an honorable means of preventing hostilities until, through the efforts of the international community, a peace with justice and honor can be achieved. . . .

The Egyptian newspaper *Al-Ahram* reported May 26 that UAR Foreign Min. Riad had rejected a 5-point peace formula by Pres. Johnson submitted May 23 by U.S. Amb.-to-UAR Richard H. Nolte. The newspaper said that Johnson's formula contained these major provisions: (a) UNEF troops would remain in the Gaza Strip and in Sharm el-Sheik; (b) the UAR would not send troops to Sharm el-Sheik until Cairo guaranteed shipping through the strait; (c) Egyptian forces would be barred from entering the Gaza sector of the UAR-Israeli border; (d) the UN would administer Gaza until the crisis was settled; (e) Egyptian and Israeli troops would pull back from the border areas. Riad was quoted as having told Nolte that "if Israel carries out aggression against any Arab country, we shall consider you [the U.S.] as partners."

(The U.S. State Department had advised U.S. citizens May 22 not to visit Israel, the UAR, Syria and Jordan in view of the crisis. The department also urged Americans not having "essential business" in those countries to leave. Another department directive called for dependents of U.S. officials to leave Israel and the UAR. About 400 were in Egypt and 120 in Israel. 500 U.S. businessmen and tourists were said to have left Egypt.)

A British Foreign Office statement May 23 upheld the international character of the Gulf of Aqaba and said it should remain open to shipping of all nations. The statement said: "If it appeared that any attempt to interfere with ships going through the waterway was likely to be made, we should support international action through the United Nations to secure free passage." British Foreign Secy. George Brown conferred in Moscow May 24 with Soviet Premier Aleksei N. Kosygin and Foreign Min. Andrei A. Gromyko. Brown urged a policy of "restraint and creative imagination" in helping to resolve the Middle East crisis. Soviet government spokesman Leonid Zamyatin said May 26, the day Brown left Moscow, that the British foreign secretary's position had shown "that the British government actually supports" Israel.

Nasser warned May 26 that an Israeli attack on Egypt or Syria could result in an all-out conflict in which the Arabs' "main objective will be the destruction of Israel." Nasser asserted that he had ordered the deployment of Egyptian troops along the Israeli border after reconnaissance photos had shown that Israel had massed soldiers on the frontier with Syria. Nasser said that the UAR and Syria were prepared for war and that Iraq, Kuwait and Algeria were sending troops. Nasser lauded the Soviet Union for its "magnificent" support of the Arab states. At the same time, he assailed the U.S. as "the No. 1 protector of Israel" and denounced Britain as "an American coattail." (Nasser was reported to have advised several world leaders that Cairo intended no aggression against Israel. His assurances were said to have been conveyed in notes to French Pres. Charles de Gaulle, Indian Prime Min. Indira Gandhi, Ethiopian Emperor Haile Selassie, Afghan King Muhammad Zahir, Communist chiefs of state and other Asian and African leaders. But after the Israeli victory in June, Israeli air force intelligence officers June 20 made public what were described as captured Egyptian documents purporting to show that the UAR had mapped detailed plans for a surprise military strike against Israel. The documents, said to have been captured by Israeli forces at El Arish and El Ser airfields during fighting in the Sinai desert, reportedly called for cutting off the southern Negev, capturing the Israeli port of Eilat and bombing Israeli airfields and radar and missile installations near Tel Aviv. The Egyptian documents, said to have been dated between May 17 and 26, cited no specific date for the attack. The Israeli air force also disclosed its possession of a Syrian map and information gathered from Syrian prisoners indicating that Syria had formulated detailed plans to attack Israel. The Israeli report said Damascus' plan had called for shelling the Safad area in Israel and capturing Ayelet Hashahar and Kfar Hanassi north of the Sea of Galilee June 6.)

The UAR May 27 adopted measures placing Egypt on a virtual war footing: a directive was issued cracking down on hording by speculators; government funds were made available for armed forces expenditures and for food purchases and production; the Economy Ministry decreed tighter controls on hard-currency expenditures abroad. The UAR was reported May 27 to have shifted some troops of its 35,000-man force in Yemen to the Sinai Peninsula. More Egyptian troops were reported moving into the Sinai border area May 28 to reinforce 80,000 already there. Additional troops and equipment reported near El Arish just outside the Gaza Strip.

Nasser May 28 ruled out a negotiated peace in the Middle East until Palestinian Arabs were returned to their homeland. Speaking at a news conference, Nasser said: "Be patient a year or 10 years until we restore these rights." If the U.S. 6th

Fleet in the Mediterranean came to the aid of Israel in the event of an Arab-Israeli military showdown, he (Nasser) would not request the assistance of the UAR's non-Arab allies, particularly the Soviet Union; although the U.S. supported Israel, the Arabs "have always extended the hand of friendship" to Washington; the UAR had not "budged one inch" from its decision to bar Israeli shipping in the Gulf of Aqaba.

The UAR National Assembly May 29 granted Nasser full powers to govern by decree. In a report to the Assembly the same day, Nasser said Soviet Premier Kosygin had promised that Moscow would support Egypt in its blockade of the Gulf of Aqaba. Nasser said Kosygin's promise had been transmitted to the UAR during the Soviet premier's meeting in Moscow May 26-28 with UAR War Min. Shamseddin Badran. Badran, he said, "relayed to me a message from Premier Kosygin saying that the Soviet Union stands with us in this battle and will not allow any country to interfere, so that the state of affairs prevailing before 1956 may be restored."

A Syrian delegation, headed by Pres. Nureddin al-Attassi, conferred in Moscow May 29-30 with Soviet officials. No communiqué was issued at the conclusion of the 2 days of talks, but Damascus radio said the Soviet Union had pledged full support for Syria. Soviet leaders participating in the talks included Premier Kosygin, Foreign Min. Gromyko and Defense Min. Andrei Grechko.

Fall & Rise in Amity with Jordan

Egypt's down-and-up cycle of political dealings with Jordan became, in retrospect, a unique barometer of the imminence of war with Israel in 1967. Relations between the 2 countries at the beginning of the year were considered by experienced observers to be cool, and they soon began to deteriorate even further.

Jordanian Premier Wasfi el-Tell accused the UAR Jan. 7 of having concluded with Israel in 1956 a "gentlemen's agreement" under which Cairo had abandoned its "role in the struggle for Palestine." Tell said the pact had been agreed to by UAR Nasser and David Ben-Gurion, then premier of Israel, with the late Dag Hammarskjöld, then UN Secretary General, acting as intermediary. The agreement resulted in the deployment of UN peace-keeping troops in the Gaza Strip between the UAR and Israel, according to Tell.

Tell said that Marxists favored peaceful coexistence between Arab states and Israel and a federation between Israel and western Jordan (formerly part of Palestine). Tell reported that Chaifi al-Hout, chief of the Cairo-based Palestine Liberation Organization (PLO) in Lebanon, had gone to Paris to discuss this matter with other Marxists. PLO Chief Ahmed Shukairy and his staff, Tell charged, were an arm of the UAR's intelligence. (Tell was regarded in Jordan as a tough pro-Hashemite installed by King Hussein to keep the Palestinian minority under control and to prevent it from becoming overly pro-Nasser.)

A UAR official Jan. 8 denied Jordanian charges of Egyptian-Israeli collusion.

In a Cairo broadcast Nov. 22, 1966, Shukairy had urged King Hussein to let the Palestine Liberation Army (PLA) defend Jordanian villages on the Israeli border with Shukairy's assurance that the PLO had no intention of seizing power in Jordan. Hussein rejected this offer. He told a correspondent for the Paris newspaper *Le Monde* Nov. 23 that "I do not see why I should offer my head to the executioner."

Shukairy, in an address carried by Radio Cairo Nov. 25, 1966, had urged Jordanian troops to remain in their barracks and "allow the popular revolution to liberate the usurped fatherland." Shukairy denounced Hussein as a "tool of imperialism," an "enemy of Islam and Arabism," an "atheist" and a "murderer." The PLO began issuing public statements advising Tell's cabinet ministers to resign at once or be prepared for any consequences.

King Hussein Nov. 29 charged the PLO with having "become a destructive factor, sowing dissension between the Arab states and stirring up subversion in this country." He added his opinion that "there no longer exists any possibility of cooperation between us and this organization." Hussein also criticized Egypt for a failure to support Jordan in its struggle against Israel, which had launched a heavy reprisal raid that included the use of Mirage jet planes Nov. 13 against the Jordanian village of Samua, believed to be a haven for Palestinian Arab commandos. Hussein said: "Why are commandos sent into Israel from Jordan, and not from Syria or Egypt?" Jordan had mobilized to support Egypt when Israel attacked in 1956, but the UAR had "failed in its duty to provide air cover for the Jordanian forces fighting at Samua, Egypt might at least have sent a squadron to bomb the Israeli air base, which to our knowledge is situated near Egyptian territory."

At an emergency meeting of the Arab Defense Council in Cairo Dec. 7–10, 1966, Jordanian Foreign Min. Aqram Zuayter became involved in a sharp verbal clash with Ahmed Shukairy, who told press representatives Dec. 9 that the PLA would enter Jordan when the time came, "whether King Hussein wants us or not," and that Hussein would have to leave Jordan. But UAR Deputy Premier (for foreign affairs) Mahmoud Fawzi at once let it be known that Shukairy spoke only for himself, not for the UAR. The council resolved to recommend the admission of the forces of other Arab countries to Jordan, which reportedly refused under any circumstances to admit the PLA.

Relations between Egypt and Jordan worsened steadily beginning early in Feb. 1967 and were suspended before the end of the monlth Matters began moving toward a climax with the landing in Aqaba, Jordan, of a Misrair (Egypt airlines) plane, one of whose passengers was Riad Kamal Hajjij, a senior UAR intelligence officer. It was announced officially in Amman, Jordan's capital, that Hajjij had requested and received political asylum.

The semiofficial Middle East News Agency in Cairo reported that Jordan had been asked to return all 41 passengers and 4 crew members of the plane, which was expected in the Egyptian Red Sea port of Hurghada. Passengers from the plane reportedly quoted the pilot as saying that Hajjij had forced him at gunpoint to change course and land in Jordan. The Cairo Newspaper *Al-Ahram* alleged that Hajjij had conspired with Israeli and U.S. intelligence operatives early in the 1960s to help the U.S. carry out planned *coups d'état* in Egypt and Syria. The newspaper asserted that Hajjij had been detained in UAR authorities' custody for 17 months before being released in 1964.

Hajjij was reported to have said in Amman Feb. 11, 1967 that he had received orders in Cairo to assassinate "a great Arab personality" and that when he had feigned illness rather than execute this assignment he was imprisoned and tortured.

The Jordanian government announced after a cabinet meeting Feb. 18 that it had withdrawn its recognition of Pres. Abdel al-Salal's Yemeni republican government because of that regime's failure to meet an official Jordanian request that (a) UAR "air raids on Yemeni villages" cease. (b) UAR forces withdraw from Yemen and (c) "measures . . . [be] taken to grant the people of Yemen the right of self-determination." King Hussein had returned earlier from a visit to Saudi Arabia, 2 of whose border towns with Yemen had been bombed 3 times in January by Egyptian aircraft.

UAR Pres. Nasser, in an evening broadcast Feb. 22, accused the Jordanian government of serving imperialist interests. He termed the Jordanian and Saudi Arabian governments "lackey and reactionary regimes." Both Jordan and Saudi Arabia had allied themselves with the outlawed Moslem Brotherhood in the UAR and the activities of both countries' leaders, together with those of Pres. Habib Bourguiba of Tunisia (which had broken off diplomatic relations Feb. 11 with Yemeni Pres. Salal's regime), were coordinated by the U.S. Central Intelligence Agency, Nasser said.

The Jordanian government Feb. 23 withdrew Abdel Moneim el-Rifai as its ambassador to the UAR and accused Egypt of "tampering with Jordan's security and misleading the citizens." The Amman government cited support for its accusation from "frank confessions made by saboteurs," who, it said were arrested by security agents after the discovery of an arms cache in the Jordanian-held Old City of Jerusalem.

PLO Chairman Shukairy proposed in Cairo in mid-March, at the 47th meeting of the Arab League Council, that Jordan be expelled from the Arab League for independently resuming relations with West Germany, which the League had condemned in mid-Mar. 1965 for recognizing Israel. The Council Mar. 18, 1967 postponed consideration of Shukairy's proposal until its next meeting (in September) and authorized League Secy. Gen. Abdel Khalek Hassouna to reestablish the League's contact with the Bonn government in order to determine how to deal with West Germany.

Jordan was one of 3 Arab countries that boycotted a 3-day conference of 9 Arab finance ministers and Iraq's Arab League ambassador in Cairo Apr. 3-5. The conference approved plans to guarantee the continuation of the PLO. As proposed by Shukairy, the League was to set up a financial organ to supply the PLO with funds to be collected regularly from popular organizations with the permission of League member-states.

Tensions continued between Cairo and Amman until late in May 1967. The Jordanian government, then apparently judging the prospect of an Egypto-Israeli war to be likely, announced May 25 that it had given official permission for Saudi Arabian and Iraqi forces to enter Jordan to assist in its defense if need be. (Nasser was reported at about the same time to have asked Jordan and Saudi Arabia to use their good offices with Iran to halt supplies of Persian oil to Israel.)

The UAR and Jordan signed a mutual defense pact in Cairo May 30 during a 6-hour visit by King Hussein, who had piloted his own twin-engined jet plane to the military airport at Almaza on the northern edge of the UAR capital for a surprise meeting with Nasser. The document was signed by Nasser and Hussein. As a further gesture of reconciliation between the 2 countries, Nasser had Ahmed Shukairy sit at Hussein's side during the ceremony. (Shukairy, at a press conference in Cairo May 21, had urged the people of Jordan to overthrow their king.) Previously, Nasser had accused Hussein of being in league with Israel. But Nasser said to Hussein after signing the agreement: "The initiative you have taken today affirms that Arabs, no matter how divided they may be, forget everything when the issue is that of the Arab destiny."

The agreement added Jordan's 55,000-man army to the UAR's 300,000 soldiers and Syria's 60,000 in the force being mustered against Israel. Under the agreement, Jordan and the UAR pledged to "use all means at their disposal including . . . armed forces, to repulse" an attack on either nation. In the event of joint military operations, the combined UAR-Jordanian force (as well as Syria's troops) were to come under the command of Gen. Muhammad Fawzi, UAR chief of staff. The treaty provided for the creation of a joint defense council (composed of UAR and Jordanian ministers of foreign affairs, defense and war) and a joint command (made up of a chiefs-of-staff council and a joint general staff). The treaty was to run for 5 years; it was automatically renewable for subsequent 5-year periods, but either nation could terminate it on notification within one year of its expiration.

Hussein June 4 announced the extension of the UAR-Jordan pact to include Iraq. A protocol extending the defense agreement to Iraq had been signed in Cairo earlier that day by Nasser and Iraqi Vice Premier Taher Yehia. Iraq had stepped up its military efforts May 30 by moving troops and armored units into Jordan to bolster Jordanian soldiers on the Israeli border. Iraqi jets June 1 took off from Habbaniyah for what was described as "front line" positions in an undisclosed Arab country—actually, Jordan.

Jordan at the time reportedly had at its disposal 2 armored brigades, 4 infantry brigades, a Royal Guards brigade and 12 combat aircraft. Iraq reportedly commanded an armored division, 2 infantry divisions and an infantry brigade and 90 combat aircraft. Egypt was said to be able to field 2 armored divisions, 4 infantry divisions, a parachute brigade, 430 combat aircraft and a navy of 6 destroyers, 9 submarines and 10 missile-equipped patrol boats. Syria, with whom the UAR had signed a mutual defense pact in Cairo Nov. 4, 1966, was reported to have ready 3 armored brigades, 5 infantry brigades, 100 combat aircraft and 4 missile-equipped patrol boats. Israel was then believed to have no more than one combat-ready armored division, 3 infantry brigades, a parachute brigade, 24 reserve brigades (8 of them armored), 230 combat aircraft, 2 destroyers and 4 submarines.

Egypt Crushed in Sinai

Egypt was subjected to a large-scale invasion and air attack by Israel early June 5, 1967. In less than 3 hours, the bulk of the UAR air force was destroyed. By the time a cease-fire went into effect June 8, Israeli troops were in control of the Sinai Peninsula as far as the Suez Canal, which Egypt had blocked during the fighting. A day before accepting the cease-fire, Gamal Abdel Nasser had announced his resignation as president of the UAR. Within 24 hours, however, he agreed to continue in office in response to great public demonstrations of popular sympathy said to have been organized by Vice Pres. Aly Sabry.

The fighting began at about 7:30 a.m. June 5 when Israeli warplanes attacked airfields in Egypt, Jordan, Syria and Iraq, destroying at least 300 of Egypt's 430 combat aircraft. At 8:15 a.m. June 5, 45 minutes after the start of the Israeli air offensive, Israeli troops began a crushing 3-pronged ground offensive against UAR forces in the Sinai Peninsula.

Egyptian commanders, anticipating a main Israeli thrust down the coast of the Gulf of Aqaba toward Sharm el-Sheik, had deployed most of their troops in the southern sector of the Sinai several days before the outbreak of hostilities. The Israelis, therefore, delivered their main blow at Egypt's weakest point, the northern Sinai coast. The Israeli drive began with 3 principal thrusts, each supported by a division of about 15,000 men. The first column, led by Brig. Gen. Israel Tal, attacked with tanks at Khan Yunis, at the southern end of the Gaza Strip, and from there headed west on the northern coastal road toward El Arish, the UAR's main military base in the northern Sinai. The 2d Israeli column, commanded by Brig. Gen. Ariel Sharon, moved on the heavily fortified Egyptian stronghold of Abu Agweigila, about 25 miles southeast of El Arish. The 3d Israeli force, headed by Brig. Gen. Avraham Yoffe, moving out between the 2 other Israeli columns, flanked the Egyptian force under attack by Gen. Tal's troops to prevent their escape to the west.

The first UAR stronghold attacked was the Gaza Strip. Its borders had been mined, lined with trenches and armed with antitank guns. The immediate target was Khan Yunis, at the southern end of the strip, and neighboring Rafah. After a preliminary bombardment of the border strip, Israeli tanks and troops crashed the Egyptian defenses and reached the coastal road. The Israeli force then split, one column heading north toward the city of Gaza and the other southwest toward El Arish. Khan Yunis was quickly captured, and Rafah fell shortly thereafter. The entire strip was thus sealed off. El Arish was captured the night of June 5, but the Israelis encountered stiff resistance in their advance into the Gaza Strip. They launched an all-out assault against the city of Gaza June 6. Aided by an air strike, the Israelis took control of the city by nightfall. During the battle, Israeli artillery shells and planes hit the UN headquarters in Gaza city and caused the death of 14 Indian soldiers and one Brazilian soldier of the disbanded UN Emergency Force (UNEF), who were awaiting evacuation from the area. 25 Indian soldiers were wounded. Thousands of Egyptian prisoners were taken by the Israelis in the battle for Gaza. Their captives included Gen. Abdul Monam Husseini, military governor of the Gaza Strip.

The fight for the Gaza Strip was the first land battle of the war. Gen. Tal said afterward: "My men knew that on this battle depended the outcome of the war—possibly the fate of Israel. More than 10 years had passed since we had clashed with the Egyptians. We could not tell what effect the Russian training, the modern Russian equipment and the new morale of the Egyptian army would have on their fighting capacity. We knew that we would be fighting forces whose equipment was superior both in quality and quantity to our own. We knew that the first breakthrough would actually be a trial between us and the Egyptian army. It was clear to all our soldiers that the attack would be carried out regardless of losses."

Gen. Sharon's forces met strong resistance in attacking Abu Agweigila in the northeastern Sinai June 6. The Egyptian position was defended by an infantry brigade, about 90 tanks and some regiments of artillery. The Israelis made a 3-pronged attack. Paratroopers stormed the artillery positions from the rear; infantry and armored troops smashed into the front-line positions; the northern side was attacked with tanks and troops. After 20 hours the Israelis finally captured Abu Agweigila June 7. Abu Agweigila's capture was vital to the Israeli advance to the west. The strongpoint commanded the junction of the roads from El Arish, Jebel Libni and El Quseima and had held up the main movement of Israeli troops in the Nitsana area to the central part of Sinai. Failure to take the stronghold would have enabled the UAR troops there to block fuel and ammunition supplies that were necessary to maintain the Israeli offensive.

Following the capture of El Arish, the forces of Gen. Tal had split in 2 again: part of one Israeli column continued west in the direction of El Mazar and El Qantara, straddling the Suez Canal, about 30 miles south of the entrance from the Mediterranean; the other column turned south to join Gen. Yoffe's forces, which were preparing to assault the UAR army's 2d defense line, stretching from Jebel Libni south to Bar Hasana. The remaining troops of the Tal-Yoffe force stayed behind to attack from the rear a strong Egyptian concentration at El Quseima. The Israeli pincer movement was aimed at crushing a force of Egyptian tanks dug in at El Quseima with their guns pointing east.

Meanwhile, an Israeli column to the south pushed out from the Negev, captured the Egyptian stronghold of Kuntilla, just over the border, seized El Thamada further south and made its way to the strategic Mitla Pass, which commanded access to the Suez Canal from the central Sinai. This

force completed its 140-mile advance in 36 hours. The battle
for the Mitla Pass started late June 7. About 1,000 tanks on
both sides were committed to the engagement, which raged
for 24 hours. The Egyptians also threw their few remaining
planes into the battle, bombing Israeli positions at Bir Gifgafa
to the northeast. Overcoming Egyptian resistance, Israeli
tanks began to move through the pass. An Israeli force was
deployed at the western end to bottle up retreating Egyptians
trying to reach the Canal through the pass. Escaping Egyptian troops, thus entrapped in the pass, became targets for
Israeli air attacks and suffered heavy casualties. The Egyptians launched a counterattack between Bir Gifgafa and the
Mitla Pass to clear a path for other retreating UAR soldiers,
but the Israelis threw back the assault after some of the fiercest fighting of the war. The Israelis then carried out a large-
scale mopping-up operation in the western and northwestern
sections of the Sinai Peninsula, where remnants of 7 Egyptian
divisions were stranded.

The road to the Suez Canal lay open to the Israelis by
late June 7. One tank column reached the east bank opposite
Ismailia early June 8; another, 2 hours later, pulled up to a
point just north of the town of Suez. The Sinai fighting
ended later June 8 as Egypt and Israel accepted a UN Security Council call for a cease-fire. The UAR had closed the
Suez Canal to all shipping June 6 after charging that U.S. and
British planes had joined Israeli forces in the war against the
Arabs. In a further act of retaliation, the UAR had orally
severed diplomatic relations with the U.S. (The UAR had
broken with Britain in 1966 in the Rhodesia dispute.) Syria,
Iraq and Sudan followed Cairo's lead and cut diplomatic relations with the U.S. and Britain; Algeria, Yemen and Mauritania severed ties with the U.S.

Egypt had lost nearly $3/4$ of its combat aircraft in the first
170 minutes of the war June 5. Taking off from airbases that
ringed Tel Aviv, the Israeli warplanes directed their main
thrust at Egypt toward the west. To avoid radar detection,

the attackers flew at altitudes as low as 150 feet in a wide curve over the Mediterranean beyond Alexandria. They then hooked inland toward the east and struck at UAR airbases extending from the Cairo area to the Suez Canal Zone and the Red Sea coast. Catching the Egyptians by surprise, the Israeli jets wreaked heavy destruction on Soviet-supplied UAR warplanes, many of them MiG-21s and MiG-19s, lined up on the fields. About 16 Egyptian airfields were put out of action in the first wave of attack. 10 of them were hit almost simultaneously: El Arish, Jebel Libni, Bir Gifgafa, Bir Thamada, Abu Suweir, Kabrit, Inchass, Cairo West, Beni Sueif and Fayid. The remaining 9 Egyptian airfields struck June 5 were: Mansura, Helwan, El Minya, Almaza, Luxor, Deversoir, Hurghada, Ras Banas and Cairo International.

Egyptian radar screens were put out of action, 16 of them in Sinai. The Israelis encountered some resistance in the air and on the ground. Only 2 flights of 4 MiG-21s managed to take to the air during the raids. The defending MiGs shot down 2 Israeli aircraft but were downed by the Israelis. UAR antiaircraft was light and inaccurate. The Egyptians fired several Soviet-made SA-2 surface-to-air missiles at the Israeli raiders, but none found their targets. The Israelis claimed that their jets, French-made Miràges, had shot down 50 UAR MiGs in 64 dogfights with no Israeli losses. It was believed that 100 of the Egyptian air force's 350 pilots were killed on the ground in the first Israeli air strike.

In a preliminary report on the number of planes downed in the first day's fighting, Brig. Gen. Mordecai Hod, commander of the Israeli air force, said in Tel Aviv the evening of June 5 that 387 Arab aircraft had been lost: 280 Egyptian MiGs on the ground and 20 in the air; 52 Syrian, 20 Jordanian and 15 Iraqi planes. Hod, who later revised these figures upwards, said 19 Israeli planes had been lost. According to Egyptian counter-claims June 5, the UAR, Syrian and Jordanian air forces that day had destroyed 161 Israeli planes. Cairo said only 2 Egyptian planes had been lost. In a further report on plane losses, Gen. Hod said June 7 that 441 Arab planes had been destroyed—410 June 5, 17 June 6 and 14 June 7.

The Arabs eventually discontinued—but did not quickly retract—unfounded charges that U.S. and British planes had aided the Israelis. A Cairo communiqué early June 6 had charged that there was "conclusive evidence" that U.S. and British carrier planes had flown cover for Israeli troops in the Jordanian and Sinai sectors and that planes with British markings had bombed Egyptian positions in the Sinai Peninsula June 5. The UAR called the alleged intervention "an actual aggressive action against the Arab nation as a whole and against its security and territorial integrity." Cairo claimed that 32 U.S. bombers had left Wheelus Air Force Base in Libya for Israel. The UAR contended that it was necessary to close Suez because Israeli attacks against shipping in the Canal threatened to obstruct the waterway.

The U.S. June 6 rebuked Cairo for charging that American planes had participated in the fighting. A protest handed to the UAR embassy in Washington called the accusation "wholly false" and "malicious." The note demanded that Cairo cease its "hostile and provocative" statements. State Secy. Dean Rusk said he believed the Egyptian charges were "invented" for the purpose of creating "difficulties for Americans" in the Middle East.

British Foreign Secy. George Brown June 7 also denied the Arab charges of British air intervention. Cairo had lied, Brown said, because the UAR "is trying to give itself an alibi for its own military failures and the extent to which its failures have let down its allies." (Brown June 8 reported the lifting of a British arms embargo imposed on the Middle East June 6 by Prime Min. Harold Wilson. Brown said Britain had been compelled to decide to "honor" its weapons contracts with undisclosed Middle East nations after other major suppliers, including the Soviet Union and the U.S., had displayed no interest in a British suggestion for a general arms ban in the region.)

The Arab charges of Anglo-U.S. air intervention were reported by Israel June 8 to have been fabricated in a radio-telephone conversation June 5 between UAR Pres. Nasser and Jordanian King Hussein. The Israelis said they had intercepted and taped the conversation, and the recording was made public by the Defense Ministry June 8. In the recording, a voice identified as Nasser's was heard saying: "I will make an announcement and you will make an announcement and we will see to it that the Syrians will make an announcement that American and British airplanes are taking part against us from aircraft carriers. . . . We will stress the matter and drive the point home." In the recording, Nasser asked Hussein: "Will we say the U.S. and England or just the U.S.?" Hussein replied: "The U.S. and England." Nasser then asked: "Does Britain have aircraft carriers?" Hussein's answer was unintelligible on the recording.

The Hussein-Nasser conversation was said by the Israelis to have taken place early June 5, after most of the Arab air forces had been knocked out by Israeli attacks. Cairo radio had reported later June 5 that Hussein had phoned Nasser to inform Nasser that he had observed on radar British planes taking off from carriers. The Israeli announcement accompanying the release of the recorded conversation said: "When the extent of the military defeat was finally clear to Nasser, he began to act to save his prestige . . . by claiming that Egyptian forces in the Sinai retreated not as a result of a clear and sharp military defeat in his war with Israel but because of imaginary foreign forces." Arabic experts differed on the authenticity of the recording.

Winston Burdett, an American journalist in Egypt at the time, reported another version of this Jordanian radar-screen origin of the Arab charge of Anglo-American air support. Burdett wrote in his 1969 book *Encounter with the Middle East* (pp. 319–20):

. . . Toward 4 a.m. on June 6 [1967], . . . [Nasser] telephoned to [King] Hussein and [Egyptian] Gen. [Muhammad] Riad at Army Headquarters in Amman [Jordan]. Their radio-telephone conversation was intercepted and taped by Israeli military monitors, and portions of it were promptly published. The Jordanians on the first day of the war had misread the signals on their highly sophisticated radar equipment. They saw masses of planes taking off on their screens, wave after wave ascending from Israel, and concluded that American or British fighters had flown in from nearby aircraft carriers to reinforce the Israelis. How else explain Israel's inexhaustible supply of planes? The Jordanians could not imagine that Israeli pilots were flying up to 8 missions a day. Hussein was full of this story, and Nasser seized on it during their early morning colloquy. The 2 rulers discussed whether they should accuse only the Americans or should extend the charge to include the British. Hussein agreed that Britain should be included in a joint denunciation. . . .

For Nasser, the story of the Anglo-American intervention was a gold mine that . . . would provide a 1956 way out of military defeat, converting the destruction of the Egyptian air force into a heroic stand against another tripartite collusion [such as the Anglo-French-Israeli alliance of Oct.–Nov. 1956]. . . .

Nasser conceded in a *Look* magazine interview published Mar. 4, 1968 (issue of Mar. 19) that he had erred in charging that U.S. planes had aided Israel in the 1967 war. Nasser acknowledged the error in an interview Jan. 28 with *Look* editor-in-chief William Attwood. Nasser said Egypt had misinterpreted the approach of Israeli planes from the Mediterranean, where American aircraft carriers were stationed. Attwood asked: "In other words, your accusation resulted from a misunderstanding based on suspicion and faulty information?" Nasser replied: "You could say that, yes." (The Cairo newspaper *Al-Ahram*, however, quoted Nasser Mar. 5 as having answered Attwood's question by saying: "You may say so, but others may say something else.") A U.S. State Department comment Mar. 4 on Nasser's remarks (as reported in *Look*) called them an "encouraging development." The U.S. had insisted that U.S.-Egyptian diplomatic relations, cut by the UAR during the 1967 war, could be restored only if Egypt publicly retracted its charges that U.S. planes had flown in support of the Israeli air attacks.

The *Times of India* correspondent in Washington reported June 8, 1967:

The West Asian [*i.e.*, Middle Eastern] war has virtually ended though the fighting continues on the approaches to the Suez Canal.

The most significant fact that has emerged is Israel's triumph in a lightning war. This massive achievement has been accomplished in about 72 hours—much sooner than in 1956.

An explanation is to be found in the structure, organization and spirit of the combatant countries and their armies. The events have confirmed the superiority of the Israeli forces in all these respects. Most Western military experts had expected the Israelis to win, but they, too, are surprised by their sweeping triumph. They had expected the Arabs to put up a better fight. The Arabs had 10 years to prepare. Numbers and military resources were on their side, and they had weeks to deploy them.

Secondly, Israeli strategy proved superior. The Israeli air force struck like lightning in the first few hours of the war and virtually destroyed the Egyptian air force as well as the air forces of the UAR's allies. Israeli trucks and tanks, therefore, moved bumper to bumper as if on a highway, unmolested by the enemy air force. In tank fighting, UAR had no air cover. The amazing success of the initial Israeli air strikes is attributed to 2 reasons. (1) Egyptian fighter pilots suffer from an aversion to fight at night. (2) The Israelis had discovered a gap in UAR radar system and exploited it by approaching their targets from the Mediterranean.

James Reston of the *N.Y. Times*, who was in Cairo and went to Tel Aviv, wrote:

The contrast between the spirit of Tel Aviv and the spirit of Cairo just a few days ago is remarkable and must have something to do with the outcome of this war. Cairo was run from the top and was full of misery at the bottom. Tel Aviv is full of lively talk and debate and personal responsibility.

. . . Both the Soviet Union and the United States have suffered setbacks.

The Soviet Union's agreement with the West not to intervene in the war and its climb-down in seeking a simple cease-fire without an Israeli withdrawal to prewar positions has brought it a harvest of openly expressed dismay from its Arab friends. The Arab countries tried very hard to secure the Soviet Union's active intervention on their behalf. Moscow stood by its pledge to Washington that . . . [nothing] could justify a confrontation between them.

The Soviet defense is that it was disappointed by the sudden collapse of the Arab forces despite its enormous military and economic assistance amounting to over $3 billion.

The switch in the Soviet stand was precipitated by the Arab accusation against the United States and Britain of intervention on Israel's behalf. The Russians knew this to be a false charge and treated it as an attempt to compel their own intervention. . . .

The United States has also emerged . . . badly mauled. A mounting number of Arab states have broken diplomatic relations with it.

The U.S. has become the victim of an unprecedented hate campaign which owes its origin to calculated misrepresentation by the UAR. . . .

According to one report, King Feisal of Saudi Arabia is privately relieved at the humiliating defeat suffered by Pres. Nasser. It would remove Pres. Nasser effectively from his self-proclaimed role of revolutionary leader of the Arab world.

The UN prestige, too, has suffered. . . . It was unable to prevent the war. It has not been able to bring about a prompt cease-fire. . . .

EGYPT AFTER DEFEAT (June 1967–Dec. 1968)

Nasser Resigns for One Day

Gamal Abdel Nasser announced his resignation as president of the United Arab Republic June 9, 1967, but he withdrew his resignation June 10 after the Egyptian cabinet and the legislative National Assembly voted not to accept it. Nasser June 11 then made major changes in Egypt's military command.

Arab informants reported July 12 that Nasser had arrested more than 150 officers in a purge of Moslem Brotherhood members because members of the outlawed but still influential brotherhood, an extremist religio-nationalistic organization, had confronted Nasser during the June 5–11 war and had demanded that he sign a cease-fire and resign. Nasser had put them off with a promise to resign when the fighting stopped. Although he honored his promise, within 24 hours he returned to power in response to massive demonstrations by his supporters.

Nasser's announcement that he was relinquishing his post was made in a TV broadcast June 9, less than 24 hours after the UAR-Israeli cease-fire had gone into effect. Nasser announced that he had called on Vice Pres. Zakaria Mohieddin (premier in 1965–6) to replace him as president so that he could "return to the ranks of the public and do my duty with them like every citizen." Conceding that Egypt's military forces had suffered "a grave setback," Nasser reiterated the charge that British and U.S. planes had entered the war on the side of the Israelis at the start of fighting June 5. Nasser said in his speech:

Brothers, we have been accustomed . . . to speak with open hearts and to tell each other the facts, confident that through this means alone we can always find our sound direction, however critical the circumstances and however low the light. We cannot hide from ourselves the fact that we have met with a grave setback in the last few days. But I am confident that all of us can in a short time overcome our difficult

39

situation. To do this we shall need much patience, much wisdom and moral courage, and ability for devoted work. . . .

We all know how the crisis began in the first half of May. There was an enemy plan to invade Syria and the statements by his politicians and his military commanders declared that frankly. The evidence was ample. The sources of our Syrian brothers and our own reliable information were categorical on this. Even our friends in the Soviet Union told a parliamentary delegation which was visiting Moscow early last month that there was a calculated intention. It was our duty not to accept this in silence. In addition to it being a question of Arab brotherhood, it was also a matter of national security. Who starts with Syria will finish with Egypt. So our armed forces moved to our frontiers. Following this came the withdrawal of the United Nations Force, then the return of our forces to the Sharm el-Sheik position which commands the Tiran Strait, which the Israeli enemy used as one of the results of the tripartite aggression on us in 1956. . . .

Our estimates of the enemy's strength were precise. . . . Our armed forces had reached a level of equipment and training at which they were capable of deterring and repelling the enemy. We realized that the possibility of an armed clash existed, and we accepted the risk.

There were several factors before us—nationalist, Arab and international. These included a message from Pres. Lyndon Johnson of the United States, which was handed to our ambassador in Washington on May 26, asking us for restraint and not to be the first to open fire; otherwise we would face serious consequences. The same night the Soviet ambassador asked to see me urgently at 3:30 and told me that the Soviet government strongly requested we should not be first to open fire.

On the morning of last Monday, June 5, the enemy struck. If we say it was a stronger blow than we had expected we must say at the same time, and with assurance, that it was much stronger than his resources allowed. It was clear from the very first there were other forces behind him which came to settle their accounts with the Arab nationalist movement.

There were significant surprises: (1) The enemy we expected to come from the east and north came from the west. This showed he had facilities beyond his own resources and exceeding the estimate of his strength. (2) The enemy attacked at one go all the military and civil airfields in the United Arab Republic. This meant he was relying on something more than his normal strength to protect his skies from any retaliation from us. The enemy was also fighting on other Arab fronts with other assistance. (3) The evidence of imperialist collusion with the enemy is clear. It sought to benefit from the lesson of the former open collusion of 1956, this time concealing itself cunningly.

What is now established is that American and British aircraft carriers were off the enemy's shores, helping his war effort. Also,

British aircraft raided in broad daylight positions on the Syrian and Egyptian fronts, in addition to operations by a number of American aircraft reconnoitering some of our positions. The inevitable result was that our land forces, fighting a most violent and brave battle in the open desert, found their air cover was inadequate in face of decisive superiority. It can be said without fear of exaggeration that the enemy was operating an air force 3 times its normal strength.

This was also faced by the forces of the Jordanian army which fought a valiant battle under the command of King Hussein, who, to be just and honest to him, adopted a fine attitude. I confess that my heart bled as I followed the battles of his gallant army in Jerusalem and other positions on a night in which the enemy and the powers plotting with him massed at least 400 aircraft to operate over the Jordanian army. . . .

The Algerian people and their great leader, Houari Boumedienne, gave without reservation to the battle. The Iraqi people and their loyal leader, Abdel Rahman Arif, also gave without reservation. The Syrian army fought heroically. . . . The peoples and governments of Sudan, Kuwait, Yemen, Lebanon, Tunisia, and Morocco adopted honorable attitudes. The peoples of the entire Arab nation, without exception, . . . struck an attitude of manhood, dignity, and determination, an attitude of insistence that Arab rights will not be lost nor will they dwindle, and that the war in defense of them continues whatever the sacrifices and setbacks along the road of inevitable and definite victory.

There were great nations outside the Arab world which gave us moral support which cannot be estimated, but the conspiracy was bigger and stronger. . . .

I realize that the development of the armed battle may not be favorable to us. I tried with others to use all resources of Arab strength. Arab petroleum played its part. The Suez Canal played its part. And there is still a major role required of Arabs everywhere, and I am fully confident they will be able to perform it. . . .

We responded to the cease-fire resolution following assurances in the Soviet draft resolution to the Security Council and following declarations by the French government that no one could achieve a territorial expansion as a result of the recent aggression. . . .

We now have several urgent tasks before us. The first task is to remove the remnants of this aggression against us and adopt, with the Arab nation, an attitude of firmness and steadfastness. In spite of the setback, the Arab nation, with all its energies and resources, is able to insist on removing the remnants of the aggression.

The 2d task is for us to learn the lesson of the setback. In this connection there are 3 vital facts: (1) The destruction of imperialism in the Arab world leaves Israel with its own strength alone. Whatever the conditions and however long they may last, the abilities of the Arabs are greater and more effective. (2) The reorientation of Arab interests in the service of Arab rights is a primary safeguard. The U.S. 6th Fleet was moving with Arab petroleum. There are Arab bases which were forcibly, and despite the will of the peoples, placed at the service of aggression. (3) What is now needed is a unified voice by the entire Arab nation. . . .

We now reach an important point in this soul-searching by asking ourselves: Does this mean we do not assume responsibility for the consequences of this setback? I tell you truthfully that I am ready to assume the entire responsibility. I have taken a decision with which I want you all to help me. I have decided to give up completely and finally every official post and every political role and to return to the ranks of the public to do my duty with them like every other citizen.

The forces of imperialism imagine that Abdel Nasser is their enemy. I want it to be clear to them that it is the entire Arab nation and not Gamal Abdel Nasser. The forces hostile to the Arab nationalist movement always try to picture it as Abdel Nasser's empire. That is not true, for the hope of Arab unity began before Gamal Abdel Nasser. It will remain after Gamal Abdel Nasser. I have always told you that it is the nation which survives. Whatever his [Nasser's] contribution to the causes of his homeland, he is but an expression of a popular will and is not the creator of that will.

In accordance with Article 110 of the Provisional Constitution promulgated in March 1964, I have asked my colleague, friend, and brother, Zakaria Mohieddin, to take over the post of president of the republic and to carry out the constitutional provisions. Consequently, and after this decision, I place all I have at his disposal. . . .

I am not thereby liquidating the Revolution. The Revolution is not the monopoly of one generation of revolutionaries. I am proud of the contribution by this generation of revolutionaries. It has brought about the evacuation of British imperialism and the independence of Egypt. It has defined [Egypt's] Arab character, fought the policy of zones of influence in the Arab world, led the Socialist revolution, and brought about a profound change in the Arab way of life. It has affirmed the people's control of their resources and the product of their national action. It recovered the Suez Canal and laid down the bases of industrial build-up in Egypt; built the [Aswan] High Dam to turn the arid desert green; extended generating power networks all over the northern Nile Valley; and extracted petroleum resources. . . .

Canceling his resignation June 10, Nasser said in a broadcast: "I wished, if the nation had helped me, to stand by my decision to resign. [But] no one can imagine my feelings at this moment in view of the people's determination to refuse my resignation. I feel that the people's will cannot be refused; therefore I have decided to say where the people want me to stay until all traces of aggression are erased. Afterward there should be a plebiscite."

Vice Pres. Mohieddin, who had declined June 9 to replace Nasser as president, explained in a radio address June 10 that "like other citizens of this nation, I accept no leadership but his leadership"; "as for myself I do not accept the presidency."

The military shake-up carried out June 11 had been approved June 10 by the National Assembly, which had empowered the president "to mobilize all the popular forces and rebuild the country politically and militarily." Nasser replaced 11 senior Egyptian commanders who resigned or who were retired. 2 top military leaders had resigned June 9: Field Marshal Abdel Hakim Amer, commander of the UAR's armed forces, and Defense Min. Shamseddin Badran. Amer was replaced by Gen. Muhammad Fawzi, 52, former chief of staff, who was given the new title of commander-in-chief. Amer's title had been deputy supreme commander; Nasser retained the title of supreme commander. The service chiefs who resigned were Adm. Soleiman Ezzat, navy commander; Gen. Abdul Mohsen Mortaga, army commander, who had led the ill-fated Sinai campaign; and Gen. Sidky Mahmud, air force commander. Their replacements: Gen. Madkour Mabulzz, air; Vice Adm. Muhammad Ahmed Fikri, navy; Gen. Saladdin Mohsen, assistant commander-in-chief.

The presidentail decree announcing the military shake-up was accompanied by a government statement that said: "We will not rest until Israel evacuates the land she now occupies. Israel will not gain any privileges through her cheap victory." (A proclamation issued by Nasser June 11 called on Egyptians to "fight the battle of production from which we shall emerge victorious to finance our military battles.")

Nasser expanded his political powers June 19 by assuming the additional post of premier, by naming a 28-member cabinet and by taking control of the Arab Socialist Union, Egypt's only legal political party. Vice Pres. Aly Sabry, who was replaced by Nasser as secretary of the Arab Socialist Union, was named a deputy premier in the new cabinet. 2 other vice presidents also were appointed deputy premiers: Zakaria Mohieddin and Hussein Mamoud el-Shafei. The 4th deputy premier was Muhammad Sidky Soliman, premier in the outgoing cabinet. Shamseddin Badran, who had resigned as defense minister June 9, was replaced by Abdel Wahab al-Bishri. Bishri was replaced as war minister July 21 by Amin Hamed el-Howeidi, 45, a longtime associate of Nasser's.

The new cabinet: *Premier*—Nasser; *Deputy Premier*—Mohieddin; *Deputy Premier for Religious & Social Affairs*—Shafei; *Deputy Premier for Local Government*—Sabry; *Deputy Premier for Industry, Electricity & the High Dam*—Soliman; *Defense*—Bishri; *Labor*—Kamaleddin Mahmoud Rifaat; *Planning*—Abdel Moneim el-Kaissouni; *Agrarian Reform & Land Reclamation*—Abdelmohsin Abu el-Nour; *Petroleum, Transport, Mineral Resources, Housing & (public) Installations*—Mahmoud Yunis; *Agriculture*—Sayed Marei; *Culture*—Sarwat Okasha; *Economy & Foreign Trade*—Hassan Abbas Zaki; *Education*—Abdul Aziz el-Sayed: *Health*—Muhammad el-Nabawy el-Mouhandes; *War & Military Production*—Howeidi; *Interior*—Sharawi Muhammad Gomaa; *Youth*—Muhammad Talaat Khairy; *Higher Education*—Muhammad Labib Shukeir; *Foreign*—Mahmoud Riad; *Justice*—Issameddin Hassouna; *Irrigation*—Abdel Khalek al-Schnawy; *Supply & Internal Trade*—Nureddin Korra; *Minister of State*—Ahmed Tewfik el-Bakry; *Minister of National Guidance*—Muhammad Ahmed Fayek; *Communications*—Kamal Henry Abadir; *Tourism*—Amin Shakr; *President's Assistant for Foreign Affairs*—Mahmoud Fawzi; *Treasury*—Nazih Ahmed Deif.

War's Economic Effects: Budget Slashed

Egypt's economic difficulties were reflected in an interim budget issued July 6, 1967. It was to remain in effect until the original 1967-8 budget was revised to meet conditions created by the postwar crisis. The provisional budget called for a reduction in public expenditures by 25% and in investment allocations by 50%. Other austerity measures included an indefinite postponement in bonuses and overtime pay for civil servants and a halt in government subsidies to private schools. These steps were announced 4 days after

Pres. Nasser, as head of the government, had opened a meeting of the cabinet to review Egypt's general, foreign exchange and development budgets.

The Egyptian development budget for 1967 was slashed to E£250 million ($575 million), or E£100 million ($230 million) less than in the first 2 years of Egypt's 2d 5 year-plan (1965–9). In its first 5-year plan, the UAR had averaged E£300 million annually on development. Planning Min. Abdel Moneim el-Kaissouny, who furnished these figures, said that Egypt's development expenditure for 1967–8 would still amount to 13% of Egypt's GNP (gross national product) and probably would generate a growth rate of more than 4%. (Nasser said at Cairo University July 23 that the June war had forced the curtailment in Cairo's development budget and that funds earmarked originally for development projects would have to be diverted to buy wheat.)

To help solve its foreign-exchange problems, Egypt had received large-scale aid since the June 8 armistice from the Arab oil states of Saudi Arabia, Lybia and Kuwait—$100 million within a month of the cease-fire (and $252 million all told by the end of 1967). Egypt used the foreign funds to shore up its own currency. Kaissouny said that Egypt had resumed repaying the International Monetary Fund at the rate of $3½ million a month, that foreign government treasury bills had been liquidated and that Egypt's assets in foreign banks came to E£14 million ($32.2 million). He put the value of gold reserves in Cairo at E£40½ million ($93.15 million).

Deputy Premier Zakaria Mohieddin disclosed some details of the revised general budget July 25. Expenditures, which created a deficit of E£41 million ($94.3 million) instead of E£78 million ($179.4 million) as originally projected, were expected to amount to E£1,941,426,000 ($4,465,279,800). Mohieddin said that, to cut the deficit, the government had undertaken (a) cuts in public spending, (b) new excise taxes and rises in certain prices not affecting essential commodities, (c) an increase—to ¾ from ½—in the amount of compulsory payroll savings of daily wages and (d) specific taxation measures such as a 50% "national security" surtax on all current defense taxes but the agricultural defense tax—on which a 25% surtax was to be imposed.

Mohieddin, revealing the prospect of prolonged economic austerity, said that the UAR had lost an important source of steady revenue with the dwindling of tourism and the closing of the Suez Canal. "Our enemies believe that we cannot bear this for a long time," he said. "The time has come for us to be put to the test. If we do not fear death, we also do not fear hunger."

The Egyptian government was reported to have informed maritime powers July 15 that the Suez Canal, blocked since June 10 by sunken ships, would not be opened by Cairo until Israeli forces were withdrawn from the Canal's east bank. Washington sources said that day that Egypt had deliberately blocked the Canal by sinking some of its ships at both ends of the 108-mile waterway. (A report from London July 11 had said that the Canal was obstructed at 3 points: 2 Egyptian ships were sunk near the north entrance, south of Port Said; 2 cement-filled floating docks were sunk between Ismailia and the Great Bitter Lake [where 14 merchant ships of 8 nations had been trapped for 5 weeks]; a small Egyptian tanker was submerged at the southern entrance, at the port of Suez.)

Nasser said at Cairo University July 23 that the closing of the Canal threatened the UAR with an annual loss of $300 million in hard currency. (The Canal's closure for 49 days thus far had cost Egypt $21 million in hard currency.) Israeli Foreign Min. Abba Eban said July 29 that Israel would be prepared to reach a separate agreement with the UAR on the Canal issue, one apart from an overall peace settlement. Such a pact, Eban said, must be conditioned on Cairo's acceptance of the Canal's use by Israel and all other nations.

But by mid-October, the resumption of Canal operations had became out of the question for at least the rest of 1967. Many important facilities of Egypt's Suez Canal Authority had been badly damaged by Israeli shelling during intermittent clashes in July and September. Many Canal employes had been moved to other jobs outside the Canal Zone, and tens of thousands of Egyptian civilians in the zone had accepted evacuation to refugee camps in Egypt's interiors. Many maritime economists had begun predicting a lessening in importance for the Canal in the transport of oil, hitherto amounting to 75% of the Canal's total traffic. They based their predictions not so much on the Canal's 2d closing in a decade as on the growing trend toward 200,000-ton supertankers which could not use the Canal because of their enormous size and draft.

Planning Min. Kaissouni had stated early in July that Egypt would be serious hurt by the effects of the 6-day war. He estimated then that the country had lost about $35 million worth of Canal dues, tourism and oil sales in the month since the war's outbreak. (Egypt had been expected to become a net exporter of oil by 1968 and to earn as much as E£100 million [$230 million] annually through oil sales by 1970. Stanley Learned, president of Phillips Petroleum, had said in Bartlesville, Okla. June 17 that [a] his company would shortly recommence drilling operations begun before the war, [b] preliminary operations were under way for drilling near Mersa Matruh and [c] WEPCO, jointly owned by Phillips and the Egyptian General Petroleum Corp., was ready to develop the Alamein field, lay a pipeline to it and transport and market the oil.)

Israel and Egypt Aug. 28 announced an agreement to suspend until further notice all movement of shipping and military activity from the Suez Canal. The announcement was delivered in a report by UN Secy. Gen. U Thant to the Security Council. The first Suez Canal agreement, whereby both Israel and Egypt concurred in a formal decision to suspend all sailing on the waterway except for Egyptian launches tending stranded freighters, had expired Aug. 27, and Lt. Gen. Odd Bull of the Royal Norwegian Air Force, head of the UN Truce Supervision Organization (UNTSO), had strongly recommended that the agreement be provisionally extended for a month.

Gen. Bull had conferred with UAR officials in Cairo July 19-24 on means of strengthening the mandate of UNTSO observers currently stationed on both banks of the Canal to supervise the UN truce between Israel and the UAR. (3 Burmese observers were posted on each side of the canal July 26, increasing the UNTSO force in the area to 26.) The Egyptians at that time had rejected Bull's traffic proposals, which called on both Israel and the UAR to refrain from operating boats in the Canal and to agree to the delineation of a specific cease-fire line along the Canal. Egypt was said to have insisted on the guarantee of "the principle of non-existence of a cease-fire line" to obviate the need for *de facto* recognition of Israel's presence on the east bank of the Canal. Israel had demanded that a cease-fire line be drawn down the middle of the Canal.

Bull reported the failure of his Cairo mission at a meeting in Jerusalem July 26 with Israeli Defense Min. Moshe Dayan. An Israeli government statement issued after the talks said Dayan had agreed to consider Bull's proposal that boats be banned from the Canal as "a feasible basis for settlement on condition that it was accepted by both sides." As for the proposed cease-fire line, the statement quoted Dayan as saying that Israel "had already shown United Nations observers the exact boundaries of the areas held by the Israeli defense forces." Dayan was said to have "requested that a map delineating the cease-fire line on the Egyptian side be sent to Israel as soon as possible." Cairo's failure to do so, Dayan asserted, "could be interpreted only as Egypt's failure to properly respect the cease-fire established by the UN Security Council."

Bull was reported July 30 to have modified his proposal for a ban on navigation by suggesting in a letter to Dayan that Egypt and Israel suspend the operation of small boats in the Canal for one month. Despite a lack of agreement then on the navigation issue, Israeli and Egyptian patrol boats were reported to be operating close to their respective sides of the Canal and avoiding provocative actions.

The Egyptian economy was damaged not only by the closing of the Canal but also by the capture or near-total destruction of the army's war matériel. Many Egyptian observers expressed fear that the expense of reequipping the army would seriously cut into the country's next 2 development budgets. (Egypt was in the middle of its 2d 5-year plan.)

Nasser appealed to the Egyptian people July 23 for total mobilization to cope with the economic hardships resulting from the military defeat. Speaking to a Cairo University gathering of 5,000 persons marking the 15th anniversary of the overthrow of King Farouk, Nasser declared that he was reequipping and revamping Egypt's armed forces to continue the struggle against Israel. He urged all Egyptians to enlist in what he called the "people's resistance organization." Alluding to the U.S.' military efforts in Vietnam, Nasser asserted: "The military struggle [in the Middle East] will have to be fought not only by the armed forces but by the whole nation. We are not inferior to the people of Vietnam." Nasser insisted that the UAR never had considered attacking Israel for fear of U.S. military reprisals. But the UAR leader charged that the U.S., aware of Israeli plans to launch a military strike against the UAR, had lulled Cairo into believing that a peaceful solution was possible until the moment war had erupted June 5. Nasser claimed that the acquisition of Arab territory was only part of Israel's military objectives; that its true goal in the June 5–10 war was to crush Arab socialism. Nasser said: "We shall never surrender and shall not accept any peace that means surrender. We shall preserve the rights of the Palestine people."

Egyptian Jews & Gazene Arabs Mistreated?

In the aftermath of the June 1967 conflict, Israel accused Egypt of abusing the Jewish minority in Egypt, while Egypt complained that the new Israeli military occupiers of Gaza were persecuting the Arab population there.

Zacharias Schuster, European director of the American Jewish Committee, reported in Geneva June 13 that 600 Jews had been arrested in Egypt. 300 were said to be imprisoned in Barrag, near Alexandria, and 300 others in a prison near Cairo. Among those seized, according to Schuster, were Jacques Nefoussi, grand rabbi of Cairo, and Chaim Douek, grand rabbi of Alexandria. A spokesman for the Joint Distribution Committee, a Jewish overseas aid organization, said all the imprisoned Jews were men under 50 years of age. They had been required to register with the police in May and were arrested when fighting broke out June 5. Schuster said many of the Jews had been beaten. (Schuster said that several Jews had been killed in Libya the previous week and that many Jewish-owned shops there had been burned by rioting mobs.)

The reports of widespread arrests of Jews in Egypt were confirmed by a London *Times* correspondent in Cyprus June 14. Egyptian Jews who had acquired Italian citizenship were permitted to leave the UAR. 43 of a group of 54 that arrived in Naples, Italy June 11 had been imprisoned by the Egyptians. The refugees were among 691 Italians and other foreign nationals who had left Alexandria on an Italian ship June 8.

By late 1968 most of the Jewish community of Egypt had emigrated. The paris office of the American Jewish Committee reported Oct. 5, 1968 that Cario had barred the departure of Egypt's remaining 1,000 Jews. Of this number, 223 to 240 Jewish men remained in 2 jails in Abu Zabaal and Turah (near Cairo) in which they had been imprisoned since the June 1967 war with no charges against them, the committee said. The UAR's Jewish population had totaled 2,500 before the 1967 war and 80,000 before the emergence of Israel.

Meanwhile, observers reported sharp resistance to the

Israeli occupation of the Gaza Strip. This tiny parcel of land had been administered by Egypt before the June war and was populated mainly by Palestinian refugees. In a message to UN Secy. Gen. U Thant (reported June 25, 1967), UAR Foreign Min. Mahmoud Riad claimed that Israel was ejecting Palestinian refugees from the Gaza Strip and that 2,402 had been driven out between June 19 and 24. Riad urged action to curb the expulsions. (It had been reported in the *Jerusalem Post* June 22 that Israel planned—merely for economic reasons and without regard to any eventual territorial adjustments—to resettle thousands of Palestinian refugees quartered before the war in the Gaza Strip and on the west bank of the Jordan River.)

Israel repatriated to the UAR Aug. 3, 1967 about 350 Egyptain women, children and men under 18 or over 50 from the Gaza Strip. Most of them were members of the families of Egyptian administrative officials or teachers there. They went home after weeks of protracted negotiations in which the International Red Cross served as intermediary.

It was reported Aug. 29 that Israel had decided to allow Gaza Strip residents to cross Israel freely to Jordan's Israeli-occupied West Bank area. Palestinian Arab refugees from the Gaza Strip soon began pouring into occupied Jordan in quest of relatives unseen for 18 years.

UN Assembly Finds No Solutions

The UN General Assembly convened an emergency special session on the Middle East June 17, 1967 but voted July 21 to adjourn "temporarily," returning discussion of the Arab-Israeli crisis to the Security Council for its "consideration." The Assembly adjourned without having taken effective measures to deal with the problems arising from the June war. The UN Security Council had met on the crisis during most of the period May 24–June 14; it was the Council's failure to adopt a Soviet resolution condemning Israel as an aggressor and demanding its withdrawal from Arab territories that had led the USSR to request the emergency Assembly session.

The Assembly's inability to approve a substantive resolution dealing with the crisis was viewed as a defeat for the Soviet Union, which had proposed the session in an effort to help the Arab states regain diplomatically what they had lost militarily. As the Assembly voted July 21 to send the issue back to the Security Council, Arab shouts of "betrayal" and "failure" were heard in the Assembly chamber. The Assembly had met and recessed July 17, then had reconvened July 20 and voted immediately to postpone the discussion for 24 hours. Finnish delegate Max Jakobson had proposed the adjournment because of "information" indicating that behind-the-scenes negotiations might succeed in working out a compromise resolution acceptable to most delegations. Jakobson's proposal was adopted without a dissenting vote. The adjournment resolution was presented to the Assembly July 21 by Sweden, Finland and Austria after it had become clear that no compromise was possible.

In the debate after the adoption of the adjournment resolution, Soviet Foreign Min. Andrei A. Gromyko charged July 21 that the Assembly had been unable to act because of the U.S.' "spirit of hostility toward the Arab states." He also charged that the U.S. had put "rude pressure" on the Latin American countries to assure the defeat of resolutions condemning Israel for alleged aggression and demanding the unconditional withdrawal of its forces. In reply, U.S. Amb. Arthur J. Goldberg declared that Gromyko knew "more than anyone in this hall" that the U.S. had "made ever effort even at the last minute . . . to arrive at a meeting of minds" on a compromise resolution that might have been expected to win acceptance. Goldberg pledged U.S. aid to the Middle East; he specifically pledged that the U.S. would attempt to assure "that the great promise of peaceful nuclear energy is applied to the problems of critical importance to the Near East—the desalting of water, the irrigation of arid deserts."

Israeli Foreign Min. Abba Eban declared: "Israel stands ready to negotiate a peace settlement with Egypt, with Jordan, with Syria and with Lebanon. All parties are free to present and examine any claims of proposals in an effort to reach mutual agreement."

Iraqi Foreign Min. Adnan Pachachi asserted that the adjournment was "an admission of failure, an abdication of responsibility and an acknowledgement of hopelessness." He reminded the Assembly that the adjournment was temporary and declared that denunciations of Israel could be expected to be heard as long as Israeli forces continued to occupy Arab territory. Algerian Foreign Min. Abdel Aziz Boutefika deplored the failure of the "3d world" countries to join forces in condemning Israeli aggression and demanding the unconditional withdrawal of its forces. He asserted that the underdeveloped countries had shown "lamentable" division on the question.

Albanian delegate Halim Budo termed referral of the issue to the Security Council "a dangerous omen for the future of this organization." He accused the Soviet Union of "collusion" with the "malicious power" of the U.S. in blocking effective Assembly action.

These developments were reported prior to adjournment of the Assembly July 21:

• In a letter July 17 (reported July 18) to Security Council Pres. Endalkachew Makonnen of Ethiopia, Soviet Foreign Min. Gromyko demanded the immediate withdrawal of Israeli forces from Arab lands "in order to prevent further military clashes and to eliminate the danger of a renewed war in the middle east. . . ." Israel's continued occupation of Arab territory, Gromyko charged, was a "flagrant violation" of the UN Charter and an "infringement of the sovereignty and territorial integrity" of Arab states. Gromyko warned that recent clashes along the Suez Canal cease-fire line, "provoked by Israel," were "extremely dangerous and could develop into a wider military conflict."

• In reply to Gromyko's letter, Israeli delegate Gideon Rafael filed a letter with Makonnen July 19. Rafael wrote that "an integral and inseparable link exists between the withdrawal and disengagement of forces, and the establishment of normal, peaceful and good neighborly relations between the states of the region." The letter declared that the withdrawal of Israeli forces without "simultaneous and parallel" action by the Arab states toward establishing peace would lead "to a renewed Arab assault on Israel at a date and in circumstances more favorable to the Arab aim of destroying Israel's independence." However, the letter continued, "conditions are ripe for the Middle Eastern states to reach agreements for the establishment of peaceful conditions free from external intervention and from the effects of great power rivalries." The letter asserted that there was no "factual basis" for the Soviet charge that Israel had violated the cease-fire. It declared that Gromyko had taken "unilateral and unconfirmed statements by the United Arab Republic" as the whole truth while "totally ignoring" the complaints Israel had raised against Egypt. A July 17 note from UAR delegate Muhammad Awad el-Kony to UN Secy. Gen. U Thant contained "a clear admission" that UAR forces had committed "grave violations" of the cease-fire, Rafael's letter stated.

• It was reported July 18 that Latin American delegates had revised a resolution they had drafted in the hope of gaining the ⅔ majority necessary for its adoption. According to the *N.Y. Times*, the amended text (a) affirmed the principle that the conquest of territory by force was unacceptable under the UN Charter and that consequently the withdrawal of Israeli forces "is expected," (b) affirmed the principles of the political sovereignty and territorial independence of UN members and of their right to be free from the threat of war, and consequently declared that the end of a state of war by all states in the Middle East "is expected," (c) called on the Security Council to continue examining all aspects of the situation and to develop solutions, particularly with respect to the refugee problem and free transit through international waterways. The draft was not presented to the Assembly, however, because the Latin delegates had ascertained in their talks with other delegations that it would not win a $2/3$ majority.

• From July 17 to July 21, the Soviet Union had attempted to develop a compromise resolution acceptable both to the U.S. and to the Arab states. Soviet Amb.-to-U.S. Anatoly F. Dobrynin had met with U.S. delegate Goldberg July 17, and further meetings were held with Goldberg during the week by Dobrynin and Gromyko. It was reported July 21 that the U.S. and Soviet Union had reached fairly close agreement on a Soviet draft based on a passage in a speech Soviet Premier Aleksei N. Kosygin had delivered June 19 to the Assembly. Kosygin had asserted that "every people enjoys the right to establish an independent national state of its own." The draft reportedly called for the withdrawal of Israeli forces to the positions they held prior to the outbreak of fighting June 5 but also reportedly asked the Arab states to end their state of belligerency with Israel. The Soviets did not present the draft to the Assembly, however, because of violent opposition to it by the Arab states, particularly Egypt, Iraq, Syria, Algerian and Sudan.

On his departure of Moscow July 22, Gromyko declared in an airport statement that the withdrawal of Israeli forces remained the "most immediate and most acute" question concerning the crisis in the Middle East. Assessing the General Assembly session, Gromyko said its positive side had been the fact that most delegations had "in one form or another condemned the aggressive actions of Israel." "The negative side," he said, was "that, mainly because of the position of the U.S. government, the General Assembly was not able at this stage to pass a recommendation for the immediate withdrawal of Israeli troops."

In a statement on his departure from New York July 22, Israeli Foreign Min. Eban said that "the solution cannot be found in parliamentary terms" but rather in the Arab states themselves. "The United Nations cannot solve problems for nations that do not want to solve them," he said, adding that the Arab states could not solve their problems "without contact with Israel."

Amer a Suicide After Coup Fails

UAR authorities in Cairo Aug. 25, 1967 arrested 50 top-ranking military and civilian officials accused of plotting a *coup d'état* against the Nasser government. Among those seized was the alleged leader of the plot, Marshal Abdel Hakim Amer, 47, former deputy supreme commander. Cairo reported Amer's suicide by poisoning Sept. 14.

Other alleged plotters arrested were ex-War Min. Shamseddin Badran, ex-Maj. Gen. Othaman Nasr, ex-Interior Min. Abbas Abdel Wahab Radwan and Salah Nasr, who was relieved of his post as head of the General Intelligence Department.

The first report of the alleged plot had emanated from Washington Aug. 29. It said about 150 officers had been arrested. The story of the conspiracy was confirmed Sept. 4 by the authoritative Egyptian newspaper *Al-Ahram.*

Amer and the other accused plotters were among military officers who had been dismissed or pensioned off by Nasser after the UAR's disastrous defeat by Israel in June. (400 to 500 officers were said to have been involved in Nasser's purge of the armed forces.) The principal objectives of the planned uprising were said to be the reinstatement of the dismissed officers and the thwarting of the government's scheduled investigation into the Egyptian armed forces' conduct of the war.

An account of the plot as described by *Al-Ahram* Sept. 13: Amer, Badran and the others had planned the coup in

Amer's Giza home. Under the plan, Amer was to fly to Suez Canal headquarters to take over the entire command facing Israeli troops on the east bank of the Canal. Amer was then to phone Nasser and demand that Nasser relinquish his additional post of supreme commander. If Nasser refused, "Amer himself would take command of the armored brigade [at the Canal] and move on Cairo."

According to Al-Ahram's earlier account of the plot, reported Sept. 4, Nasser had been aware of the conspiracy and had urged Amer to abandon his plans. When Amer refused, Nasser decided to end "this long nerve-racking wait" and smash the plot, the newspaper declared. Al-Ahram said that Amer and the others had gone Aug. 27 to armed forces headquarters in Cairo, where Amer produced a forged presidential decree. The document called for turning the supreme command over to Amer. The field marshal, according to the newspaper, then issued an ultimatum demanding that Nasser turn over the command to Amer and halt inquiries into the conduct of the war.

According to Cairo's account of Amer's death: Government authorities came Sept. 13 to Amer's home, where he had been placed under house arrest Aug. 25, to question him about the plot. But Amer slipped into his bedroom and swallowed "poisonous material." Amer recovered enough to be taken to another house, where he was placed under a doctor's care. The following day, Sept. 14, Amer was found on the bathroom floor after having taken more poison, which he had taped to his body. He was taken to the armed forces hospital in Cairo, and he died later Sept. 14 of "a large quantity of narcotic poisoning."

Al-Ahram reported Sept. 16 that Amer had attempted to kill himself 4 times in recent months. The first attempt had been made June 9, after Egyptian forces had been routed by the Israeli army, Al-Ahram said. Nasser, the newspaper disclosed, had then stayed by Amer's side through the night to comfort him. According to testimony released in Cairo Oct. 11, Amer had last tried to take his own life 3 weeks before his death. (The testimony was that of one of Pres. Nasser's younger brothers, Air Force Maj. Hussein Abdel Nasser; it was published in *Al-Ahram* along with the testimony of 34 other witnesses.)

Amer had been one of Nasser's oldest friends. Nasser often addressed him by the nickname "Abdu" and, more jocularly, "Robinson." Amer sometimes called Nasser "Jimmy." Amer played an important role in the 1952 coup that overthrew King Farouk and ultimately brought Nasser to power. Several years after the 1952 coup Amer, at the age of 38, was appointed Egypt's military commander-in-chief with the rank of field marshal. He served as first vice president of the Egyptian Republic and was known for his intense loyalty to Nasser. In 1959, during the formation of the Syro-Egyptian union, he received full powers in Syria. Observors have said that Amer had vigorously opposed Nasser's challenge to Israel in late May and early June. Amer apparently had believed that, should Nasser's bluff be called, the Egyptian army was too ill-prepared and outnumbered to face an all-out war with Israel. Many younger officers, among them members of the Moslem Brotherhood or sympathizers of the brotherhood, apparently had agreed with Amer.

Al-Ahram Sept. 16 payed this editorial tribute to Amer: "The latest events cannot erase the role played by . . . Amer in the service of the nation and the long years of struggle together with his friend and brother Gamal Abdel Nasser." Amer "was worth a thousand times more than most of those surrounding him. . . . The adventure in which Marshal Amer engaged recently could be considered by some psychiatrists as another form of suicide."

The following points were made by the *Egyptian Gazette*'s Cairo correspondent: Amer's suicide "is not likely to have an adverse effect on Egypt's reputation in the Arab world at

large, but within Egypt, it probably will have adverse consequences. In the other Arab countries the event is seen as a
personal tragedy—perhaps more for Pres. Nasser than for the
deceased—but for some time popular feeling about . . . Amer,
who suffered a string of defeats as much in the political as in
the military field, has been that if he was not incompetent he
was at least very unlucky. It was also widely known that he
had been addicted to drugs and that his private life, to put it
mildly, was not above reproach. Indeed, some puzzlement
was felt at the long continuance of the incongruous friendship between the calm, shrewd, puritanical Pres. Nasser and
his tense, unpredictable military colleague. However, to the
man on the street, Amer continued to be one of the original
heroes of the revolution which overthrew King Farouk. The
news of his attempted coup and now of his suicide will
produce bewilderment and some disillusionment. More important is the repercussions it is bound to have in the armed
forces. Having been the military chief for 15 years, there are
a number of officers who have feelings of personal loyalty to
him, despite his professional incompetence. It is their dis-
gruntlement, added to that of the 600 officers who were
sacked. after the June defeat, that could prove dangerous in
the next few months."

Salah Nasr, ex-director of the intelligence service, was
named early in Oct. 1967 as one of the alleged participants in
the plot: Under house detention since the smashing of the
conspiracy, he was arrested Oct. 4. *Al-Ahram* reported Oct.
5 that Nasr had been arrested for possible connection with
Amer's suicide. According to reports, Nasr had ordered the
poison tablets that Amer had used to take his life. But
official Egyptian spokesmen said Oct. 18 that all investigation
into the circumstances of Amer's death had been shelved.
Prosecutor-General Muhammad Abdel Salem announced that
the evidence showed conclusively that the field marshal had
committed suicide.

(A UAR government source had reported Sept. 19 that 181 military officers and civilians had been arrested for security reasons since the outbreak of the war in June. Among those seized were the 50 officers and civilians who had been arrested Aug. 25 for alleged involvement in Amer's plot. The total arrest figures were said to have been submitted to Nasser at a cabinet meeting Sept. 17. The release of the total Sept. 19 was aimed at refuting a *N.Y. Daily News* report Sept. 15 that 70,000 Egyptians had been arrested by security police since the end of the war and that arrests were taking place at the rate of 1,000 a day. *Al-Ahram* Sept. 19 assailed the *Daily News* report as "seditious and ferocious propaganda against the UAR.")

A revolutionary tribunal Aug. 26, 1968 handed down life sentences against Salah Nasr, ex-War Min. Shamseddin Badran, ex-Interior Min. Abbas Abdel Wahab Radwan, Maj. Gen. Othaman Nasr (a former army divisional commander) and Lt. Col. Galal el-Haridy, ex-commander of the army shock troops school, for their parts in the plot to overthrow Nasser. 2 other officers—Lt. Col. Ahmed Abdullah of the army's shock troops and Flight Col. Tahsin Zaki, a former air-base commander—received sentences to 15 years at hard labor for their roles in the Amer *putsch.*

These 7 alleged ringleaders had been indicted in Oct. 1967. They also were charged with having converted Amer's home into an arsenal in which they cached a great deal of arms and ammunition in preparation for the putsch. The court imposed sentences varying from 10 years at hard labor to one year in prison on 30 other defendants, ordered 3 others dismissed from military service and acquitted 14 persons.

In a separate trial before Deputy Premier Hussein el-Shafei, Salah Nasr received an additional sentence of 15 years at hard labor for "deviations" in official conduct—indecency, blackmail and torture—and, together with Radwan, was ordered to repay $23,900 in missing state funds given them by Amer for safekeeping.

Arab Summit Meetings

Leaders of the UAR and 12 other Arab states attended a conference in Khartoum, Sudan, Aug. 29–Sept. 3, 1967 for the purpose of formulating a joint policy against Israel.

The conference had been arranged at meetings of the states' foreign ministers in Khartoum Aug. 1–5 and Aug. 27–28. The foreign ministers had met in Kuwait June 17–18 to elaborate a joint political strategy with which to counter the Arabs' military defeat.

The Kuwait conference's final statement, issued by Kuwaiti Foreign Min. Sheik Sabah al-Ahmed al-Jaber, had made no mention of any definitive Arab joint policy but had merely condemned "Israeli aggression" against the Arab states. In a speech opening the conference, Jaber had said that the "deep hurt" inflicted by Israel "requires us to start a new era in Arab relations, an era of solidarity based on absolute confidence in each other." Jaber charged that Israel sought to use its occupation of Arab territories "as a means for bargaining a solution that guarantees [the] aggressors permanent settlement in our homeland." A Kuwaiti official informed the conferees that Kuwait, which had suspended oil shipments June 6, had resumed them June 8, "except to Britain and the U.S." (Saudi Arabia had announced June 15 that it was resuming oil exports but not to "countries which backed Israel.") Algerian Foreign Min. Abdel Aziz Bouteflika told the conferees that at a meeting with Soviet officials in Moscow June 12–13, he and Algerian Pres. Houari Boumedienne had been given a "firm commitment" by the USSR to assist "in wiping out the traces of aggression."

Several other strategy meetings of Arab leaders were held after the Kuwait session and prior to the Khartoum conference. Jordanian King Hussein had conferred with Nasser and Boumedienne in Cairo July 10–11. The king reportedly had urged an Arab summit conference. Boumedienne flew to Damascus later July 11 and conferred with Pres. Nureddin al-Attassi and other Syrian leaders. In a speech broadcast over Damascus radio, Boumedienne urged Syria to press its "fight against Zionism and America." He vowed that Algeria would join "in the forefront of coming battles" against Israel.

A 2-day strategy conference was held in Cairo July 15–16, 1967 by the presidents of 5 Arab states. A communiqué issued at the conclusion of the meeting announced joint agreement on "the necessary effective steps to eliminate the consequences of imperialist Israeli agression in the Arab homeland." The statement was signed by Presidents Nasser of the UAR, Boumedienne of Algeria, Attassi of Syria, Abdel Rahman Arif of Iraq and Ismail el-Azhari of Sudan. The communiqué warned that the Arab states would reconsider their relations with all countries suspected of aiding Israel. The conferees accepted Azhari's suggestion that Arab foreign ministers meet in Khartoum, Sudan, to pave the way for a summit meeting of Arab heads of state. *Al-Ahram* of Cairo had reported June 12 that Sudan had won Nasser's agreement in principle to attend a summit meeting of Arab heads of state to consider possible political action aimed at nullifying Israel's military gains.)

Boumedienne and Arif left Cairo for Moscow and conferred there July 18 with Soviet Premier Aleksei N. Kosygin and Communist Party Gen. Secy. Leonid I. Brezhnev. A communiqué issued after the talks paralleled the language of the Cairo conference; it said the Moscow meeting had dealt with "ways of liquidating the aftermath of Israel's aggression." Boumedienne and Arif returned to Cairo July 19 to brief Nasser on their meeting with the Soviet leaders.

The conferees at the Khartoum summit meeting adopted resolutions (a) pledging a continued nonmilitary struggle against Israel, (b) announcing the creation of an Arab fund to assist the war-ravaged economies of Jordan and the UAR, (c) lifting the Arab oil boycott against the West and (d) announcing a UAR-Saudi Arabian agreement designed to end the Yemeni civil war.

The anti-Israel resolution, adopted at the conclusion of the formal leaders' talks Sept. 1, stated that the conferees had "agreed to unified efforts at international and diplomatic levels to eliminate the consequences of aggression and to assure the withdrawal of the aggressor forces of Israel from Arab lands, but within the limits to which Arab states are committed: No peace with Israel, no negotiations with Israel, no recognition of Israel and maintenance of the rights of Palestinian people in their nation." It was disclosed that Nasser had said at a closed-door meeting that Egypt was willing to fight Israel but could do so only if financed by the other Arab states. He was reported to have warned that without such Arab aid, a political solution would have to be found. He was quoted as saying: "Surrender [to Israel] is out of the question, but to carry on the struggle involves certain responsibilities, military, political and economic. The question is: Are we ready to shoulder these responsibilities? That is what we must agree on."

The proposed Arab fund, agreed to at the Aug. 31 session, was to provide £95 million ($266 million) to the UAR and £40 million ($110 million) to Jordan.

With regard to the oil embargo, the Khartoum conferees agreed in principle Aug. 31 to permit each Arab state to decide independently how it would act on the recommendations made by Arab finance and petroleum ministers at an Aug. 15–19 meeting in Baghdad. This agreement, in effect, allowed the lifting of the oil embargoes that had been imposed against the U.S. and Britain in retaliation for their alleged military assistance to Israel in the June war. (Saudi Arabia announced Sept. 2 that it had ended tis oil embargo and that it would start pumping oil "to all countries without exception." The Algerian Foreign Ministry said Sept. 2 that Algeria would continue to bar the shipment of oil and gas to the U.S. and Britain. Kuwait decided Sept. 3 to resume oil shipments to Britain, the U.S. and other countries boycotted since the start of the Arab-Israeli war.)

The agreement on Yemen had been negotiated Aug. 31 by Nasser and Saudi Arabian King Faisal at the residence of Sudanese Premier Muhammad Ahmed Mahgoub. Mahgoub announced at the conclusion of the Nasser-Faisal talks that the agreement called for the formation of a 3-country committee to supervise the withdrawal from Yemen of Egyptian troops who had been fighting on the side of republican forces since late in 1962. The committee was composed of Iraq (chosen by the UAR), Morocco (chosen by Saudi Arabia) and the Sudan. The committee was to consult the UAR and Saudi Arabian governments "on all matters impeding implementation" of the original cease-fire plan that had been negotiated at Jidda, Saudi Arabia in 1965 by Nasser and Faisal. Unlike the Jidda agreement, the new proposal made no mention of a plebiscite to determine the type of regime that should govern Yemen. In order to overcome the objections of Yemeni Pres. Abdel (Abdullah) al-Salal, the new plan did not set a time limit for the withdrawal of the Egyptian troops.

Salal, who represented his country at the Khartoum conference, denounced the UAR-Saudi Arabian agreement Aug. 31. He said that it constituted "interference in our internal affairs" and that it was an "illogical revival of a rejected document [the Jidda agreement] to which Yemen was never a party." Salal also rejected "plans and good offices that detract from our revolutionary gains." Like the Jidda agreement, Salal said, the latest UAR-Saudi Arabian proposal was not "in any way binding on the Yemeni republic, because Yemen is not a party to its resolutions."

Only 8 heads of state of the 13 Arab countries attended the Khartoum conference. Algerian Pres. Boumedienne and Syrian Pres. Attassi, who opposed compromise on Israel, boycotted the meetings. Boumedienne was represented by Foreign Min. Bouteflika. Syrian Foreign Min. Ibrahim Makhos had attended the Aug. 27–28 foreign ministers meeting, but he and the entire Syrian delegation boycotted the formal conference after the ministers rejected Syrian demands

for a specific agreement on action to "remove the consequences of Israeli aggression." The Syrian government newspaper *Al Thawra* Sept. 2 assailed the Khartoum conference
resolutions on the ground that they would "consolidate rather
than eliminate Israeli aggression."

The heads of state who attended the conference were
Kings Faisal of Saudi Arabia and Hussein of Jordan, Presidents
Nasser of the UAR, Salal of Yemen, Abdel Rahman Arif of
Iraq, Charles Hélou of Lebanon and Ismail el-Azhari of Sudan
and Emir Sabah al-Salam as-Sabah of Kuwait. Crown Prince
Hassan el Ridha of Libya represented King Idris.

Tunisian Pres. Habib Bourguiba, whose country boycotted
the Khartoum conference, had already reiterated his plea for
an end to the Arab countries' state of belligerency against
Israel. Speaking Aug. 23 to leaders of the Tunisian Students
Union, Bourguiba had described the Arab position as a "dead-
end policy." He declared: "Policies adopted hitherto have
deprived [the Arabs] of all sympathies. . . . The state of
Israel has been recognized by both the United States and the
Soviet Union. . . . Its existence is challenged only by the
Arab countries. In these circumstances it is useless to continue ignoring the reality and claim to wipe Israel off the
map. In so doing, one drives himself into near-isolation."
The June war was started, Bourguiba asserted, because,
"deliberately and without weighing well the risks, steps had
been taken to bar Israel from access to the Gulf of Aqaba."
He noted that until then "Israel was satisfied with its
frontiers."

Israeli Premier Levi Eshkol declared Sept. 3 that the
Khartoum conference decision against recognizing Israel was
"against the real interests of the people of the region and is
against the principles" of the UN Charter. Eshkol said: "We
also have noted the security and political implications of
these resolutions" adopted at the Arab parley; "they make
the prospects for peace in our region dimmer"; "in contrast
to the aggressive intentions of the Arab heads of state, we

will stand stanchly in the positions vital to the security and undisturbed development of Israel." Israeli Foreign Min. Abba Eban said Sept. 5 that Israel had detected no signs of moderation in the resolutions adopted in Khartoum. He asserted: "The Arab leaders . . . voted in favor of immobility. Their decision strengthened Israel's need and right to maintain her present position until a new situation is negotiated between herself and her neighbors."

Eshkol visited Israeli positions on the east bank of the Suez Canal Sept. 6. Later Eshkol toured an Israeli base in the Sinai desert and told troops: "When I stood on the bank of the Suez, I said to myself, here I stand, not far from the ruler of Egypt. If I could talk to him as premier of Israel to the president of Egypt, I would propose that we seek the way to an understanding. But the summit conference at Khartoum determined irresponsibly that there is to be no peace with Israel. If Khartoum is their proclaimed position, our reply is, 'We are here.' "

Fighting Renewed in Canal Zone

Despite the stationing of UN Truce Supervisory Organization (UNTSO) observers along the Suez Canal, Israeli and Egyptian ground and air forces continued to fight in the vicinity of the waterway. The clashes were particularly intense between Aug. 26 and Sept. 21, 1967. *Among reports of major actions:*

● An Israeli army spokesman reported that Israeli anti-aircraft guns Aug. 26 had shot down an Egyptian Soviet-built Sukhoi-7 fighter-bomber in the Sinai Peninsula at Bir Gifgafa, about 50 miles east of the Canal. Israeli and Egyptian troops later August 26 engaged in a one-hour exchange of gunfire along the Canal after UAR troops opened fire on an Israeli position opposite Ismailia.

● Israeli and UAR forces Sept. 4 fought their most serious clash since the June war across the Canal just north of the Gulf of Suez. One Israeli soldier was killed and an Egyptian boat was sunk in 8 hours of sporadic shelling that was halted by the intervention of UNTSO observers.

According to the Israeli report of the incident: UAR guns near the west bank town of Suez had opened up on an Israeli torpedo boat and and a landing craft that were cruising south of Israeli-held Bûr (Port) Tewfiq, on the Gulf of Suez. Israeli guns returned the fire, which lasted for an hour. The Egyptian shelling resumed an hour later and was stopped by the first of 3 UN-arranged truces. UAR artillery resumed firing 5 minutes later on Port Tewfiq and from another gun position 4 miles to the north. UNTSO observers arranged a cease-fire, but UAR guns opened up again ½ hour later. Egyptian antiaircraft at the same time fired at an Israeli army helicopter over Port Tewfiq, but the plane was not hit. Before the 3d and final cease-fire, Israeli guns sank the Egyptian torpedo boat near the west bank of the Gulf of Suez.

Egyptian authorities contended that the Israelis had provoked the fighting by attempting to enter the Canal with "an armed launch, a trawler and carrier" in defiance of a UN agreement that barred military activity in the Canal. But Egypt was accused by the UNTSO of instigating the clashes. In a report filed with the UN in New York Sept. 6, Lt. Gen. Odd Bull, UNTSO commander, said that after Egyptian forces had opened fire on an Israeli motorboat about 2 miles south of Port Tewfiq, "the incident accelerated rapidly into an exchange of fire where tanks and mortars were used by both sides."

● An Israeli communiqué Sept. 20 claimed that Israeli tank shelling that day had sunk 3 Egyptian troop-carrying boats in the Canal less than one mile from the southern end of the waterway near Israeli-held Port Tewfiq. Israel charged that the presence of the UAR craft was in violation of the Egyptian-Israeli agreement that banned small-craft navigation in the waterway. (The agreement, negotiated early in August under UN auspices, first barred Israeli and UAR ships from the canal for one month. When renewed Aug. 27, the agreement imposed the ban for an indefinite period.)

Israel's account of the incident: Israeli tanks opened fire after spotting 6 Egyptian boats, carrying 8 to 15 soldiers each, which had left a breakwater on the west bank and were heading toward the east-bank town of Port Ibrahim. 2 of the boats were hit and sunk. Israeli machinegun and tank fire was directed 2½ hours later against 2 other Egyptian ships allegedly making their way out of the same area. One ship was sunk and the other was driven off. An official Egyptian letter delivered to the UN Security Council Sept. 6 asserted that Egyptian forces had fired in self-defense when 2 Israeli motorboats and a tug had forcibly sought to enter the Canal from the Gulf of Suez. Cairo claimed that the Israeli shelling that followed had destroyed Port Tewfiq and killed 42 civilians and wounded 161 persons in the city. A subsequent Egyptian report said that the casualties totaled 44 dead and 172 wounded.

● Cairo reported Sept. 6 that Egyptian positions had been fired on Sept. 5 by Israeli guns at the Israeli base at El Tina, south of Port Said.

The UAR communiqué reported no Egyptain casualties in the ½-hour exchange.

• In another Suez Canal clash, reported by the Israelis, Egyptians in the west bank town of Ismailia Sept. 6 fired on Israeli positions on the east bank with machineguns, heavy mortars and artillery. The Israelis replied with similar fire, and the fighting was ended 2 hours later by UNTSO observers. Firing broke out again around Ismailia Sept. 7.

• Israeli and Egyptian forces exchanged fire Sept. 12–13 in the vicinity of the Israli-held east-bank part of El Qantara. Tel Aviv said Israeli troops opened fire on Egyptian forces on the west bank Sept. 12 after UAR antiaircraft guns fired at an Israeli jet. Israeli authorities reported that in the 2-hour exchange an Egyptian artillery battery was set afire and an Egyptian tank destroyed. The report said Egyptian fire damaged UNTSO observers' cars, a church and a mosque in El Qantara. The Egyptian high command claimed that UAR antiaircraft fire had shot down an Israeli jet at El Qantara. Israel claimed that the Sept. 13 fighting had started when Egyptian machineguns opened fire on an Israeli patrol along the east bank of the Canal about 5 miles north of El Qantara.

A UAR Foreign Ministry statement Sept. 20 asserted that no Egyptian ships had been sunk in the Canal and that "our armed forces had [made] no embarkations."

• Israel charged that Egyptian tank shelling and machinegun fire from the west-bank part of El Qantara Sept. 21 had killed 4 Israelis and wounded 6 in the Israeli-occupied part of the town on the east bank. Israeli guns retuned the fire. The one-hour exchange was halted after 2 cease-fire agreements were arranged by UNTSO observers in El Qantara. The Egyptian newspaper *Al-Ahram* reported Sept. 22 that 23 Israelis had been killed in the Qantara shellings. An Egyptian spokesman in Cairo reported Sept. 23 that 2 civilians had been killed and 12 wounded in the Qantara clash. 3 UAR soldiers were said to have been slain and 7 wounded.

On instructions from UN Secy. Gen. U Thant, Lt. Gen. Odd Bull, UNTSO commander, arrived in Cairo Sept. 22 from Norway to investigate the Sept. 20 and 21 Suez Canal clashes. Bull conferred Sept. 23 with UAR Foreign Affairs Undersecy. Salah Gohar and UNTSO observers.

• Israeli and Egyptian forces exchanged machinegun fire in the Ismailia sector Sept. 27. The fighting quickly spread along the entire length of the Canal from El Qantara to Suez. An Israeli communiqué said 14 persons had been killed on the east bank during the ensuing 9-hour tank and artillery duel. 10 of those slain were said to be civilians. UNTSO observers had made 6 attempts to halt the fighting. Ismailia Gov. Mobarik Rifai charged Sept. 27 that the Israelis had shelled

Ismailia for 7 hours that day and had killed 36 civilians and seriously injured 85. A Cairo communiqué confirmed the heavy firing along the Canal and asserted that Israeli troops and equipment had suffered heavy losses. Reporters in Ismailia reported heavy damage to the city.

The fresh outbreak of fighting along the Canal was reported Oct. 2 to have spurred the further evacuation of civilians from the city of Suez. 60,000 of the city's 250,000 inhabitants had left previously. Civilians were being evacuated also from Ismailia. The UAR government Oct. 4 announced plans for providing food and shelter for evacuees fleeing Suez and Ismailia, and $100,000 was made available to help evacuees resettle in rural provinces away from the Canal. The government said that more than 150 civilians had been killed and at least 500 wounded in mortar and artillery shelling that had started along the Canal July 14. The seriousness of the situation had been pointed up by the appointment Sept. 30 of Vice Pres. Aly Sabry as resident minister for the Suez Canal Zone.

In one of the most violent post-war clashes, missiles fired from UAR naval craft Oct. 21, 1967 sank the 2,300-ton Israeli destroyer *Eilat* off the northern coast of the Sinai Peninsula. 47 Israeli sailors lost their lives, and 91 were wounded. The sinking of the *Eilat* was followed by Israeli shelling of Egypt's major oil installations at Suez Oct. 24 during a 3-hour artillery exchange across the southern end of the Suez Canal. The 2 incidents led to the convening of an emergency meeting of the UN Security Council in New York Oct. 24 to prevent a possible renewal of large-scale warfare.

The Israeli version of the Oct. 21 naval incident was provided Oct. 22 by Commodore Shlomo Erel, naval commander. Erel said: The *Eilat* was on routine patrol in international waters and was 13½ miles off UAR-held Port Said when it was hit amidships by a missile. A few minutes later a 2d missile struck the engine room, and 1½ hours later a 3d rocket smashed into the burning destroyer and sank it. A 4th missile exploded in the water a few minutes later and caused more casualties. 19 Israeli sailors were killed in the attack, and 28 were reported missing and presumed dead. 155 crew members were rescued.

Erel said the rockets had been fired from Soviet-made missile patrol boats of the *Komar* class believed to have been positioned inside Port Said. He said the rockets were Russian, "the most advanced type," but he expressed doubt that they had been fired by Russians. Israeli military leaders said this might have been the first time sea-to-sea missiles were used in combat.

Israeli Premier Levi Eshkol charged in a nationwide address Oct. 22 that the Egyptian attack on the *Eilat* was unprovoked and was a violation of international navigation laws and of the truce agreement. Israeli Defense Min. Moshe Dayan asserted Oct. 23 that UAR Pres. Nasser had "renewed hostilities" with Israel by sinking the *Eilat*. Dayan held that "there was only one reason" for the attack: "the desire to renew hostilities exactly as they existed 5 months ago," when Egypt closed the Strait of Tiran to Israeli shipping.

The Egyptian newspaper *Al-Ahram* had reported Oct. 22 that the *Eilat* had been "hit and sunk by 2 Egyptian rocket-launching vessels that surprised the Israeli destroyer while trying to enter Egyptian territorial waters northwest of Port Said." (In a speech to the National Assembly Nov. 23, Nasser said that Egypt would not permit Israeli navigation in the Suez Canal: "We must not be provoked by the enemy before the time is propitious. We must choose the time and place. The naval battle off Port Said shows what we can do. Our missile craft were able to destroy an Israeli warship with the most up-to-date equipment.")

In Washington Oct. 23 U.S. officials identified the missile used as the Soviet-made ship-to-ship type called the Styx by the Western allies. The Styx, about 20 feet long and shaped like an airplane, traveled at subsonic speed, was equipped with a 1,000-pound high-explosive warhead and had a range of 20 to 25 miles. The Egyptians had acquired the missiles in

1962 when the Soviet Union gave Cairo 3 *Komar*-class guided-missile vessels. The 75-ton attack vessel traveled at a top speed of 40 knots and carried 2 launchers for Styx missiles.

Israel reported Oct. 24 that its artillery had pounded the UAR Canal port city of Suez that day and destroyed about 80% of Egypt's oil-refining capacity there. The announcement said that during a 3-hour artillery duel across the southern end of the Canal, Israeli guns had set ablaze fuel tanks and 2 refineries. The tanks had a capacity of 590,000 tons and the refineries had a combined annual production of 5 million tons, although it was believed the plant had not been operating at capacity. The plant at Alexandria became Egypt's only intact oil installation. The Israeli communiqué said that the fighting had started when UAR artillery north of Port Tewfiq, just south of Suez, opened fire on Israeli units on the eastern bank of the Canal. The communiqué added: Israeli forces "returned the fire." One Israeli soldier was reported slightly wounded. The firing stopped 3 hours after a cease-fire call issued by UN observers.

A UAR communiqué accused the Israelis of starting the Suez shooting. It said that "the enemy lost heavily in arms and men": one Israeli jet was downed, and 10 Israeli tanks, 4 armored cars and 5 rocket launchers were destroyed. (A Cairo report Oct. 25 said that 8 Egyptian civilians and 3 soldiers had been killed and 60 civilians and 32 soldiers wounded in the shelling.)

Soviets Rearm Egypt

The Soviet Union promised the defeated Arabs continued support against Israel, and Soviet weapons were soon en route to rearm Egypt and Syria. A statement supporting the Arab cause was issued June 22, 1967 by the Soviet Communist Party's Central Committee at the conclusion of a 2-day Moscow meeting on the Middle East. The statement said: "The most important task is to prevent the aggressor from taking advantage of the results of its perfidious action, to achieve an immediate unconditional withdrawal of the troops of the interventionists from the territories occupied by them behind the truce line, and the payment of indemnity to the United Arab Republic, Syria and Jordan for the damage inflicted by the aggressor."

The Yugoslav news agency Tanyug reported from Cairo June 23 that the UAR and the Soviet Union had signed a military agreement "of great importance." According to Tanyug, the agreement had been concluded June 22 following talks between the chief of the Soviet General Staff, Marshal Matvei Zakharov and Egyptian military leaders. The 2 countries had come to terms on concrete forms of military cooperation but gave no details of their agreement, Tanyug reported.

The London *Sunday Telegraph* reported July 1 that the Egyptians had begun installing heavy missiles along the west bank of the Suez Canal. The newspaper said: "A number of launching ramps are being hastily constructed in the area of the Canal. On June 27, an experienced military observer reported seeing 25 heavy missiles with considerable capacity and sufficient range to reach Israel. They were being moved on a road north of Cairo towards the Canal Zone."

4 Soviet destroyers and 2 submarines arrived in the Egyptian port of Alexandria Sept. 4, the Egyptian Middle East News Agency reported. The 6 Russian warships replaced a Soviet squadron that had left Alexandria and Port Said Sept. 2. The latter ships had arrived at the 2 ports July 10 in an apparent show of support for Nasser. Most of the Soviet warships that had arrived in Egyptian waters during and shortly after the June war had begun to leave the Mediterranean for Russian Black Sea ports June 24.

It was reported in the U.S. magazine *East Europe* of Feb. 1968 that the Soviet bloc up to that time had reequipped the defeated Arab countries with more than $150 million worth of arms and ammunition.

Israeli Foreign Min. Abba Eban condemned the Soviet Union before the UN General Assembly Sept. 25, 1967 for encouraging "extremist Arab policies" and for attempting to "restore the conditions which have led to war." (In General Assembly debate Sept. 29, UAR Foreign Min. Mahmoud Riad accused the U.S. of violating its stated policy of supporting "the political independence and territorial integrity of the states in the Middle East." Riad said that the U.S. had stated such a policy many times prior to the outbreak of hostilities June 5 but that afterwards the U.S. had "adopted a position of alignment with Israel and hostility toward the Arab people." Riad said that the Assembly's emergency session had failed to condemn Israeli aggression because of the U.S.' "negative position." He lauded the USSR, which "has stood closely by our side in difficult times," and he reiterated that the UAR would not negotiate with Israel. Speaking in reply, U.S. Amb. Arthur J. Goldberg termed Riad's description of the U.S. role "distorted and incomplete." The U.S., he said, had contributed economically to the Arab states as well as to Israel and had taken the lead in trying to prevent the war and, later, to bring about a cease-fire.)

Unrest, War Trials & Cabinet Shake-Up

Egypt experienced in 1968 a massive official and social reaction to the events of 1967. This took the forms mainly of recriminations and riots; there were 2 major military trials, in February and in August, and 2 serious outbreaks of student and worker unrest in February and in November. Pres. Nasser, however, had enough popular support and political control to enable him to change the government and outlast the criticism of his domestic enemies.

A 5-man military tribunal in Cairo Feb. 20, 1968 convicted 2 former high-ranking UAR air force officers on unpublished charges of negligence in connection with the air force's poor performance in the June 1967 war. Following a trial that had started Oct. 31, 1967, the former air force commander, Air Marshal Muhammad Sidky Mahmoud, received a 15-year prison term, and Air Vice Marshal Ismail Labib was given a 10-year sentence. 2 codefendants in the trial were acquitted: Air Marshal Gamal Afifi, air force chief of staff, and Air Vice Marshal Hamud el-Dogheidy, ex-commander of the air force's eastern sector. But the government Feb. 25 intervened and decreed the retrial of all 4 air force commanders. A military court Aug. 29 upheld the acquittals of Afifi and Dogheidy but increased Mahmoud's sentence to life imprisonment at hard labor and Labib's to 15 years at hard labor.

The government had ordered the new trials after widespread violent demonstrations in protest against the alleged leniency of the verdicts. The demonstrations, staged in Helwan, Cairo and Alexandria, had an anti-government tone in general and were the first such disorders in the country since the 1952 revolution that ultimately brought Nasser to power. The first outbreak occured in Helwan (25 miles south of Cairo), where about 2,000 workers demanded death sentences for all 4 officers. Police fired into the crowd. According to a report of the incident, released Feb. 27 by Interior Min. Sharawi Gomaa, 23 persons were wounded. Unofficial accounts claimed 17 person had died. The demonstration was organized by the Arab Socialist Union, the UAR's only political party. The AP reported that the union's role was attacked in the National Assembly, which met Feb. 29 to discuss the riots.

The Helwan disturbances spread to Cairo and Alexandria. In Cairo, thousands of persons, mostly students, marched Feb. 24 in a government-authorized demonstration, threw stones at buses and gathered in front of the National Assembly. Police later broke up the gatherings with tear gas and clubs following charges that the march had been infiltrated by "outside elements." More than 50 policemen and 20 civilians were injured in the clashes. About 50 persons were arrested. Scattered demonstrations continued through Feb. 27. More than 100 students staged a sit-in at Cairo University but agreed Feb. 27 to end the sit-in on a promise by authorities that the 4 military officers would be retried and that a number of arrested demonstrators would be released. The government Feb. 26 had announced the closing of 5 universities and other institutions of higher learning.

In a speech in Helwan Mar. 3, Nasser dismissed the disturbances as a "misunderstanding." He said that "reactionary elements" had attempted to foment demonstrations that would result in the "butchery" of marchers by the police.

Another Cairo military court Feb. 20 had sentenced several army officers for their role in the war. Maj. Gen. Sidky Awad el-Ghoul, ex-commander of an armored division, received a 15-year prison term, and 2 colonels were sentenced to hard labor for life.

Nasser Mar. 20 named 14 civilians to an expanded cabinet of 32 members. Deputy Premiers Zakaria Mohieddin and Aly Sabry resigned from the cabinet, but Sabry remained as head of the UAR's only political organization, the Arab Socialist Union. Power & High Dam Min. Muhammad Sidky Soliman was dropped from his deputy premier's position; only one deputy premier remained—Hussein el-Shafei.

The new cabinet: *President and Premier*—Nasser; *Vice President and Minister of Waqfs* (responsible for the administration of Moslem charitable foundations)—Shafei; *Power & the High Dam*—Soliman; *Labor*—Kamaleddin Mahmoud Rifaat; *Industry, Petroleum & Mineral Wealth*—Aziz Sidky; *Local Administration*—Abdelmohsin Abu el-Nour; *Culture*—Sarwat Okasha; *Justice*—Muhammad Abou Nosseir; *Agriculture & Agrarian Reform*—Sayed Marei; *Economy & Foreign Trade*—Hassan Abbas Zaki; *Health*—Muhammad el-Nabawy el-Mouhandes; *War Production*—Muhammad Abdul al-Bishri; *Higher Education*—Muhammad Labib Shukeir; *Foreign Affairs*—Mahmoud Riad; *Interior*—Sharawi Muhammad Gomaa; *State*—Amin Hamed el-Howeidi; *National Guidance*—Muhammad Ahmed Fayek; *Communications*—Kamal Henry Abadir; *War*—Gen. Muhammad Fawzi; *Education*—Muhammad Helmy Murad; *Supply & Internal Trade*—Muhammad Abdullah Marazban; *Irrigation*—Ibrahim Zaky Kennawy; *Transport*—Aly Zein el-Abedin Saleh; *Scientific Research*—Ahmed Mustafa Ahmed; *Planning*—Gaballah el-Sayed; *Housing & Utilities*—Hassan Hassan Mustafa; *Land Reclamation*—Muhammad Bakr Ahmed; *Treasury*—Abdul Aziz Muhammad Hegazy; *Tourism*—Muhammad Hafez Ghanem; *Youth*—Muhammad Safieddin Abul Ezz; *Social Affairs and State Minister for National Assembly Affairs*—Diaeddin Muhammad Daoud; *Deputy Minister of Waqfs*—Abdel Aziz Kamel.

Nasser Apr. 30 appointed Gen. Talat Hassan to replace Gen. Abdel Moneim Riad as chief of staff of the Arab Unified Command. Riad had been appointed chief of staff of the Egyptian armed forces.

A reform program proposed by Nasser received overwhelming support in a nationwide referendum held May 2, 1968. According to results announced May 3 by Interior Min. Sharawi Muhammad Gomaa, 7,315,734 voters approved, 798 voted "no" and 887 ballots were voided. The program, announced by Nasser Mar. 30, called for (a) "liberation of the land" captured by Israel in 1967 and (b) a new constitution that would reform the Arab Socialist Union (ASU), establish a supreme court, grant parliamentary control over the executive and provide greater personal and press freedom. Under the ASU reform, popular elections would be held for the first time for party candidates for National Assembly seats, with half the seats going to farmers and workers. Party members would elect a new ASU National Congress, which in turn would vote for the party's Supreme Executive Committee. Nasser had proposed the reforms as a result of the factory-worker and student riots in February.

At least 15 persons were killed and 84 wounded in student rioting in Egypt's major cities Nov. 21-25. The demonstrations were precipitated by a government decision to upgrade the UAR's educational system, ostensibly to compete with Israel's technical superiority. The unrest quickly took on an anti-government tone as the demonstrators protested against the regime's alleged authoritarian rule. The government had enacted a new educational law (effective in 1969) that would, among other things, bar automatic promotion of elementary school students and deny the reexamination of students who twice failed secondary school final examinations.

The unrest first erupted Nov. 21 in Mansura (75 miles northeast of Cairo), where 4 civilians were killed and 43 wounded when police opened fire. Most of the injured were policemen. The Interior Ministry said the outbreak had occurred after "nonstudent elements" had infiltrated a student march protesting the educational law. The ministry said the action of the infiltrators had forced security police to fire in the air. The rioting spread Nov. 23 to Alexandria where students protested against the police treatment of the Mansura rioters. At least 7 students were said to have been hospitalized as a result of injuries incurred in clashes with police.

The government Nov. 24 ordered the indefinite closing of all universities in the country "in the light of events and to avert any clash that might harm the interest of the majority of students, who have faith in their country." Secondary schools in Alexandria were closed Nov. 25 as younger students joined the demonstrations. The student rioting had spread to Cairo Nov. 24. Hundreds of youths gathered outside Cairo University and stoned police before being forcibly dispersed. Disturbances erupted in Alexandria Nov. 25, and at least 11 civilians were killed in the city in clashes with police. Order was restored by Nov. 26. Alexandria students were said to have evacuated most of the university buildings, where they had staged sit-ins.

At an Arab Socialist Union meeting held in Cairo to discuss the riots, Nasser declared Dec. 3 that his government had broken up an Israeli spy ring operating in Egypt. Nasser said

several Egyptians had been "caught red-handed." One of
those cited by Nasser was an Egyptian war veteran, identified
as Muhammad Mahmoud el-Haddad, who had been accused
of having fomented the Alexandrian unrest at Israel's behest.
(Justice Min. Muhammad Abou Nosseir had charged Dec. 2
that Haddad, a prisoner of war in Israel in 1967, had been
enlisted as a spy by an Israeli of Alexandrian origin.) Nasser
offered a one-month amnesty to Israeli agents currently
operating in Egypt. He pledged that if they surrendered to
police "you will not be punished for your past activities."
The amnesty did not apply to Haddad.

SEARCH FOR PEACE (Nov. 1967-Feb. 1969)

UN Urges Withdrawal & Peace

The UN Security Council Nov. 22, 1967 unanimously approved a British-proposed resolution aimed at bringing peace to the Middle East. The British resolution, one of several suggested, called for the eventual withdrawal of Israeli forces from Arab areas captured in June and for an end to the Arabs' state of belligerency with Israel. It empowered UN Secy. Gen. U Thant to send a representative to the Middle East "to establish and maintain contacts with the states concerned in order to promote agreement and assist efforts to achieve a peaceful settlement in accordance" with the provisions of the resolution. Thant Nov. 23 announced the appointment of Swedish Amb.-to-USSR Gunnar V. Jarring as his special envoy to the Middle East.

The adoption of the British resolution climaxed nearly 6 weeks of Security Council public debate and private consultations. The Council had resumed efforts to seek a formula to end the Arab-Israeli impasse after the General Assembly had ended its debate on the Middle East Oct. 13. During Council debate Nov. 2, Israeli Foreign Min. Abba Eban had stated the Israeli position that an Israeli military pull-back prior to a peace settlement was "irrational."

The Council's 10 nonpermanent members Nov. 3 had turned over the task of drafting a resolution to the body's 5 permanent members—the U.S., Britain, France, the USSR and Nationalist China. The nonpermanent members, led by India, Canada and Denmark, had passed the problem to the permanent members after reporting that they had been unable to agree on a proposal to send a special representative to the Middle East to seek a solution within generally agreed principles. The main stumbling block remained the goal of balancing Israeli withdrawal from captured Arab territory with an end to belligerency.

79

Israeli Foreign Min. Eban Nov. 8 had expressed opposition to 3 suggested resolutions on the ground that they failed to support sufficiently Israel's call for direct negotiations with the Arab states. The 3 resolutions had been proposed by India, the U.S. and the USSR. Eban particularly criticized the Indian resolution, which proposed that an Israeli military pull-back precede negotiations. Eban noted that the resolution had been drawn up in close consultation with the UAR whereas Israel had not been consulted. Eban also said: Israel would not "return to an armistice or to any other than permanent peace. We shall not go back to the back to the vulnerable demarcation lines which the Arab governments have undermined and destroyed by continuing belligerency. After the cease-fire line, our only possible destination is an agreed, secure, permanent frontier."

In Council debate Nov. 9, UAR Foreign Min. Mahmoud Riad asserted that the Council had "the duty to suppress the Israeli aggression and to force the aggressive Israeli forces to return to the positions they held before June 5."

The U.S., Indian and Soviet delegations eventually decided not to request a vote on the draft resolutions they had submitted. The Soviet delegate, Deputy Foreign Min. Vasily V. Kuznetzov, said, however, that he would insist that Israel adhere strictly to that part of a resolution put forward by Great Britain that called for Israeli withdrawal from all Arab territories. The U.S., Indian and Soviet draft resolutions were essentially alike. They all called for Israeli withdrawal from Arab territories, an end to the state of belligerency, the right of all Middle East states to a guarantee of their territorial inviolability and political independence, the right of all states to innocent passage through international waterways and a resolution of the Arab refugee problem. The Soviet resolution differed from India's and the U.S.' in suggesting that Israeli troops be withdrawn "without delay" and in not proposing a UN envoy to the Middle East.

Eban told the Council Nov. 13 that Israel was in favor of

a special UN envoy to the Middle East to help search for a peaceful solution. But Eban insisted that the UN representative must not block any prospects for direct Arab-Israeli discussions. The Israeli delegation repeated this view in accepting the British resolution Nov. 15.

The UAR and Jordan also expressed approval of the British resolution Nov. 15 but reiterated their demands for immediate and complete Israeli withdrawal from Arab territories. Syria rejected the resolution before it was adopted. The Arab states argued that negotiations could start only after an Israeli withdrawal to positions held prior to the outbreak of war June 5.

The following text is the English-language version of the British resolution on Mideast peace adopted by the UN Security Council unanimously Nov. 22. Clause 1.(i.), "withdrawal of Israeli armed forces from territories of recent conflict," does not specify the date of withdrawal or the precise territories to be evacuated by Israeli troops. UN editions in foreign languages read somewhat differently. The French-language text, for example, uses the phrase "*des territoires occupées,*" which may be translated either "*from all occupied territories*" or "*from occupied territories.*" The English-language version:

THE SECURITY COUNCIL,

EXPRESSING its continuing concern with the grave situation in the Middle East,

EMPHASIZING the inadmissibility of the acquisition of territory by war and the need to work for a just and lasting peace in which every state in the area can live in security,

EMPHASIZING FURTHER that all member states in their acceptance of the Charter of the United Nations have undertaken a commitment to act in accordance with Article 2 of the Charter,

1. AFFIRMS that the fulfillment of Charter principles requires the establishment of a just and lasting peace in the Middle East which should include the application of both the following principles: (i) Withdrawal of Israeli armed forces from territories of recent conflict; (ii) Termination of all claims or states of belligerency and respect for and acknowledgment of the sovereignty, territorial integrity and political independence of every state in the area and their right to live in

peace within secure and recognized boundaries free from threats of acts of force;

2. AFFIRMS FURTHER the necessity (a) for guaranteeing freedom of navigation through international waterways in the area; (b) for achieving a just settlement of the refugee problem; (c) for guaranteeing the territorial inviolability and political independence of every state in the area, through measures including the establishment of demilitarized zones;

3. REQUESTS the Secretary General to designate a special representative to proceed to the Middle East to establish and maintain contacts with the states concerned in order to promote agreement and assist efforts to achieve a peaceful and accepted settlement in accordance with the provisions and principles in this resolution;

4. REQUESTS the Secretary General to report to the Security Council on the progress of the efforts of the special representative as soon as possible.

The Israeli government Nov. 23 expressed satisfaction with the Security Council resolution. An Israeli diplomat said: "We can live with it. . . . It's probably the best resolution we could have hoped for under the circumstances."

Describing the Council resolution as "insufficient" and "unclear," UAR Pres. Gamal Abdel Nasser called Nov. 23 for an Arab summit meeting to discuss it. In an address at the opening of the UAR National Assembly's 5th session, Nasser said: "The British resolution is not enough for a settlement of the Middle East crisis. The Soviet resolution was clearer in its interpretation of the situation. There were clarifications before the voting on the British resolution, and without them, the resolution would have been inadequate." Nasser took issue with the British call for "freedom of navigation through international waterways" in the Middle East. He pledged that Egypt would continue to bar Israeli ships from the Suez Canal "no matter what the cost." Nasser said that Arab policy remained: no recognition of Israel, no negotiations with Israel, no armistice and no "liquidation of the Palestine question." Nasser confirmed that 80% of Egypt's military equipment had been destroyed in the June war. 10,000 soldiers and 1,500 officers had been killed and 5,000 soldiers and 500 officers had been captured, Nasser said. But the UAR, he asserted had recouped its losses and was stronger than it had been before the conflict. Nasser cautioned, however, that "we must not be provoked by the enemy before the time is propitious. We must choose the time and place."

Syrian Pres. Nureddin al-Attassi charged Nov. 23 that the British UN Security Council resolution "rewards Israel for her aggression."

The Soviet Communist Party newspaper *Pravda* Nov. 24 praised the British resolution as one that "can be a step on the path of the Middle East crisis if the terms . . . are carried out."

Jarring Goes to Mideast as UN Envoy

Gunnar V. Jarring of Sweden, UN Secy. Gen. U Thant's special envoy to the Middle East, visited Lebanon, Israel, Jordan and the United Arab Republic Dec. 13–26, 1967 to determine the prospects for peace. Thant had dispatched Jarring to the area in compliance with the Security Council's Nov. 22 resolution, which had requested that he designate and send a representative to the Middle East to promote a political solution. Syria, which had denounced the resolution, barred Jarring.

Jarring conferred with Lebanese officials in Beirut Dec. 13–14. Then he proceeded to Israel, where he met with Foreign Min. Abba Eban Dec. 14 and with Premier Levi Eshkol Dec. 15. On arriving in Amman Dec. 15, Jarring conferred with Jordanian King Hussein and stayed in Jordan until Dec. 18. Jarring's presence in Jordan precipitated a demonstration Dec. 17 of 600 students and some faculty members of Jordan University, 7 miles from Amman. The demonstrators carried placards demanding that Israel return the Old City of Jerusalem and the Jordan River's West Bank area to Jordan. Hussein Dec. 19 expressed hope that Jarring's mission and a forthcoming Arab summit meeting would produce "a permanent settlement" of the Middle East impasse. Otherwise, he said, "there will be a scope for all sorts of emotions."

Jarring flew to Cairo Dec. 18 and conferred with Nasser and UAR Foreign Min. Mahmoud Riad.

The UN envoy then flew to Cyprus for a respite. He was reported Dec. 22 to have reported to Thant that in his talks with Arab and Israeli leaders he had received "expressions of willingness to cooperate with his mission." Jarring conferred again with Eban in Israel Dec. 26–27 and with Egyptian officials in Cairo Dec. 27–28.

Muhammad Hassanein Heykal, a close associate of Nasser's and editor of the Cairo newspaper *Al-Ahram*, had stated in an editorial Dec. 15 that Jarring's mission was "almost foredoomed to failure." But he said the UN envoy's political endeavors would help Egypt by keeping "the crisis alive" and by providing Cairo with needed "breathing space" to reequip and retrain its army for another round of fighting with Israel. "The Middle East crisis should always remain a hot and lively issue and should never be left for a minute to cool down or stagnate," Heykal declared. Heykal said in an editorial Jan. 26, 1968 that Jarring's mission "has not achieved any progress," and "we are bound to enter a military battle with Israel."

Jarring held additional talks with Egyptian and Jordanian officials in Cairo and Amman in January and February 1968. In a report to the Security Council Jan. 17, Secy. Gen. Thant had said that Arab and Israeli leaders were cooperating with Jarring in his search for a peaceful solution.

Tito's Peace Plan

Pres. Tito of Yugoslavia visited Nasser in Cairo Feb. 4–8, 1968. At a press conference in Cairo Feb. 7, Tito declared that the solution to the Middle East problem lay in the U.S.' hands. He called on the U.S. to urge the Israelis to withdraw from the territories captured in June 1967. "It is difficult to believe that Israel would not obey the United States if Washington told Tel Aviv that the crisis must be settled peacefully to the advantage of both sides and not simply to the detriment of the Arab countries," Tito said. He proposed that an Israeli withdrawal from the occupied territories be followed by a formal declaration ending the state of hostility between Israel and its Arab neighbors. Negotiations would then follow. The Yugoslav leader also insisted that the Arab nations most directly involved had already accepted the principle that an Israeli withdrawal would be followed by an Arab declaration of non-belligerency and of the right of Israeli free passage through the Suez Canal.

It was reported in Belgrade Feb. 8 that Tito had received the consent of Nasser and of other Afro-Asian leaders for a new plan for the solution of the Mideast conflict. The "Tito plan" called for: (a) a demilitarized zone along Israel's frontiers; (b) Israeli withdrawal from all occupied territories; (c) a solution of the refugee problem; (d) the ending of the state of war between Israel and the Arabs; (e) freedom of navigation for Israel in the Suez Canal and the Strait of Tiran.

The "Tito plan" was immediately and totally rejected by Israel. Israeli spokesmen ridiculed Tito for suggesting a new peace plan without consulting both the belligerents.

Egypt Bars Direct Talks with Israel

UAR Foreign Min. Mahmoud Riad told UN Middle East peace envoy Gunnar Jarring in Cairo Mar. 7, 1968 that Egypt "categorically" refused to meet with Israeli representatives in Cyprus "in the present and the future" to discuss the possibilities of establishing peace in the Middle East.

Jarring had arrived in Cairo Mar. 7 after reporting on his 3-month mission to UN Secy. Gen. U Thant in New York Feb. 29–Mar. 4; he returned to his headquarters in Nicosia, Cyprus Mar. 5 before leaving for the Egyptian capital. According to a report from UN headquarters Mar. 1, Jarring had proposed inviting Egypt, Jordan and Israel to send representatives to Cyprus to negotiate a peace settlement. Israel accepted the proposal; Jordan had not yet responded.

Reporting on Riad's reaction to Jarring's plan, the Cairo newspaper *Al-Ahram* said Mar. 8 that Egypt would not attend any meetings with Israel that could be interpreted as "negotiations," whether they were conducted face-to-face or through intermediaries. The newspaper said Riad had complained to Jarring of Israel's decision to redesignate Israel-occupied Arab territories from "enemy territory" to "militarily occupied" areas. This action, Riad was quoted as asserting, showed Israel's "aggressive and expansionist" designs and proved that Israel was not prepared to accept the UN Security Council's resolution of Nov. 22, 1967.

The designation of Arab areas captured by Israel in June 1967 had been changed from "enemy territory" to "militarily occupied territory," Feb. 28 by Israeli Interior Min. Moshe Haim Shapiro. The order also designated the Allenby Bridge over the Jordan River as an official exit and entry point between the Jordan River's Israeli-occupied West Bank and Jordan. The text of the ministry order was not made public, but Israeli officials confirmed that the directive labeled the West Bank as Samaria and Judea, the Biblical names of the northern and southern parts of the area. Israeli Foreign Ministry officials insisted that the move had not altered the status of the territories, that it was essentially a legalism required to make dealing with the conquered areas possible despite the bans against visiting or trading with "enemy territory."

The Israeli action was assailed by Arab governments as an expansionist move that would undermine Gunnar Jarring's peace efforts. In a speech at a workers' rally in Helwan Mar. 3, Nasser warned that Israel's "decision shall cost her a lot." "We swear," he said, "that we shall liberate" former Arab areas "inch by inch regardless of the cost or sacrifice. We shall be one front, the army and the people, for the sake of the struggle for the liberation of occupied territory." He said that Egyptian accomplishments in rebuilding the shattered UAR armed forces "could be regarded as a miracle."

Nasser had said, in an interview with William Attwood published Mar. 4 in the American magazine *Look*: If a negotiated settlement could not be arranged, Arabs would "have to fight" to regain lands captured by Israel. Arms limitation in the Middle East could not be discussed "when our country is occupied and our army and air force were destroyed." The rebuilding of Arab armies was imperative because the "Israelis are reluctant to settle things, and they will be willing only when they feel we have an effective fighting force." The Arabs would not negotiate directly with Israel. Israeli withdrawal from Arab areas "must be the first step before any kind of meeting."

Iraqi newspapers Mar. 1 called the Israeli redesignation of occupied Arab territories an outright annexation of the West Bank, the Sinai Peninsula and the Golan Heights. Radio Cairo said the Israeli measures reflected "Zionist expansionist ambitions." Jordan's semiofficial newspaper *Al Destour* (*the Constitution*) said Arab cooperation with Jarring's mission was futile in the face of the Israeli actions. Radio Damascus charged Israel with "a gross violation" of the UN Charter.

The Arabs had insisted that the holding of peace talks was conditioned on Israeli acceptance of the UN Security Council resolution. Israel had neither accepted nor rejected the resolution but had expressed a willingness to declare that it "responds affirmatively" to it.

Israel's approval of Jarring's proposal for Arab-Israeli talks had been confirmed by Foreign Min. Abba Eban in a report to the Israeli Knesset (parliament) Feb. 26 on his talks with the UN envoy. Eban added: "We shall regard the readiness of the Arab government to sit down with us face to face as a test of their actual desire to make peace. A refusal to meet us face to face is to be interpreted as a refusal to make peace. . . . You can, of course, have negotiation with-

out success, but you cannot have success without negotiation." Eban blamed Egypt for the political impasse. He
charged that Cairo's intention was only to pledge support for
implementing the Security Council resolution provided there
was no contractual agreement with Israel. "In other words,"
Eban said, "the Egyptians are saying, 'We will implement it
verbally provided we are free to violate all its central
provisions.' "

Premier Levi Eshkol Mar. 2 affirmed Israel's readiness to
meet with the Arabs, but, unlike Eban, he did not insist on
direct talks. Eshkol said: "If it helps for us and the Arabs to
sit at first with [Jarring] . . . as chairman, by all means we
will sit with him as chairman. If this is the road to peace, we
will take it."

Nasser Mar. 12 reiterated his government's refusal to
negotiate with Israel. He said: "There does not appear to be
progress toward a political solution. What is taken by force
can only be regained by force. Strength means that we
should benefit from previous lessons."

Nasser asserted again Apr. 29 that another war with Israel
was inevitable. Addressing officers at a military barracks, he
said the UAR might have to fight alone because other Arab
states were not yet able to integrate their military plans. The
Egyptian president, warning that Israel might mobilize in a
"desperate" showdown with Egypt, said he had informed Lt.
Gen. Muhammad Fawzi, the UAR war minister, "that he and
our other officers should calculate on this basis" and be prepared to eliminate "the consequences of Israeli aggression."
Nasser assailed Israel for planning its independence day parade
for May 2 in Jerusalem in defiance of a UN Security Council
resolution of Apr. 27.

Jarring continued to confer in the Mideast with Arab and
Israeli leaders and representatives of the major powers
throughout the first quarter of 1968. But by April, UN
officials were suggesting that the mediation site be trans-
ferred to UN headquarters in New York. Jarring relayed the

recommendation to the parties concerned, and Egypt, Israel and Jordan agreed to the proposed shift to New York. Their agreement was coupled with their acceptance in principle of the Nov. 22, 1967 resolution and its main points: Israeli withdrawal from captured Arab territories, an end to the Arab countries' state of belligerency and guaranteed and safe borders for Israel. The UAR agreed May 9; Israel and Jordan had approved previously. UAR Foreign Min. Riad, who had given Jarring his government's reply, said later at a meeting of all Arab ambassadors that he had reaffirmed to the UN envoy that Cairo "is not prepared to give up one inch of Arab territory."

Jarring had held 41 meetings with Israeli and Arab leaders in Jerusalem, Cairo and Amman since the start of his mission in Dec. 1967. His efforts to end the political deadlock, however, appeared to be fruitless. The impasse centered on Israeli insistence on direct talks with the Arab states, while Egypt refused to participate in such negotiations. Jordanian Foreign Min. Abdel Moneim Rifai had said Apr. 21 that the Arab states were prepared to start "indirect negotiations" immediately with Israel if Israel made a "simple declaration of intention to implement" the Nov. 22 resolution. King Hussein was reported to have appealed to Nasser Apr. 30 to continue discussions with Jarring. Hussein's plea was handed to Nasser by Jordanian Premier Bahjat al-Talhouni.

The text of a letter sent by Pres. Johnson to Nasser May 13 was made public June 7. The message discussed prospects for peace in the Middle East. It was in response to a May 1 letter in which Nasser thanked Johnson and other chiefs of state for the Apr. 27 approval by their UN Security Council representatives of a resolution urging Israel not to stage a military parade in Jerusalem May 2. In his letter, Johnson said: "For the first time since 1948 there is an opportunity to move toward peace. For the sake of all peoples concerned, that opportunity should be seized." Jarring's peace mission "provides the best means for reaching a solution."

(At a meeting with Israeli Foreign Min. Eban in Jerusalem Feb. 1, Jarring had said that he did not have the jurisdiction to help solve a Suez Canal controversy. Although Jarring had been instrumental in overcoming an impasse that led to the initial Canal agreement in July 1967, the negotiations had been handled by Lt. Gen. Odd Bull, UNTSO commander. Eban said Feb. 3 that the Israeli-Egyptian deadlock over the Canal would not compromise Jarring's mission to promote peace in the Middle East. The operation to release the trapped vessels in the Suez Canal, Eban said, "has only a marginal relationship" to Jarring's peace efforts.)

U.S.-Soviet Rapprochement, Nonproliferation Treaty

In an action widely interpreted as having deep signifi-cance for Egyptian relations with the U.S. and the Soviet Union as well as for the world in general, 62 countries, among them the UAR, Iran, Iraq, Lebanon, Morocco, Syria and Tunisia, signed an international nuclear nonproliferation treaty July 1, 1968 as it was opened for signature in Washing-ton, Moscow and London. The treaty had been approved by the UN General Assembly June 12. Algeria, Israel, Jordan, Libya and Saudi Arabia were among countries that did not sign the treaty.

U.S. Pres. Johnson announced in Washington July 1 that the U.S. and Soviet Union had agreed to begin talks "in the nearest future" on means of limiting and reducing their arsenals of offensive and defensive nuclear weapons. Johnson made the announcement at the White House during signing ceremonies for the treaty. Soviet Foreign Min. Andrei A. Gromyko, in a wide-ranging foreign policy address to the Supreme Soviet in Moscow, June 17, had announced that the USSR was "ready for an exchange of opinion" on the question of a "mutual restriction and subsequent reduction of strategic vehicles for the delivery of nuclear weapons— offensive and defensive—including anti-missile." Gromyko declared that the Soviet Union was ready to sign "immediately" an international convention prohibiting the use of nuclear weapons and, as in the past, to implement "a program of general and complete disarmament."

A 9-point disarmament and arms control plan was issued in Moscow July 1 by Soviet Premier Aleksei N. Kosygin. The plan, which Kosygin disclosed had been distributed to all of the world's governments, was made public during signing ceremonies for the nuclear nonproliferation treaty. Among the Soviet proposals was one for the establishment of "denuclearized zones in various parts of the world" and the "implementation of measures for regional disarmament and for the reduction of armaments in various regions of the world, including the Middle East." The memo added: "The question of such measures for slackening the arms race in the Middle East, of course, could be considered only in conditions of elimination of the consequences of the Israeli aggression against the Arab countries and, above all, the full evacuation of the Israeli forces from the territories of Arab countries occupied by them."

UAR Pres. Nasser had maintained in an interview published Mar. 4 in the American magazine *Look* that although Cairo was more friendly toward the USSR than toward the U.S., Egypt still pursued a policy of nonalignment. There was "no coordination of policy" with the Soviet Union, Nasser maintained. The USSR had fewer than 1,000 military advisers in Egypt; British and American estimates of 1,200 to 2,000 were exaggerated, he said. (Israeli officials estimated that 3,000 Soviet military instructors, technicians and advisers were operating in Egypt, as compared with 500 to 700 before the June 1967 war.)

Peace Prospects Seem Brighter

By mid-May 1968 some observers reported signs of Egyptian willingness to make concessions in the interest of peace. The UAR government indicated May 15 that it would seriously consider a peace settlement that could precede the withdrawal of Israeli troops from Arab areas captured in June 1967. Cairo's position was enunciated by Dr. Muhammad H. el-Zayyat, the government's chief spokesman. Zayyat disclosed a report by UN peace envoy Gunnar Jarring, who had informed the UN that Egypt and Israel had accepted the terms of the UN's Nov. 1967 resolution and "intend to devise arrangements under my auspices for the implementation of the provisions of the resolution."

Western diplomats said in Cairo May 16 that Egypt was prepared to end its state of belligerency with Israel and let Israeli ships use the Strait of Tiran if Israel pledged to quit Arab areas. But Israeli officials May 17 discounted the purported Egyptian concession as meaningless. The officials said that in addition to free passage through the Strait of Tiran, Israel insisted on use of the Suez Canal, demilitarization of the Sinai Peninsula, an end to the Arab state of war and Arab recognition of Israel.

Israeli Foreign Min. Eban said May 29 that Israel would implement the Nov. 1967 UN resolution after the Arab states signed peace treaties with Israel incorporating all elements of the resolution. As for the withdrawal of Israeli troops from Arab areas, Eban said: "The definition of the agreed border and agreed security arrangements would obviously determine the deployment of armed forces in conditions of peace." Eban said the resolution should be executed in 4 phases: negotiation, agreement, treaties and implementation.

Jarring discussed the Mideast situation with Soviet Premier Aleksei N. Kosygin and Foreign Min. Andrei A. Gromyko in Moscow June 28. He met with Israeli and Arab representatives in London July 8–9, conferred with U Thant in Geneva July 10 and met again with Kosygin during the latter's visit to Stockholm July 11–14. Sources at UN headquarters in New York said July 12 that Jarring had expressed "cautious encouragement" on the results of his talks.

There were several further indications early in July that the UAR was taking a more conciliatory approach. The developments coincided with a visit by Nasser to Moscow. UAR Foreign Min. Riad, on a Scandinavian tour, was reported to have said in Copenhagen July 3: "We recognize the realities and one of the realities is Israel. Now we want peace." The Arabs, he said, had made a "big mistake in demanding the annihilation of Israel," but "this kind of propaganda has stopped since the June war." But Dr. Muhammad el-Zayyat, chief UAR government spokesman, said in Cairo July 7 in response to queries concerning the Riad statement: "We know Israel exists, but this does not mean Egypt is ready to accept diplomatic links with her." A UAR statement July 7 accused news services of "distorting and misreporting" Riad's statement.

Diplomatic sources in London said July 4 that the UAR had indicated to Gunnar Jarring that Cairo would be willing to permit the return of UN peace-keeping forces to Egyptian territory. The report was confirmed July 6 by Zayyat, who told reporters in Cairo: "If implementation of the Security Council's November [1967] resolution necessitated the presence of UN peace-keeping forces, we should have no objection." Zayyat asserted that such a position represented nothing new in UAR policy.

Israeli officials, however, had indicated July 5 that their government would never agree to the return of UN forces in the absence of a peace treaty between Egypt and Israel. One official said: "The biggest mistake we made after the 1956 Sinai campaign was to agree to withdraw on the basis of all sorts of international guarantees, while failing to get the one that counted—Pres. Nasser's." An official of the Foreign Ministry noted that "our experience with the United Nations as a means of protection does not make the reported Egyptian proposal terribly inviting for us." The allusion was to U Thant's compliance, in May 1967, with Nasser's demand that the UN forces be withdrawn.

Diplomatic sources in Cairo said July 8 that Egypt would be willing to permit Israeli cargo vessels to use the Suez Canal if Israeli troops pulled back from the east bank of the Canal. The sources, described as friendly to the Nasser government, said that such a concession would be part of an Egyptian effort to obtain a settlement. But an Israeli official said in Jerusalem July 8 that Israeli troops would withdraw from the Canal only under a peace treaty with the UAR. The official said: "We want to see the Canal opened to everyone, including ourselves. That can be accomplished through United Nations intermediaries if the Egyptians prefer, but we would remain where we are . . . . As far as pulling back is concerned, that should be part of an over-all peace treaty. Otherwise we are back to 1956."

UAR Accepts Soviet Guidance in Return for Aid

The Soviet Union, by its policy of gradually rearming Egypt after the June 1967 war, was said to have retained over Cairo a measure of influence unavailable to the U.S. or any other world power. (France, though it had supported the Arab and Soviet positions against Israel's occupation of conquered Arab territories, did not go as far as to extend military aid. The countervailing, anti-Soviet influence of Communist China, then still in the throes of its "cultural revolution," remained dormant.) The implied advice of the USSR was that Egypt should avoid another early clash with Israel.

Israeli Defense Min. Moshe Dayan, analyzing the Soviet-Egyptian relationship, suggested that the USSR preferred to improve its position through diplomatic rather than military means. "Russia would not send in so much new equipment and risk another Egyptian defeat nor will Egypt risk another round without full Russian backing," Dayan said. By Apr. 1968, the Soviets were known to be pressing for a détente with the United States, which, it was held, they did not want upset by a new Mideast explosion.

UAR Pres. Nasser then told his countrymen July 23, 1968—less than 2 weeks after his return from a visit to the

Soviet Union—that "we still have not reached the capability of a sweeping military offensive" and that Egypt must avoid premature war with Israel. A *N.Y. Times* dispatch from Cairo July 24 quoted informed Arab sources as saying that Nasser had told Jordanian King Hussein that Egypt's armed forces would not be capable of war against Israel before 1970.

U.S. officials in Washington had reported Apr. 23 that the Soviet Union for the first time had supplied Egypt with short-range ground-to-ground missiles. The missiles, which had started arriving in Egypt in the previous few weeks, had a 45-mile range and were a modification of the 28-foot Kennel air-to-ground missile, adapted by Egypt for surface operation. But despite the new Soviet military equipment, the UAR had not yet replaced the losses it had suffered in the 1967 war, according to American sources.

The current number of UAR warplanes was said to total about 300 jet fighters and fewer than 50 bombers, compared with 365 fighters and 69 bombers prior to the war. The UAR also had fewer advanced Soviet planes than it had before the 1967 conflict. It had (pre-war figures in parentheses): MiG-21s—90 to 115 (163); SU-7s—50 (55); TU-16s—12 (26). (Despite the French government's arms embargo against Israel, a French arms manufacturer [Marcel Dassault] was continuing to develop a ground-to-ground missile for Israel, U.S. sources said. The weapon, designated MD-620, was capable of carrying a 1,000-to-2,000-pound warhead.)

Soviet aid to the UAR was not restricted to the military area, however. The Egyptian government announced May 15 that the USSR had agreed to help build an $800 million industrial project at Helwan, 15 miles south of Cairo. The agreement, signed in Cairo that day, called for facilities that would increase the production of iron and steel 6-fold and provide jobs for about 12,000 workers. The annual capacity of the new mills, scheduled for completion in 1976 was projected to be 1¾ million tons of cast iron and 1½ million tons of steel.

Nasser made his visit to the Soviet Union July 4–10. The talks were held amid press reports that he was dissatisfied with the level of Soviet military aid to the Arab world. Nasser was accompanied by Lt. Gen. Abdel Moneim Riad, UAR chief of staff. They arrived in Moscow July 4 and held 5 official meetings with Gen. Secy. Leonid I. Brezhnev of the Soviet Communist Party, Premier Aleksei N. Kosygin and Pres. Nikolai V. Podgorny before leaving for Belgrade, Yugoslavia July 10. Nasser conferred with Yugoslav Pres. Tito before returning to Cairo July 12.

In an exchange of toasts with Brezhnev at a Kremlin luncheon July 5, Nasser had asserted that Israel was a Western "bridgehead" in the Middle East that "separates Arab unity." He pledged that the Arabs would "liberate the occupied Arab territories" "whatever the costs and sacrifices." Nasser assailed Zionism as a "religious myth that strives for territory at the expense of other people" and therefore stood "concretely with imperialism." Nasser declared that the Arabs were for peace but that "peace based on the *status quo* is simply surrender." In his toast, Brezhnev warned that there should not be the "least doubt" that the Soviet Union would "always side with the Arab nations in the struggle for the withdrawal of Israeli troops from all the Arab lands occupied as a result of the June [1967] aggression."

In remarks made at a luncheon July 6, after 2 days of Soviet-Egyptian talks, Nasser said: "We have become convinced once again that the Soviet Union supports the Arabs and the rights of the Arab nations." In reply, Soviet Pres. Podgorny pledged that the Soviet Union would "continue assistance" to Egypt, but he did not elaborate on the form the assistance would take.

Nasser vacationed at a country house outside Moscow July 7–8 and returned to the capital July 9. He conferred once more with the Soviet leadership before leaving for Belgrade July 10. A joint communiqué issued July 10 stated that both sides had exchanged views "frankly" and in a "friendly and cordial atmosphere." There had been a "coin-cidence of views on the most important international prob-lems," particularly "armed U.S. aggression in Vietnam," the communiqué said. The communiqué condemned "Israel and the imperialist forces supporting it" and asserted that "the strengthening of peace in the Middle East area must be based on respect of the lawful rights of the Arab peoples, including the Arab population of Palestine."

The communiqué noted the UAR's "readiness to fulfill in the nearest future" the UN resolution of Nov. 22, 1967, but it cited only the part of the resolution calling for a with-drawal of Israeli forces from captured Arab territory, not the call for Arab recognition of Israel's sovereignty and its right of free access to international waters. The communiqué pledged that the USSR would continue to support Egypt po-litically and economically and would continue "strengthening its defense potential." In conjunction with the latter point, Riad remained in Moscow to consult further with Soviet leaders.

After his return to Cairo, Nasser July 23 cautioned the Arab states not to be provoked into premature war with Israel. Speaking to the new National Congress of the Arab Socialist Union, Egypt's only legal party, Nasser declared that "we must have patience in order to score victory in the end." But he pledged that Arabs would recapture the territory lost to Israel "even if we have to sacrifice a martyr for each inch." The Egyptian president, asserting that "it is we who will make the decision" about renewing hostilities, said that "our troops are working day and night, but they must have time in order to achieve what they are expected to achieve"—"liqui-dation of the traces of the June [1967] defeat."

With the weapons the Soviet Union was sending and the record $690 million a year Cairo was spending on arms, Egypt's forces were stronger than before the 1967 war, Nas-ser said. The president confirmed that much of the Soviet arms delivered since the war was to be paid for in long-term installments. The remainder of the shipments, he said, were free. In his talks with the Soviet leaders in Moscow, Nasser said, he had "spent hours asking for things." He said he had told the Soviet chiefs that he "was embarrassed to be always asking for something, and I asked if they wanted anything from me, and they said no." He asserted again that he would not negotiate directly or sign a peace treaty with Israel.

Israeli Defense Min. Moshe Dayan said July 24 that Nasser had presented Israel with the alternative of "war or peace," not "territory or peace." Nasser had made clear that he would not recognize or accept Israel's borders even if the Israelis withdrew from the Arab territories they had captured in 1967, Dayan said. Israeli Foreign Min. Abba Eban said July 24 that Nasser was seeking "a new war in the Middle East for the purpose of bringing about Israel's complete liquidation."

The Soviet repression of the nationalist Dubcek regime in Czechoslovakia in Aug. 1968 placed Egypt in an uncomfortable position. Many highly-placed Egyptians were sympathetic to the Dubcek government, but they also regarded Soviet aid to Egypt as indispensable.

Bernard Lewis, University of London professor of history of the Near and Middle East, wrote in the July 1969 issue of the American quarterly *Foreign Affairs:* "The invasion of Czechoslovakia brought a new shock. Arab governments in general felt obliged to support or at least excuse the Soviet action, and some spokesmen even went so far as to rejoice that the Soviets had now demonstrated their readiness and ability to defy the world and occupy a country in a few hours. This, it was said, was how they could deal with Israel, when the time came. More perceptive Arabs, however, were deeply alarmed by the Czechoslovak affair and the memories of Hungary which it evoked. This kind of action, they observed, was taken by the Soviets, not against their enemies, but against their allies. It was a profoundly disturbing thought."

The first official UAR reaction to the Czechoslovak crisis came Sept. 4 when Muhammad H. el-Zayyat, government spokesman, said that "no people should be coerced or victimized by aggression." Zayyat said Cairo had "sympathy for people who have stood with us against aggression, among them the Czechs."

Nasser declared Sept. 14 that Egypt had completed the first stage of rebuilding its armed forces and that in the next 2 stages it would "stand firm" and then "liberate our occupied land." Speaking at the opening of the National Congress of the reorganized Arab Socialist Union, he asserted: "A year ago our enemy had great superiority, but now our forces can repel and have repelled aggression." He called "the liberation" of Arab territories captured by Israel "a sacred duty in fulfillment of which we cannot hesitate." Nasser informed the National Congress Sept. 15 that action was being taken to establish a "joint Arab front" against Israel. He said also that the Arabs were attempting "to consolidate the Jordanian front" along the Jordan River "to strengthen it against Israeli aggression and provocation."

Cairo Sept. 18 elaborated on a Sept. 8 directive providing for "preventive defense operations" against Israeli positions on the east bank of the Suez Canal. Muhammad el-Zayyat, the government spokesman, explained that "when the Israelis fire a shot on the Canal, everything in our defense system will reply from now on."

UN envoy Gunnar Jarring met Dec. 2 with Israeli Foreign Min. Abba Eban in Nicosia, Cyprus and with UAR Foreign Min. Mahmoud Riad in Cairo Dec. 5. Riad said after the meeting that Jarring's mission was at an impasse "because Israel continues to raise side issues and avoids the crux of the [Nov. 22, 1967] Security Council resolution, which calls for the Israeli withdrawal from Arab territories."

Soviet Foreign Min. Andrei A. Gromyko conferred with Nasser in Cairo Dec. 23–24. A communiqué on the talks Dec. 24 reiterated the Egyptian and Soviet condemnation of

Israel's alleged expansionist policy and demanded that Israel withdraw from all Arab territories it had occupied in 1967. Israeli Foreign Min. Abba Eban said Dec. 24 that the Soviet-UAR communiqué showed "rigidity in thought, in policy and in formulation." Eban added: "By condoning Egyptian aggression in the past and by refusing to make peace in the present, the Soviet Union is contributing to the perpetuation" of the Middle East deadlock.

It was reported Dec. 28 that Gromyko's trip to Cairo had been prompted by alleged Egyptian military plans to invade the Israeli-occupied Sinai Peninsula. Gromyko was said to have urged Nasser to defer such an attack for at least 3 months to give the Soviet Union time to pursue a peaceful settlement in cooperation with the U.S. Nasser was said to have agreed to delay the Sinai operation but reportedly told Gromyko that "If I do not do something soon, the people will hang me." The Soviet government newspaper *Izvestia* had reported Dec. 26 that antiaircraft guns had been placed around the Soviet-built Aswan Dam and its approaches to protect it against possible Israeli commando attacks.)

U.S. State Department officials Dec. 31 confirmed the receipt of a Soviet offer Dec. 19 to consult on a joint U.S.-Soviet move to promote peace in the Middle East. The department said Washington was drafting a reply.

French Foreign Min. Michel Debré Dec. 30 repeated his government's call for joint U.S.-French-Soviet-British peace efforts in the Middle East. Debré said that France sought negotiations and discussions, not a summit meeting. He said that the 3 principles to the dispute—Egypt, Israel and Jordan—should participate in the discussions.

Israelis Shell Suez

Gov. Hamid Mahmoud of the city of Suez reported Sept. 19, 1968 that thousands of civilians had been evacuated from the Canal town since it had been heavily shelled by Israeli forces Sept. 8. Mahmoud said that all state employes had been removed from the city, that gas masks had been issued and that more trenches were being dug. Less than 60,000 of Suez' 260,000 inhabitants remained, most of them working at essential services.

Israeli Amb.-to-U.S. Itzhak Rabin, the former general, had warned in a speech in New York Sept. 14 that Israel would continue its policy of military reprisals for Arab attacks on its territory. Calling the attacks "a nuisance which interferes with our nation's development," Rabin said that "we will have to fight with different means and these means include reprisals which will continue despite condemnations in the UN."

The UN Security Council, by 14–0 vote (one abstention, Algeria) Sept. 18, adopted a resolution calling on Israel and the Arab states to "rigorously" respect the Council's cease-fire orders and to cooperate with the Middle East peace mission of UN envoy Gunnar Jarring. The Council had been meeting since Sept. 4 to consider Israeli charges that Egyptians had abducted an Israeli soldier after killing 2 others in an ambush along the Suez Canal.

Israeli delegate Yosef Tekoah denounced the resolution, asserting that it "discriminated" against Israel and its right to self-defense. Charging that the resolution was another example of the Council's "double standard," "We now leave the Security Council table disappointed again and disenchanted," Tekoah said. "The outcome of the deliberations can under no circumstances be regarded as a satisfactory response to our just complaint. . . ." Tekoah said that Israel would cooperate with the Jarring mission and would respect the cease-fire, but he insisted that Israel would "continue to fulfill its obligations to protect its citizens, military and civilian, and the territories under its control."

Algeria had abstained on the ground that the resolution had failed to deal with what it regarded as the root of the problem–Israel's refusal to withdraw from Arab territories. Although Soviet delegate Yakov A. Malik voted for the resolution, he deplored the Council's failure to condemn Israel.

Sporadic clashes also occurred along the Suez Canal cease-fire line. Israel reported Sept. 23 that an Egyptian force the previous day had infiltrated the Israeli-held east bank, ambushed an Israeli vehicle and planted mines and then had withdrawn. An Israeli protest filed with the UN Security Council said that 2 Israeli soldiers had been wounded in the incident, about 3 miles south of Small Bitter Lake. Another Israeli soldier was seriously wounded in the same region Sept. 25 when his patrol vehicle hit a mine. 3 Israeli soldiers were killed Sept. 26 when a mine blew up in their ammunition carrier in the Negev. 2 other soldiers were seriously injured.

The search for an Egypt-Israel peace had been marred by several clashes at the Suez Canal earlier in 1968. Israeli and Egyptian forces had exchanged gunfire across the Canal Jan. 30. The clash resulted in the cancellation of a UN-negotiated bilateral agreement to clear the southern end of the waterway to permit the exit of 15 foreign ships trapped there since the June 1967 war. The UAR, which had started a survey Jan. 28, preparatory to removing sunken wreckage in the Canal, announced Jan. 30 that it would suspend the operations indefinitely as a result of the clash.

Israel had charged that the UAR had provoked the fighting by sending 2 patrol boats northward from Lake Timseh in violation of the accord, which, Israel claimed, limited the exploratory work to the area south of the lake. Egypt had completed a survey of the southern end of the Canal and insisted that it had the right to inspect the northern sector as well. The UN had not made public the details of the Israeli-Egyptian agreement on the clearance of the Canal; Israel and Egypt had given different versions of the pact. According to the Israelis: their forces opposite Ismailia had fired warning shots over the 2 Egyptian boats proceeding north of Lake Timseh; UAR troops on the west bank then opened fire on

Israeli positions with small arms and artillery; Israeli troops returned the fire, and the exchange quickly spread northward to Qantara and southward to Great Bitter Lake; UN observer intervention halted the fighting 2 hours later.

Israel reported that 5 Israeli soldiers were wounded and 2 Egyptian tanks destroyed in the Jan. 30 clash. Cairo claimed that its artillery had knocked out 9 Israeli tanks and had destroyed Israeli artillery, anti-tank and antiaircraft equipment. The UAR report said that the Israelis had fired at a Suez Canal Authority boat leading 3 other vessels north from Ismailia. Israeli shelling caused light damage to the authority's buildings in Ismailia, the Egyptians said.

UN Secy. Gen. U Thant said Feb. 1 that the Jan. 30 clash might permanently stop the clearing of the Canal. In a report to the Security Council based on a survey of the UN Truce Supervision Organization (UNTSO), Thant said that "the difficulties encountered by this operation demonstrate graphically the complexities and hazards involved in seeking solutions even to relatively noncontroversial matters on which the parties themselves are agreed in principle." Confirming the UAR's decision to halt Canal clearance work, Thant said the "future possibilities for its completion are in serious doubt."

An exchange of artillery fire across the Canal took place in March.

A number of clashes between Israeli and Egyptian forces erupted in June and July along the Canal cease-fire line: Israeli and Egyptian units fought a 2½-hour artillery and tank duel June 14 in the Suez-Port Tewfiq area at the southern end of the Canal. The fighting halted after UN observers arranged a cease-fire. Israel reported that one of its soldiers had been wounded in the clash. According to Israeli military authorities, the fighting had started when Egyptian troops opened small-arms fire on Israeli soldiers on the east bank. About an hour later the Egyptians began directing tank, mortar and artillery fire across the Canal, and the Israelis replied in kind.

Soviet & Israeli Peace Plans Rejected

Soviet and Israeli formulas for peace in the Middle East were made public in September and October 1968, but both were rejected almost immediately.

The 4-point Soviet plan to end the impasse between Israel and the Arab states was disclosed by U.S. spokesmen Sept. 25 and rejected by Israel Sept. 26. Soviet representatives had submitted the plan to U.S. officials in Washington 2 weeks previously. Although American authorities declined to publicize the details, other sources, according to the *N.Y. Times*, said the Soviet proposal called for: (a) Israeli withdrawal from areas captured in 1967; (b) a UN presence in the areas evacuated by Israel; (c) an end to the Arabs' "state of belligerency" with Israel, in existence since the 1949 armistice; and (d) a guarantee of future peace in the Middle East by the USSR, the U.S., Britain and France.

Israeli Foreign Min. Abba Eban rejected the USSR proposal Sept. 26 on the ground that it was "identical to a plan presented by the Soviet Union" to the UN Security Council Nov. 22, 1967. Speaking at a news conference in Paris after meeting with French Foreign Min. Michel Debré, Eban noted that Israel, "with the majority of governments, rejected this [1967] plan." Moscow's latest proposal, Eban complained, called for Israeli withdrawal from the cease-fire lines "without the possibility of sure and recognized frontiers." Asserting that it neither insured peace nor guaranteed Israel navigational rights, Eban said Israel "is called on to renounce its security without obtaining peace under the proposed Soviet plan. That is why we reject it."

Commenting on the Soviet plan, Muhammad H. el-Zayyat, the chief Egyptian government spokesman, said Sept. 26 that Cairo had agreed to implement the Nov. 22, 1967 UN Security Council resolution, which "excludes the annihilation of the Israeli state." "Therefore, if the Israelis say that the peace proposals do not require us to abandon the goal of annihilating their state, they simply mean they do not want peace," Zayyat said.

Israeli Defense Min. Moshe Dayan Sept. 25 had expressed fear that a resumption of war in the Middle East was more likely than it had been a few months previously. Commenting on increased guerrilla raids on the truce borders, Dayan said that the UAR probably was not ready to begin open warfare and had decided to help Jordan by increasing border tensions.

Israeli Premier Levi Eshkol warned Sept. 26 that continued Arab forays on Israel's borders could precipitate war. He discounted Arab claims that these raids did not have the approval of Arab governments. "Even if that were so," Eshkol said, "the Arab rulers would be like reckless parents who allow delinquent children to play with matches near barrels of gasoline."

A 9-point peace plan providing for the withdrawal of Israeli troops from Arab territories in exchange for a permanent peace treaty was presented by Israeli Foreign Min. Eban in an address to the General Assembly Oct. 8. The Israeli plan called for secure and recognized boundaries, a mutual nonaggression pledge, open frontiers, freedom of navigation, a solution of the Arab refugee problem, new arrangements for Jerusalem's religious shrines, mutual recognition of sovereignty and regional cooperation.

The Israeli proposal was denounced by the UAR Oct. 9 as "really a proposal for the surrender of the Arab nations." Muhammad el-Zayyat, spokesman for the Cairo government, ruled out any direct peace talks with Israel. Zayyat explained: "Israel was not established in the Middle East as the result of direct negotiations between the Arabs and Israel but as a result of force and of a resolution of the United Nations. Therefore any peace negotiations must be through the United Nations." The newspaper *Al Missaa*, owned by the Arab Socialist Union, Egypt's only legal political party, said Oct. 9 that the Israeli proposal was "nothing new" and was a "deceitful maneuver." *Al Missaa* charged that Eban "knows that the demand for direct negotiations is the rock on which all earlier attempts at a peaceful settlement have been smashed."

Details of the Israeli proposal:

(1) Israel and the Arab states should negotiate a peace treaty that would "lay down the precise conditions for our coexistence, including an agreed map of the secure and recognized boundary." The treaty would commit "both parties to the proposition . . . that their 20-year-old conflict is at a permanent end."

(2) Under terms of the projected treaty, the current cease-fire would "be replaced by permanent, secure and recognized boundaries between Israel and each of the neighboring Arab states, and the disposition of forces will be carried out in accordance with the boundaries under the final peace."

(3) Israel and the Arab states would "discuss other agreed security arrangements to avoid the kind of vulnerable situation which caused a breakdown" in 1967. The peace treaty "should contain a pledge of mutual nonagression."

(4) The "freedom of movement now existing in the area [captured by Israel in 1967], especially in the Israel-Jordan sector, should be maintained and developed."

(5) Israel must be guaranteed freedom of navigation by arrangements "founded on absolute equality of rights and obligations" between Israel and the Arab states and "indeed all members of the maritime community."

(6) "A conference of Middle Eastern states should be convened, together with the governments contributing to refugee relief and the [UN] specialized agencies . . . , in order to chart a 5-year plan for the solution of the refugee problem. . . . This conference can be called in advance of peace negotiations."

(7) Israel would be willing to work out arrangements giving Christians and Moslems complete control of their holy places in Jerusalem. "Israel does not seek to exercise unilateral jurisdiction" in this area.

(8) "Recognition of sovereignty, integrity and right to national life" "should be fulfilled through specific contractual engagements to be made by the government of Israel and of each Arab state to each other—by name. It follows logically that Arab governments would withdraw all the reservations which they have expressed on adhering to international conventions, about the nonapplicability of their signatures to their relations with Israel, or about the nonexistence of Israel itself."

(9) Israeli-Arab peace talks should deal with "an examination of a common approach to some of the resources and means of communication in the region in an effort to lay foundations of a Middle Eastern community of sovereign states."

In a move to promote peace talks, Eban said that Israel would "continue to be ready to exchange ideas and clarifications on certain matters of substance, through" UN Middle East peace envoy Gunnar Jarring "with any Arab government willing to establish a just and lasting peace with Israel."

UAR Foreign Min. Mahmoud Riad said at a news conference at UN headquarters in New York Oct. 10 that Cairo would agree to a "timetable," if arranged by Jarring, for the implementation of the UN Security Council's Nov. 22, 1967 resolution. Riad had reaffirmed Egypt's support of the resolution in a speech to the General Assembly earlier Oct. 10. He disclosed that Cairo had formally advised Jarring May 9 of its willingness to accept a timetable for putting the resolution into effect. Riad said that in talks with Jarring, Egyptian officials had affirmed "that the faithful implementation of the Security Council resolution represents the road to peace and that, on our part, we are ready to implement" it. Riad said Cairo supported the resolution's call for free navigation through the Suez Canal and other international waterways.

In his address to the General Assembly, Riad charged that Israel's "traditional policy of unilaterally renouncing its signature[s] to international agreements . . . make it all the more imperative for us, and for peace in the Middle East, to secure the supervision and guarantee of the Security Council in the implementation" of the Nov. 22 resolution. The remainder of Riad's speech reiterated Arab charges of Israeli aggression and of Israel's "campaign of terror and oppression against Arab citizens in the occupied territories." Riad asserted that U.S. military supplies to Israel enabled Israel "to continue its policy of aggression and defiance of the United Nations and its resolutions."

Israel Seeks U.S. Jets

After the 1968 U.S. Presidential election campaign had begun, Israel renewed its request for American jet warplanes. The *N.Y. Times* quoted U.S. Administration sources Sept.

14 as saying that Pres. Johnson had decided to bar the sale of
50 supersonic F-4 Phantom jet fighter-bombers to Israel at
least "in the near future." Israel had been seeking the planes
since 1967. Johnson's decision reportedly had been based on
the belief that the jet sale would: (a) damage prospects for a
U.S.-Soviet summit conference; (b) jeopardize possible arrangements for arms limitation in the Middle East; (c) damage the efforts of UN Middle East peace envoy Gunnar
Jarring.

But in a message Sept. 14 to the Washington convention
of the Zionist Organization of America, Vice Pres. Hubert H.
Humphrey, the Democratic Party's Presidential candidate,
renewed his pledge "to support United States military aid to
Israel, including Phantom jet aircraft, to maintain a balance
of power in the area."

Pres. Johnson directed State Secy. Dean Rusk Oct. 9 to
start negotiations with Israel on the warplanes. The President
acted under a Foreign Aid Authorization Act amendment expressing Congress' desire that Johnson "should" sell the
planes to Israel. The amendment stressed the need "to provide Israel with an adequate deterrent force" to prevent
"future Arab aggression by offsetting sophisticated weapons
received by the Arab states [from the USSR] and to replace
losses suffered by Israel in the 1967 conflict." In signing the
act, the President said he had taken note of the amendment
and was thus instructing Rusk "to initiate negotiations with
the government of Israel and report back to me." Although
Johnson did not specify what type of planes were involved in
the projected deal, it was presumed they were the 50 supersonic Phantoms that Israel had been requesting for a year.

The proposed plane sale was assailed by Egypt Oct. 10.
Al Goumhouria, the newspaper of the UAR's ruling Arab
Socialist Union, said that "these aircraft symbolize nothing
but aggression and the ambitions of expansionism and
racism."

Israeli and Egyptian jets clashed Dec. 10, 1968 over the

Sinai Peninsula for the first time since the June 1967 war. An Israeli military spokesman said that one UAR jet had been shot down into the Red Sea near Sharm el-Sheik and another had been hit but had headed back to Egypt.

Israeli Premier Levi Eshkol disclosed Dec. 15 that in his meeting with Pres. Johnson Jan. 7–8, Johnson had assured him that Israel would start getting the first of 50 U.S. Phantom jets in 1970 or sooner. Eshkol, interviewed over the state radio, made the statement when asked to comment on ex-Gov. William W. Scranton's remark that it might be 3 years before Israel got the jets. Scranton, former governor of Pennsylvania, had conducted a 6-country fact-finding tour of the Middle East Dec. 4–10 for Richard M. Nixon, who had won the U.S. Presidential election.

The U.S. Dec. 27 announced its agreement to sell Israel 50 Phantoms at a cost of more than $200 million. The State Department said that "deliveries will begin before the end of 1969 and will continue through 1970."

Israeli Premier Eshkol Dec. 28 expressed "deep appreciation" for the planes. But he cautioned that "even with the delivery of the Phantoms, the arms balance in the Middle East is a far cry from being balanced."

Nixon Hints at New U.S. Mideast Policy

American policy in the Mideast took a new turn with the election of Richard M. Nixon to the U.S. Presidency Nov. 6, 1968. As a Republican, Nixon was considered less receptive to the pressure of American Jewry, which had voted predominantly Democratic, and more open to pressure from the traditionally pro-Republican Mideast oil lobby. The Republican Party already had a position, dating back to Dwight D. Eisenhower's role in the 1956 Suez crisis, of so-called "even-handedness" in dealing with Arabs and Israel.

Ex-Gov. William Scranton reported the findings of his 6-country Mideast tour to Pres.-elect Nixon in New York Dec. 13. Scranton had aroused controversy with a statement urging a "more even-handed" U.S. policy in the Middle East. His remark raised concern in Israel and among its supporters that Washington's attitude toward Israel might become less favorable under the Nixon Administration.

After meetings with UAR Pres. Nasser and Foreign Min. Mahmoud Riad in Cairo Dec. 6–7, Scranton said before leaving Egypt Dec. 8 that as a result of these talks, he was "more encouraged about a possible peaceful agreement than when I came here." He had also met with a group of 4 Palestinian leaders. He flew to Riyadh Dec. 8 and was received by Saudi Arabian King Faisal. It was reported Dec. 8 that Nasser and Faisal had specifically reiterated to Scranton the Arab claim to Jerusalem.

Scranton conferred in Amman Dec. 8 with Jordanian King Hussein, Premier Bahjat al-Talhouni and Foreign Min. Abdel Moneim Rifai. He said later that the Arab leaders he had met with on his tour were looking to the Nixon Administration "for what they call a change." However, they were "not completely specific" about the policy shift they hoped for, he said.

Scranton's suggestion for a "more even-handed" U.S. policy in the Middle East was made Dec. 9 after he had crossed the Jordan River to the Israeli-held West Bank. When asked by newsmen at Jericho to explain his statement, Scranton said: "I think it is important for the United States to take into consideration the feelings of all persons and all countries in the Middle East and not necessarily espouse one nation over some other." He said he had found that Jordanian leaders were "reasonable in their thinking and wanted a just settlement" of the Middle East impasse.

In a communiqué issued after a meeting later Dec. 9 with Israeli Premier Eshkol, Scranton was quoted as saying that he believed that U.S. policy in the Middle East remained unchanged and that Washington's stand on Israel was consistent. Jerusalem Mayor Teddy Kollek told newsmen after meeting

Scranton Dec. 10 that Nixon's representative had agreed with him that Jerusalem "must not be divided again."

Nixon's press spokesman, Ronald Ziegler, Dec. 11 dissociated Nixon from Scranton's call for a "more even-handed" policy in the Middle East. Ziegler said Scranton "was in the Middle East strictly as a fact-finder. His remarks are Scranton remarks, not Nixon remarks."

On returning to New York Dec. 11, Scranton said: "The impression in the Middle East is widespread that the United States is only interested in Israel. I do not think that is true of the present Administration or of Americans. I think we have other interests." In his meeting with Nixon Dec. 13, he again urged the forthcoming Administration to adopt an "even-handed" approach toward the Arabs and the Israelis to help ease Middle East tensions, which he called "extremely explosive." Meeting later with newsmen, Scranton said Arab leaders suspected that the U.S. was "interested in only one thing—the state of Israel and its security. We are interested . . . in Israel and we should be. But it is important to point out to the Middle East and to people around the world that we are interested in other countries in the area and have friends among them."

Israeli Defense Min. Moshe Dayan met with Pres.-elect Nixon in New York Dec. 14. Dayan told newsmen later that "after this morning's meeting" he was not worried about a possible reduction in U.S. support of Israel under Nixon's Administration. He conceded that Israelis "didn't exactly like" Scranton's suggestion for a "more even-handed" policy in the Middle East. But he said he did not object to Scranton's call for improved U.S. relations with Arab states. Dayan said that he "personally would like to see more influence of the United States in Arab countries," particularly in the UAR, Iraq and Syria, to counter Soviet influence. He also said that he had been misquoted by newsmen on his arrival in New York Dec. 13. He was reported to have said that Scranton's remarks in Israel on American policy "weren't quite proper."

Dayan had come to New York to address the annual banquet of the United Jewish Appeal. Speaking at the UJA gathering the evening of Dec. 14, he said that the "key to the resumption of war in the Middle East is in the hands of the Soviets." The U.S., he asserted, could prevent another major conflict and pave the way to peace by "providing 2 elements which Israel cannot do itself—supplying weapons, which we cannot produce ourselves, and discouraging the Russians from intervening."

UAR Champions Palestinian Cause

The UAR, blocked by its military condition and its Soviet allies in its efforts to recover Egyptian territories occupied by Israel, turned in the autumn of 1967 to the Palestinian Arab guerrilla movement as a political instrument for furthering its aim. Even though the guerrilla movement was headquartered in Cairo, Egypt did not acknowledge supporting militarily the guerrillas' activities until mid-Apr. 1968, after having been discovered by the Israeli army to be controlling and conducting those operations.

The formation of a joint Arab military command comprising 8 Palestinian organizations aimed at stepping up terrorist raids on Israel had been announced in Cairo, Jan. 20, 1968 after a 3-day closed-door meeting. Announcing the action, a conference Palestinian spokesman, Dr. Isam Sartawi, said infiltrators would intensify their attacks to bring about the "liquidation of the Zionist state." Opposing a peaceful solution of the Middle East dispute, Sartawi said that "through our guns we are going to establish an independent Palestine." He disclosed that "for purposes of military expediency," the terrorist army would be divided into 3 corps: Al Asifa (Storm), Al Saiqa (Lightning) and Khaled Ibn Walid (a famous Arab commander of medieval days).

The Cairo meeting had been called by Al Fatah, the most

militant of the Palestinian terrorist groups. The other organizations participating were the Palestine Liberation Front, the Organization for Support Action, the Palestinian Revolution, the Palestinian Revolutionary Youth Movement, the Vanguard for Palestine Liberation, the Palestinian Revolutionaries Front, the Popular Front for the Liberation of Palestine and the Vanguard of the People's War of Liberation. The Palestine Liberation Organization (PLO), recognized by Arab governments as representing all Palestinian Arabs, did not attend the Cairo conference.

Al Fatah, in a statement issued in Beirut Feb. 6, said that its commandos had established "many well-hidden, well-stocked bases" in Israel or in Israeli-occupied Arab territories and were "now operating daily." Al Fatah said its guerrilla actions were "in no way aimed at the Jewish people as such." It denied "a Zionist insinuation that this 'terrorist' movement is inspired and directed from outside by such countries as Syria, Jordan or Algeria."

In its first broadcast, Al Fatah announced May 11 that its ultimate aim was to free all of Palestine and not only to terminate Israeli occupation of Arab areas seized in June 1967. The announcement, apparently beamed from Cairo, said that Al Fatah would broadcast an hour a day and direct its messages largely at Palestinian Arabs under Israeli rule.

Israeli army authorities had reported Apr. 8 that a few dozen Israeli helicopter-borne soldiers had crossed 18 miles into Jordan that day to pursue Arab *fedayin* infiltrators. All of the guerrillas, "about half a dozen," were killed and the Israelis suffered no casualties, the report said. According to the Israelis, the guerrillas had been spotted east of the Israeli Negev settlement of Ein Yahav, near the Jordanian border, 35 miles south of the Dead Sea. After firing at a circling Israeli helicopter, the Arabs fled back to Jordan. Several other helicopters joined the chase, and some landed behind the fleeing band to bar their escape. The operation culminated in a gun clash between the Arabs and their pursuers on the cliffs of the Hills of Moab. In addition to wiping out the infiltrators, the Israeli patrol destroyed a granite house reportedly used as a terrorist base. The infiltrators were identified as Jordan-based members of the Egyptian 141st Commando Battalion, receiving its orders from the Egyptian embassy in Amman, Jordan. The Israelis also claimed to have found documents telling of imminent attacks against the Israeli Negev towns of Elath, Sdom and Timna.

A report from Cairo Apr. 12 said that the UAR had begun to help Arab guerrillas attacking Israel by giving them arms, training and intelligence information. The report followed an Egyptian statement Apr. 10 in which Pres. Nasser had declared that Egypt was "fully prepared to support, train and arm the Palestine resistance movement because it is part of the battle for destiny."

Israeli military authorities May 28 sealed off the Gaza Strip to Arab traffic to counter a violent Arab civil-disobedience campaign that had erupted in the area May 22. The disturbances, in protest against Israeli rule, had broken out after the Israelis May 22 had imposed a curfew on the Saya Reyeh quarter of the city of Gaza and had ordered all its Arab men between the ages of 18 and 70 to gather in the square for questioning. It was believed the area was being used as a refuge by terrorists responsible for a mine explosion that had caused the deaths of 2 Israeli farmers in a jeep May 21 and for the wounding of 5 others at nearby Nahal Oz, just outside the Strip.

About 200 Arab women, shouting anti-Israeli and pro-Nasser slogans, marched on the military governor's headquarters to denounce the men's detention. The demonstrations continued despite the release of the detainees May 23, and the unrest spread to other parts of the Gaza Strip. Israeli security forces confronted the demonstrators in several of the incidents: They fired into the air May 25 to scatter a crowd of 400 persons marching in the city of Gaza's main street. The troops May 26 broke up a demonstration by Arab pupils who paraded through the streets after going on strike against 4 high schools. 5 girls were wounded slightly, reportedly by an Israeli civilian who fired a submachinegun after his car was blocked and stoned. Israeli troops fought with high school boys May 27 in the courtyard of their school in the city of Gaza. About 200 Arab women May 28 blocked a highway in Muzirat, 10 miles south of the city of Gaza, but ended the demonstration as Israeli troops approached.

An Egyptian letter to UN Secy. Gen. U Thant (made public May 18) charged that Israel was harassing the Arab residents of the Gaza Strip in a deliberate attempt "to empty the Strip." The UAR note, filed by Egyptian Amb.-to-UN Muhammad Awad el-Kony, called for an "on-the-spot investigation." According to Kony, 3,000 to 4,000 Arabs were forced to leave the Gaza Strip each week because of arrests, detention without charges, intensive interrogation and 24-hour curfews. This alleged harassment, Kony asserted, was in violation of the 1949 Geneva Convention on the treatment of civilians as well as Security Council resolutions. Kony claimed that as the Gaza Arabs left for the east bank of the Jordan River, the Israelis had "ordered them under extreme conditions of intimidation and harassment to sign statements relinquishing their inalienable right to return to their homes."

Arabs June 5 staged demonstrations and general strikes in Jerusalem, the West Bank of the Jordan River and the Gaza Strip to mark the first anniversary of the 1967 war. Demonstrations also took place in Arab countries. Jerusalem demonstrators clashed with police, and similar violence took place there June 6 and 7. Arab shops and schools in Jerusalem as well as in the Gaza Strip and the West-Bank cities of Nablus, Jenin and Tulkarm were closed by general strikes. A mass rally held in Amman, Jordan included members of Al Fatah. Baghdad radio reported a general strike call in Iraq and a rally in Baghdad. Demonstrations were held in Beirut and southern Lebanon.

In an address in Cairo June 5, Nasser called "the resistance on the West Bank of the Jordan and in the Gaza Strip" "the glory of the Palestinians and a challenge" to Israel. In Damascus, Syrian Pres. Nureddin al-Attassi called for immediate military unity of Syria, the UAR, Iraq and Algeria.

The Egyptian newspaper *Al-Ahram* reported Dec. 16 the formation of a new Arab guerrilla group called the Organization for the Liberation of Sinai, whose members, it said, had already had encounters with Israeli soldiers. The newspaper said the guerrilla force would "assume responsibility for resistance against the Israeli imperialist presence" in the Sinai.

New Soviet Peace Proposal Rejected

The French government announced Jan. 3, 1969 that it had received a "5-step" Soviet plan essentially similar to Moscow's previous calls for implementing the UN Security Council's resolution of Nov. 22, 1967. The new element in the Soviet plan, the French government said, provided for an active role by Britain, the U.S., the USSR and France in seeking to break the Arab-Israeli impasse.

The U.S., which had received the Soviet proposal Dec. 19, 1968, responded to it publicly Jan. 2, 1969 but only in a general way and without going into detail. But Israeli Foreign Min. Abba Eban Jan. 2 expressed opposition to having the Big 4 impose a settlement. He conceded that once Israel and the Arabs negotiated their dispute and reached an agreement, "it would be natural for that agreement to be reinforced by the support of the international community, not only by the 4 powers but by all the powers."

U.S. officials disclosed Jan. 8 that a note dated Dec. 30, 1968 from Moscow contained a new Soviet approach toward a Middle Eastern settlement. The message, handed to State Secy. Dean Rusk, hinted at the possibility of an "agreed" solution rather than an "imposed" one and of a package solution dealing with all outstanding Israeli-Arab problems, the U.S. officials said.

The details of the latest Soviet plan for the Middle East, first made public in a Beirut newspaper Jan. 10, were publicized by the Kremlin for the first time Jan. 25. The text, appearing in the Soviet Communist Party newspaper *Pravda*, was coupled with a warning that "there is no certainty that a conflict would not blow up with new force, threatening peace not only in the Middle East." In this connection, the newspaper said, "the present moment offers definite possibilities for movements toward a peaceful settlement of the Middle East problem." *Pravda* complained that such efforts were being impeded by the "aggressive treacherous policy of Israel's ruling forces, supported by certain outside imperialist circles."

The U.S. replied Jan. 14 to the Dec. 30, 1968 proposal. In its reply, the U.S. made clear that it found the Soviet plan unsatisfactory. The text of the U.S. reply was published by the Cairo newspaper *Al-Ahram* Jan. 19, and U.S. officials Jan. 20 confirmed its accuracy. The U.S. said in its reply:

• Russia and other states should "use all other influence to stop the grave increase of Arab terrorist operations" against Israel since these acts "inevitably lead to retaliatory operations." "The terrorist activity, supported or permitted by some governments, and the retaliatory actions" violated the UN Security Council's cease-fire resolutions and endangered the chances of achieving peace.

• Contrary to Soviet contentions, the U.S. believed that Israel had accepted and agreed to implement the Security Council's Nov. 22, 1967 resolution. Since the Arab states "interpret these clauses differently from the Israelis," both sides should clarify their positions.

• The U.S. supported the Soviet call for cooperation with UN envoy Gunnar V. Jarring's efforts "to reach a peaceful and acceptable settlement." It would be useful if Jarring helped the Arabs and the Israelis reach an agreement that would "include all elements for a settlement . . . as a 'package deal' " before any steps were taken toward implementing the plan.

• The 1967 war had been precipitated by "the question of rights of navigation through the Strait of Tiran." Therefore, there was no possibility of a peaceful solution "except through maximum security arrangements to guarantee these rights."

• The U.S. doubted whether the Soviet proposal for partial demilitarization of the Sinai Peninsula "provides the necessary security measures for the establishment of peace, especially in view of "events" there that had led to war in 1956 and 1967.

• The U.S. regretted that the Soviet plan made no mention of limiting the export of arms to the Middle East. "This question should be considered as an indispensable element in the peaceful settlement of the Middle East crisis."

Israeli Foreign Min. Eban Jan. 17 lauded the U.S. statement as "fully revealing the political, moral and intellectual weakness of the Soviet" proposal.

Al-Ahram, which reflected Nasser's views, charged that the U.S. reply to the Soviet proposal parroted Israeli policy. The newspaper asserted that outgoing U.S. Pres. Johnson, "more hated than any other modern politician, has ended his rule in an anti-Arab stance, a stance that invites more hatred." *Al-Ahram* said that Washington's answer to Moscow had been drafted by State Undersecy. (for political affairs) Eugene V. Rostow, whom it described as "not only a Jew but also a Zionist extremist."

In a speech to the Egyptian National Assembly Jan. 20, Nasser said that he supported UN peace resolutions on the Middle East. But he also indorsed Arab commando attacks against Israel. Nasser pledged that "we will not give up one inch of Arab territory," "nor will we ever sit down to negotiate with an enemy who is occupying our territory." He asserted that the Arabs were stronger militarily than they had been before the June 1967 war, and he expressed the conviction that "the enemy will not retreat unless we are able to force him to retreat by fighting." He lauded the USSR for its aid and described French Pres. Charles de Gaulle as "one of the greatest men of our century."

Nasser Offers Peace Plan, Warns Israel

Nasser granted interviews to 2 American news publications in Feb. 1969. In these interviews he specified his conditions for peace and warned Israel that Egypt was prepared to fight for its lost territory. Both statements drew sharp comment from Israeli Foreign Min. Abba Eban.

In an interview published in the Feb. 10 issue of *News-week* magazine, Nasser proposed a 5-point plan for a peaceful solution of the post-1967-war crisis and conditioned it on Israeli military withdrawal from Arab territories overrun in the 1967 war. Nasser said that if the Israelis removed their troops from the captured areas, the Arab states would favor: "(1) A declaration of nonbelligerence; (2) the recognition of the right of each country to live in peace; (3) the territorial integrity of all countries in the Middle East, including Israel, in recognized and secure borders; (4) freedom of navigation on international waterways; (5) a just solution to the Palestinian refugee problem."

Other statements made by Nasser in the interview with *Newsweek's* senior editor, Arnaud de Borchgrave:

• There could be direct talks between Arab and Israeli representatives. "We sat down with the Israelis after the 1948 war under the armistice agreement until the 1956 war, and we are prepared to do so again."
• Cairo could resume diplomatic relations with the U.S. if Washington changed its policy on Israel's retention of Arab territories. "If you give Israel Phantom fighter-bombers while they are occupying Arab lands, this can only mean you support this occupation. Otherwise, you would make delivery contingent on withdrawal." The U.S. "supports Israel 100%. Every day Israel says the occupation will continue and there is no reaction from the U.S. Does this mean the U.S. agrees? If you don't, all you have to do is say so. That would be a good start."
• As for the Palestine refugees, "the United Nations has said over and over again 'the right to return or compensation'" was essential for a settlement of the problem.
• Egypt had no intention of starting a war with Israel. It was Israel that "was preparing for a 4th round" against the Arabs. "So we must be prepared, too . . . the Soviet Union wants a peaceful settlement. . . . As for us, we do not want to go on mobilizing everything for war. We crave peace. . . . The Israelis have said many times their country stretches from the Nile to the Euphrates."
• Cairo supported the Arab commando attacks against Israel because Israel refused to support the UN Security Council's Nov. 22, 1967 resolution on peace in the Middle East, while Egypt accepted it. "So really what choice do I have but to support courageous resistance fighters who want to liberate their lands?"
• Egypt opposed the presence of U.S., Soviet, French and British troops in the Sinai Peninsula as part of an agreement on Israeli withdrawal, but it would accept units from smaller countries serving under

the UN flag. Soviet military personnel currently in Egypt were there as "advisers, not in uniform, and they take orders from us."

Israeli Foreign Min. Abba Eban Feb. 4 rejected Nasser's proposal as "a plan for liquidating Israel in 2 stages." "First, Israel is to withdraw to the previous armistice line with Egyptian troop and air forces reoccupying Sinai. Then, with Egyptian support, the so-called 'resistance fighters' will move to 'liberate their homeland.'" Eban said that "the only new element in Nasser's proposal is the explicit statement of the intention to remilitarize Sinai and encourage terrorist groups." Eban derided Nasser's assertion that Israel considered its borders to stretch from the Nile to the Euphrates. This statement, he said, showed Nasser to be "a man whose discourse lies outside the boundaries of reason or truth."

Nasser warned in a *N.Y. Times* interview Feb. 26 that there was a possibility of another full-scale war between Israel and the Arab states if Israel did not withdraw from Arab territories it had occupied since June 1967. Speaking to *Times* correspondent C. L. Sulzberger, Nasser said: "We are striving to end the occupation of Arab territory in Egypt, Jordan and Syria . . . by peaceful means." If that fails, "one has to fight." But withdrawal of Israeli forces alone would not bring a settlement, Nasser declared. Israel, he insisted, must permit the return of the "more than one million Arabs" who had been expelled from Palestine since 1948 if there was to be "lasting peace." "I don't mean that Israel should gain part of our Arab territory and then say in exchange it would accept Arabs," Nasser explained. Permitting the "expansion of Israel" "would merely be a step to achieve the dreams of some of the leaders of Israel to have Israeli territory expand between the Nile and the Euphrates," Nasser said. He stated that the Arabs would agree to recognize Israel's frontiers as of June 1, 1967, just prior to the outbreak of the war. Nasser also said:

Egypto-American ties—Cairo was "ready to resume relations with the United States" but could not do so "as long as the United States supports the Israeli occupation of our territory and as long as the United States supplies Israel with planes while it is occupying our territory. . . ."

Nuclear war—There would be a danger of nuclear war in the Middle East as long as Israel failed to sign the nuclear nonproliferation treaty. "We have signed it. But if they begin, there will be a race also. If they tried to build nuclear weapons, we would try to have our own."

Arab commandos—"I admire" the Arab guerrillas attacking Israel "because they are fighting for their rights." There was no danger that Al Fatah, one of the Arab commando groups, would take over the government of Jordan or of other Arab states in which it was based. Al Fatah "has as one of its main principles not to interfere in the internal affairs of any of the Arab countries. . . . It concentrates on planning on the Palestine question and how Palestinians can end the occupation and achieve their rights in their homeland."

Jews in Arab countries—About 5,000 Jews lived in Egypt. About 100 of them were "under arrest because they are Zionists and are in contact with Israel and were put under arrest after the war. Those who want to leave the country can leave. . . . The rest live as Egyptians and have all rights." The hanging of alleged spies by Iraq was not directed against Jews. "Some were Moslems, some Arab, some Christian. . . . It was the hanging not of Moslems, Christians, Jews, but of spies."

Soviet presence in Egypt—Cairo did not provide naval bases for the USSR or any other foreign country. The Soviet ships in Egypt "were visiting our ports before the [1967] aggression against our country, and they visit our ports also now. However, no single ship is here right now. . . . We welcome visits because the Soviet Union helped us after the aggression. . . ." Less than 1,000 Soviet technicians were in Egypt, "but I am asking for more."

Israeli Foreign Min. Eban Mar. 2 assailed Nasser's remarks as a "startling rejection of political truth and human values." Nasser's policy, he said, was "no peace, no recognition, no negotiation, no establishment of secure and recognized boundaries, no acknowledgment of Israel's sovereignty, no freedom of Israeli navigation in the Suez Canal, no agreement on arms limitation."

The Egyptian leader's interview with the *Times*, Eban declared, "confirms what I said after his *Newsweek* interview. He envisages a policy in 2 stages: first, the restoration of the fragile and insecure armistice lines of June 4, 1967, 2d, the effective liquidation of Israel through terrorist action combined with the introduction of enough Arabs into what remains of Israel to insure our country's conversion into an Arab state. His encouragement of those who murder people in supermarkets and passengers in civil aircraft is a true index of his character." Eban said that it was evident that Nasser "effectively rejects the Security Council's resolution of Nov. 1967, for the establishment of permanent peace with Israel in secure and recognized boundaries. We must regard all contrary declarations by Egyptian spokesmen as null and void."

Eban reported Mar. 5 that governments close to Israel had "told us very frankly that they do not believe that the United Arab Republic is ready for peace with us on terms that Israel would accept or that those friendly governments would advise us to accept." Eban said that the conclusion drawn by Israel from public statements made by Nasser and reports of his position relayed to Israel by UN envoy Gunnar V. Jarring was that Cairo would conclude peace with Israel only if it became an Arab state with a Jewish community, or "a sort of Lebanon." "This is so clear, . . . that to assume Nasser wants peace with Israel as a Jewish sovereign state . . . is utterly frivolous," Eban said.

Egyptian Airmen Fight in Nigeria

Egyptian fliers, said to be members of the UAR air force, helped the Federal Republic of Nigeria in subduing the Ibo secessionist state of Biafra.

By early 1968 observers in West Africa had reported the presence of Egyptian air force flight crews in Nigeria. It was said that they were flying missions for Nigeria against Biafra as part of a crash training program. Their aircraft—Soviet MiGs and Ilyushins and Czechoslovak Delfins—were serviced by Soviet maintenance crews.

Reports from Biafra claimed that federal air attacks on civilian population centers had resulted in the deaths of several hundred people during January and February and of nearly 300 persons Apr. 21-27, 1968. The planes used were reported to be MiGs and Delfins, and the pilots were said to be Egyptians and Sudanese. Many of the air raids allegedly were aimed at schools and hospitals, causing many civilian casualties.

According to Biafran charges and foreign press reports, Port Harcourt and other Biafran towns were subjected to air raids in late April by MiGs and Ilyushins piloted by Egyptians.

The Biafrans Aug. 16, 1968 reported air raids on villages around Abagana, killing 12 persons. Biafra radio charged Aug. 30 that 22 persons were killed when the planes bombed a Biafran hospital. Foreign medical personnel who had been in Biafra reported Sept. 6 that MiGs also had bombed hospitals at Ihiala, Ozubulu and Nnewi, killing many persons. The Ihiala central marketplace was also reported bombed and about 100 persons killed.

(The Biafrans capitulated Jan. 12, 1970 as Ilyushin-28 bombers piloted by Egyptians bombarded Biafra's Uli airstrip, which international relief agencies had been using in an effort to airlift food to starving civilians.)

WAR OF ATTRITION (Mar. 1969-Aug. 1970)

As prospects of a peace settlement in the Middle East began to dim in the early months of 1969, there was a noticeable upsurge in shooting incidents across the Suez Canal. Ultimately the clashes escalated into a series of encounters described as an Egyptian "war of attrition" against Israel.

Suez Canal Clashes

Israeli and Egyptian forces engaged in their biggest artillery duel in 4½ months across the Suez Canal Mar. 8 and 9, 1969. The clashes, following weeks of sporadic gunfire along the waterway, resulted in heavy damage to Egyptian oil storage installations at the city of Suez and in the death of Lt. Gen. Abdel Moneim Riad, 49, the chief of staff of the Egyptian armed forces.

An announcement from Cairo said that Riad was killed in Ismailia Mar. 9 when an Israeli shell "hit the position" where he stood. The Cairo newspaper *Al-Ahram* said that Riad was taken to a hospital in Ismailia but died shortly after his arrival. Riad had gone to Ismailia to inspect damage caused by Israeli shelling near the city the previous day. A statement issued by Nasser said: "It was an honor that Abdel Moneim Riad had given his life in martyrdom on a heroic day in which the armed forces were able to inflict upon the enemy losses which are considered the most severe it has suffered." A state funeral was held for Riad in Cairo Mar. 10. Riad had been appointed chief of staff shortly after the June 1967 war, replacing Gen. Muhammad Fawzi, who had resigned after the Egyptian defeat. (Maj. Gen. Ahmed Ismail Ali was appointed chief of staff of the Egyptian armed forces Mar. 13.)

Israel and Egypt blamed each other for having started the latest fighting along the canal. According to the Israeli version of the Mar. 8 clashes: Egyptian artillery opened fire on Israeli positions along a 60-mile front extending from El

125

Qantara to Suez in the south, and Israeli guns replied. Under a cease-fire arranged by UN truce observers, both sides stopped firing in the northern sector 2¼ hours later, but the Egyptians kept up the shooting on a 15-mile front in the southern area. Israeli forces resumed shelling in the south after 20 minutes, suspended the firing for 20 minutes and opened fire again 40 minutes later when the Egyptians refused to stop.

Cairo's account of the Mar. 8 fighting: Israeli forces had started the firing with an artillery attack on the Ismailia sector, and the shooting then spread along the entire canal. The UN truce observers negotiated a cease-fire, but Israeli forces broke the truce 10 minutes later by shelling petroleum installations at Suez. Egyptian guns replied, and the artillery duel resumed. (Israel claimed that the Suez oil installations were not a deliberate target of its gunners, that they had been hit inadvertently.)

The artillery exchanges came 6 hours after an air clash over the Suez Canal. The Egyptian high command reported that 4 Egyptian fighter planes, on a training flight over the Great Bitter Lake, were intercepted by 8 Israeli Mirage jets and that they shot down one of the Israeli planes. An Egyptian plane also was shot down in the dogfight. An Israeli report on the aerial clash said that an Egyptian MiG-21 fighter was downed and that the pilot was taken prisoner.

Ahmed Mahmoud, governor of the Suez District, said Mar. 9 that about 300 Israeli shells or rockets had struck the Suez refineries and nearby areas Mar. 8. He said 10 residential buildings and a movie theater had been hit in Suez but that there had been no civilian casualties. The Egyptian command said that one UAR soldier had been killed and 15 wounded in the 2 days of fighting. The command claimed that counterfire had destroyed 5 Israeli rocket emplacements, 12 tanks and other vehicles and troop positions.

In a report filed Mar. 9 with UN Secy. Gen. U Thant, Lt. Gen. Odd Bull, chief UN observer, said that 15 of the 16 truce teams along the Canal had observed the Egyptians firing from one to 32 minutes Mar. 8 before Israeli fire responded. Some of the first shots came from Egyptian positions at Ismailia, the report said.

Israeli Defense Min. Moshe Dayan, commenting Mar. 8 on that day's clashes, had said: "We aren't as weak along the Suez Canal as the Egyptians believe, and we have the capacity to hit back hard and painfully. War is war and if the Egyptians don't want to observe the cease-fire, they'll get back what they need to open their eyes."

According to an Israeli account of the Mar. 9 clashes: Egyptian forces precipitated the fighting by firing a machine-gun at an Israeli tractor working at El Shatt, opposite Suez. Israeli forces responded with light-weapons fire. 10 minutes later the Egyptians opened fire on El Shatt with a heavy artillery barrage, and the exchange quickly spread along the entire Canal to El Qantara; both sides used tanks, rockets and artillery. The fighting halted following 2 cease-fires arranged by UN observers. During the 3½-hour exchange, Israeli forces set 3 oil tanks ablaze at Suez (6 had been hit the previous day). Israeli shells also hit 3 Egyptian ships in Port Ibrahim (opposite El Shatt), a fertilizer plant in Suez and army installations. Israel acknowledged the loss of an observation plane to Egyptian antiaircraft fire; it crashed in Israeli-held territory, and the pilot was killed. One Israeli soldier was killed and 13 wounded; Israeli losses Mar. 8 were one soldier killed and 9 wounded.

An Egyptian communiqué on the Mar. 9 fighting said that 2 Israeli artillery-spotter planes had been downed by Egyptian gunners. Egyptian convoys headed eastward Mar. 9 to reinforce and resupply UAR artillery bases facing Israeli forces. The Interior Ministry announced a partial blackout of Egyptian cities as a precaution against possible Israeli aerial strikes.

Reporting to U Thant Mar. 10 on the previous day's fighting, Gen. Bull said that the exchange of fire had started with "mortar and artillery fire by Egyptian forces from an area northeast of Port Tewfiq against Israeli positions on the east side of the Canal."

Israel's Acting Premier Yigal Allon and Defense Min. Dayan visited Israeli positions along the Suez Canal Mar. 10. Allon said later that Israel would respect the UN-arranged cease-fire "on a basis of mutuality" and that it was "in Egypt's interest as well as ours to respect the cease-fire." Allon said he was "particularly impressed with the effectiveness of Israeli counterfire" during the exchanges with the Egyptians.

Israeli and Egyptian forces resumed artillery fire across the Suez Canal Mar. 11-13, 18 and 24. The heaviest clashes occurred Mar. 11 and 13. Each side blamed the other for starting the attacks, which were halted by cease-fires arranged by UN truce observers. The clashes reportedly were lighter than the sharper artillery duels along the waterway Mar. 8-9.

Israel reported that in the 3½-hour engagement Mar. 11, one of its soldiers had been killed, bringing to 5 the number of Israelis killed since Mar. 8. Israel charged that Egypt had started the fighting with sniping at Israeli tractor drivers on the east bank of the Canal south of Small Bitter Lake. According to Israel's account, its forces replied with machinegun fire and the Egyptians responded with artillery fire along the Canal between the lake and the Gulf of Suez. The firing stopped after UN truce observers had twice called for a cease-fire.

The Egyptian high command claimed that an Israeli artillery spotter plane had been shot down in the Mar. 11 clash. Egyptian Foreign Min. Mahmoud Riad was reported to have cautioned Gen. Bull, commander of the UN truce observers, that Egypt reserved the right to intervene against any move by Israel to reinforce its military positions on the east bank of the Canal.

Yigal Allon asserted Mar. 11, after the shooting, that "if

the Egyptians decided to interfere with our entrenchment work, they made a mistake. They are too late. We are already well fortified along the Canal and in Sinai." Allon warned that "if Egyptian aggression continues, we shall take countermeasures of the kind we have already employed, and some hitherto not used."

The heaviest of the latest series of shellings occurred Mar. 13 when, for the first time, the firing extended north of El Qantara and to within 12 miles of Port Said on the Mediterranean Sea. Israel claimed that the oil storage tanks at Port Suez had been hit again and that an Egyptian tank had been destroyed near the Firdan Bridge, just south of El Qantara. Egypt's high command claimed that 3 Israeli helicopters had been shot down during the battle. The Egyptians said that Israeli forces had started the attack with small arms fire and then with rockets, mortars and artillery near the towns of El Qantara, El Firdan, Tusun and Ismailia. Hamed Mahmoud, governor of the Suez district, said that 20 Egyptians had been killed and 52 wounded in the past 3 days of Suez shellings.

A new commando group, called the Arab Organization of Sinai, was reported by Cairo to have carried out its first raids behind Israeli lines in the Sinai Peninsula Mar. 23. In one engagement, the attackers, using portable rockets, were said by Cairo media to have destroyed an Israeli command center and radar site at El Borg, 10 miles east of the Suez Canal in the northern part of the peninsula. In another raid, the guerrillas reportedly struck at Israel artillery and supply positions at Ein Moussa, on the eastern shore of the Red Sea near the southern entrance to the Canal. The raids were said to have precipitated an exchange of artillery fire across the Canal Mar. 24.

Israeli army officials indicated Mar. 26 that they considered the Sinai commando group ineffectual. The Israelis said that the March clashes along the Suez Canal had paralyzed the Egyptian port of Suez and that the destruction caused by Israeli artillery and tank shelling had made it impossible to ship cargo or oil through the port.

Pres. Nasser warned Mar. 27 that "the day will come when the shelling and bombing of our civilians" in Suez Canal towns by Israeli artillery "will be answered by the bombing and shelling of [Israeli] civilians on our part." Speaking at the opening of the 4-day national congress of the Arab Socialist Union, Nasser said: "A new stage was emerging in the Arab struggle" to recover the territories captured by Israel in June 1967; Egypt's armed forces were preparing to "launch the battle of liberation" against Israel; the war would not be started prematurely, nor "24 hours too late." He assailed a U.S. document circulated at the UN in preparation for the forthcoming Big-4 talks on the Middle East. He said that its terms, not yet officially disclosed, showed "continuing United States support for Israel." Rejecting an imposed settlement by the 4 major nations, Nasser said: "There will be no negotiations with the enemy. We shall not give up one inch of land, and there will be no bargaining over the Palestinian land, which belongs to the Palestinian people."

At the closing session of the Arab Socialist Union congress Mar. 30, Nasser reiterated his threat to use force to oust Israel from the seized territories. The delegates had approved a resolution to expand the guerrilla activities of the Arab Organization of Sinai. The congress' executive body said Mar. 30 that Arab states would reject Big-4 settlement proposals if they did not require the evacuation by Israel of all the captured land.

Egyptian and Israeli tanks and artillery exchanged fire across the Canal Apr. 4. A Cairo communiqué claimed that Egyptian gunners had destroyed an Israeli tank and 6 observation posts, had damaged others and had shot down an Israeli helicopter. Israeli authorities denied the Egyptian claims. Israel reported that its forces had scored direct hits on Egyptian gun positions and had set a tanker afire at Port Suez.

Israeli and Egyptian artillery exchanged fire for 5 hours along the Canal Apr. 8. 4 Israeli soldiers were injured, 2 critically. Israel claimed that the Egyptians had started the clash with shelling in the Port Tewfiq area, then had extended the firing north to the Mitla region and Ismailia. The shelling stopped after 3 cease-fires arranged by UN truce observers.

Peace Terms Hardened

Diplomatic sources at the UN said Apr. 8, 1969 that Egypt and Jordan had hardened their positions in reply to detailed questionnaires, submitted to them in March by UN envoy Gunnar Jarring, asking their conditions for a peace settlement. (Israel answered Jarring's queries Apr. 2.) The questions posed by Jarring were published in Beirut Apr. 3 and confirmed by UN sources. The questions asked of the UAR were:

- Would Egypt accept the right of Israel to live in peace within secure and recognized boundaries free from belligerent acts or threats? If so, what borders would Egypt accept?
- Would Egypt agree that the territorial integrity and political independence of countries in the area should be guaranteed by the establishment of demilitarized zones and through additional measures?
- Would Egypt agree to the establishment of a demilitarized zone on its territory from which Israeli forces would be withdrawn? Would Egypt agree to UN supervision of such zones?
- Would Egypt accept as a final act of agreement all provisions of a mutually signed multilateral document that would incorporate the agreed conditions for a just and lasting peace?

In their replies on the questions of boundaries, Cairo (and Amman) were said to have insisted that Israel's frontiers should be rolled back to the area defined by the UN General Assembly's resolution of Nov. 29, 1947 on the creation of the state of Israel. These boundaries would reduce Israel's territory to about 60% of the land it had held before the 1967 war. (Israel claimed that this was the first time the

Arabs had raised the question of the 1947 boundaries in discussion of a peace settlement.)

Israel's reply to Jarring's question about the withdrawal of forces from Arab areas reportedly stated that its troops would be pulled back in accordance with whatever pact was reached with the Arabs on secure and recognized boundaries.

Israel's intention to retain at least some areas captured in 1967 were reiterated in separate statements Apr. 6 by Deputy Premier Yigal Allon and Defense Min. Moshe Dayan. Allon called for the establishment of Israeli settlements in the occupied areas to assure safe borders, which, he said, would eventually be accepted and recognized. Dayan, also calling for the establishment of border settlements, said that Israel "must take action to remain in the occupied areas despite the Big 4, the United Nations and the hostile populations of those areas." He specifically proposed the application of Israeli laws to the West Bank of the Jordan River, the introduction of Israeli currency and other measures to promote the area's economic integration with Israel. Israel's "return to the previous borders and the return of the [Arab] refugees of 1948 is suicide," Dayan said.

Egyptian Offensive & Israeli Retaliation

Israeli Defense Min. Dayan said Apr. 10, 1969 that the Arab guerrilla rocketing of the Israeli port of Eilat before dawn Apr. 8 and the rash of Egyptian artillery attacks on Israeli positions along the Suez Canal in previous weeks represented a new phase in an Arab political and military drive to obtain conditions better than those existing before the 1967 war. Dayan charged that "the Egyptians and their Soviet advisers are, day and night, studying, planning and organizing for the possibility of fording the Suez Canal, for the sake of a potential invasion of Sinai." He vowed to double Israel's retaliation for any future attack on Eilat.

The rocketing, for which the Palestinian Arab guerrilla group Al Fatah claimed responsibility, had consisted of 30 to 40 salvos. Israeli authorities reported that 10 civilians were wounded, 3 seriously, and one house destroyed and others damaged in the attack. Israeli jets, retaliating later Apr. 8, struck the launcher positions in the Jordanian port of Aqaba 4 miles east of Eilat. Jordanian authorities said that 8 civilians were killed and 10 injured in the air strikes. Observers considered the incidents, the first in the Gulf-of-Aqaba port area in 20 years, to be a gesture of defiance toward King Hussein on the part of Al Fatah and the swiftest sort of retaliation by Israel. The *N.Y. Times* Mar. 24 had reported on what appeared to be a "tacit agreement" between Israel and Jordan to "avoid" such incidents because of the area's "economic importance" to both countries.

Israeli and Egyptian forces engaged in sharp clashes along the Canal Apr. 10, 11 and 14. Following the Apr. 11 clash, the Egyptian army was placed on full alert along the waterway. In the Apr. 10 clash, one Israeli soldier was reported killed and 4 wounded by Egyptian fire in the Port Tewfiq area. Intermittent fire continued along the Canal throughout the day, Israeli authorities reported. Egypt claimed that in the Apr. 11 artillery duel, extending from El Qantara in the north to the Ismailia region in the south, 3 Israeli tanks were destroyed and several Israelis were killed or wounded. Israel denied suffering losses. In the Apr. 14 incident, said to be the sharpest since Mar. 8, Israeli losses totaled 2 killed and 2 wounded in fighting that included tank, artillery and small-arms fire across the Canal, as well as air clashes. Israel claimed the destruction of an Egyptian MiG-21 near the town of Suez and denied Cairo's claim that an Israeli plane had been shot down and another damaged. In 2 separate shellings, each lasting about 2 hours, Israel claimed its forces had destroyed or damaged several Egyptian antitank positions, bunkers and vehicles.

Muhammad Hassanein Heykal, editor of the Egyptian newspaper *Al-Ahram*, in an article published Apr. 11, called for an attack across the Suez Canal in which "Arab forces

may, for instance, destroy 2 or 3 Israeli divisions, kill between 10,000 and 20,000 Israeli troops and force the Israeli
army to pull back to other positions" in Sinai. This would
convince the U.S. that it should change its friendly policy
toward Israel and would prove that the Israelis were not
invincible, Heykal said. The current artillery duels along the
Canal were only "the beginning and far from the real showdown," he said. (*Al-Ahram* Apr. 16 confirmed previous
speculation that the escalation of Egyptian artillery attacks
along the Suez Canal was aimed at prodding the Big 4 to
reach an early decision on a Middle East peace settlement.)

Israeli Defense Min. Dayan Apr. 17 scoffed at Egyptian
claims of heavy Israeli losses along the Canal and elsewhere.
Dayan said that since the end of the June 1967 war Israel
had suffered 1,600 dead and wounded, compared with
3,600 casualties in the 1967 war. Contrary to Egyptian
claims that Israel had incurred 744 casualties in the March-
April attacks along the Canal, losses in that period had only
totaled 4 killed and 48 wounded, Dayan said. Dayan also
dismissed Egyptian claims of heavy destruction of planes,
tanks and fortified positions. Dayan conceded that some
Israeli tanks had been damaged, but he said "they have all
been returned to action." As for plane losses, Dayan said
that since the 1967 war Israel had lost 7 jets and one Piper
Cub, all downed by ground fire. Egypt had lost 15 jets and
Syria 3, he said.

It was reported in Cairo Apr. 19 that the Egyptians had
deployed Soviet-supplied long-range artillery along the west
bank of the Canal, apparently to implement the UAR's declared aim of destroying Israeli fortifications in the area.
Cairo reported that many Israeli positions had been destroyed and that the Israelis had suffered heavy casualties
since the start of the intensive artillery exchanges. Commenting on Egyptian strategy, the Cairo newspaper *Akhbar
al-Yaum* said Apr. 19 that the Israeli fortifications "could
have been one of the elements that would impede the progress

of Egyptian forces if they thought of crossing the Canal into Sinai to deal with the enemy."

Fighting between Israeli and Egyptian forces along the Canal entered a new phase as Egyptian commandos crossed the waterway Apr. 19, 21 and 22, 1969 to attack Israeli positions on the east bank.

Reporting on the Apr. 19 foray, the Israelis said that 15 Egyptians had landed at Lake Timsah, in the middle section of the Canal, but were forced to return to the west bank after a brief clash. The Israelis reported that several of the raiders were wounded. According to Cairo's version, 30 Israelis were killed or wounded and one tank was destroyed in the commando attack, made opposite the Egyptian-held town of Ismailia. The commandos returned safely to their base, Cairo said. The Egyptian report said that after the Suez raid another commando force, the Arab Organization of Sinai, operating behind Israeli lines in the Sinai Peninsula, had penetrated to a point near the Mitla Pass, 18 miles east of the Canal. The unit reportedly fired rockets at an Israeli camp, setting fire to tents and supplies.

An Egyptian spokesman said that 5 Israeli soldiers had been killed in the Apr. 21 raid. The report did not specify the location of the attack. But the Israelis said that the attack occurred 20 miles north of El Qantara and that the raiders were forced back to the western bank after an exchange of fire with an Israeli patrol. Israel listed its losses as 3 slightly wounded and a vehicle damaged.

Israel reported Apr. 22 that a 15-man Egyptian raiding force had been intercepted that day south of Little Bitter Lake and that 3 Israeli soldiers were killed in the clash. 2 Israelis were wounded and one was missing and possibly captured. The Israelis said another "boatload" of Egyptians was spotted later Apr. 22 heading for the east bank 4 miles north of El Qantara but was prevented from landing after being fired on by an Israeli patrol.

In a report to the UN Security Council Apr. 22, Secy.

Gen. U Thant said that "a virtual state of active war" existed between Israel and the UAR along the Canal. Security Council cease-fire orders "had become almost totally ineffective," Thant said. The secretary general's report was delivered as Israeli and Egyptian forces exchanged heavy fire along the Canal for the 14th consecutive day. Thant proposed no specific action, and the Council agreed that there would be no purpose in meeting to consider his report. Thant said that UN military observers along the Canal, "operating under great danger and difficulty, in each instance exert every effort to bring a quick end to the firing, with varying degrees of success, but no later than the following day, firing erupts again."

A U.S. State Department statement appealed Apr. 22 to Israel and Egypt "to take effective measures to insure maintenance of the ceasefire" along the Canal and "to avoid all actions which aggravate the tense situation in the area." The statement said the Nixon Administration was "increasingly concerned at the growing violence" and associated itself "in a very meaningful and material way" with Thant's report. The department warned that the continued fighting would "only delay and hinder" Big 4 efforts to achieve a peace settlement through the mediation of UN envoy Gunnar Jarring.

Clashes on the Jordanian front were marked by Israeli jet attacks Apr. 21 and 22. The targets in the Apr. 22 strike were 2 Egyptian-operated radar installations in southern Jordan and 2 Palestinian guerrilla camps in the north, near Irbid and Ashtafina. A Jerusalem communiqué said that the radar bases at Mazar and at Jebel Juwaissat, further south, had been completely destroyed. An Israeli official said that the Egyptians had established the radar bases in Jordan to make up for the loss of their Sinai radar installations in 1967.

The Egyptian government announced Apr. 23 that it regarded the 1967 cease-fire agreement ending the war with Israel to be void. The statement was followed by a report from Cairo Apr. 25 that Egypt no longer considered the Suez

Canal to be a truce line between Egyptian and Israeli forces. The Apr. 23 statement was issued by Muhammad H. el-Zayyat, chief government spokesman. In responding to UN Secy. Gen. U Thant's statement Apr. 22 that "a virtual state of active war existed" along the Canal, Zayyat said: "A cease-fire agreement must be followed by something—an armistice, a withdrawal, fighting or surrender. There must be something."

Following the Cairo statement, Israel called on the UN Apr. 23 to get Egypt to abide by the cease-fire agreement. A note submitted to Thant by Yosef Tekoah, Israeli representative to the UN, stated that "faithful and scrupulous observance of the cease-fire is the policy of Israel." Tekoah accused Egypt of carrying out "deliberate assaults," shelling Israeli positions on the east bank of the Canal, where UN observers were stationed to maintain the cease-fire. Another Israeli note, submitted to Council Pres. Padma Bahadur Khatri of Nepal, urged him to use his good offices to have Egypt "abide effectively by its obligations to maintain the cease-fire." Israeli officials contended Apr. 23 that there was nothing new in the Egyptian policy statement, that it was merely a reiteration of Cairo's long expressed belief that it was not bound by the cease-fire agreement.

The Egyptian newspaper *Al-Ahram* reported Apr. 25 that Cairo had informed Lt. Gen. Odd Bull, chief of the UN truce observers, that Egypt did not recognize the truce line along the Suez Canal.

Israeli helicopter-borne commandos struck deep inside Egypt the night of Apr. 29, attacking the area of the Idfu and Nag Hammadi Bridges across the Nile River and a power station west of Luxor. The targets were more than 300 miles south of Cairo and 200 miles from the nearest Israeli base in the Sinai Peninsula. Israeli forces had carried out a similar thrust deep in Egypt Oct. 31, 1968. Israeli authorities claimed the striking force had damaged the Nag Hammadi dam and bridge and the smaller Idfu Bridge, about 60 miles south, and destroyed 2 of the 6 pylons at the high-voltage power station at Isna, near Luxor. The power station carried electricity from the Aswan Dam to Cairo and other parts of the north. An Israeli radio statement said that "the severe blow to Egyptian morale and self-confidence was more important than any material and economic damage caused by the raids."

The Egyptian government Apr. 30 denied that any damage had been caused by the attackers. The government said that this had been confirmed by foreign newsmen who flew over the area. Muhammad H. el-Zayyat, chief government spokesman, said that Israeli planes had attempted to bomb a bridge under construction at Idfu and targets at Nag Hammadi but were driven off by heavy antiaircraft fire. Zayyat denied "that there was a commando operation. No Israeli soldier touched Egyptian soil last night." An Egyptian protest filed with the UN Securtiy Council Apr. 30, however, accused Israel of a "grave act of aggression against civilian installations hundreds of miles from the military front."

A separate statement issued by the office of Premier Golda Meir Apr. 30 said that the raid was in retaliation for recent UAR commando attacks across the Suez Canal. The Israeli attack on Egyptian territory, the statement said, was intended to remind the Egyptians "of their responsibilities for violating the cease-fire agreement" and "to make them aware that their acts of aggression cannot continue without being reacted to." The Israeli statement charged that the "intensification" of Egyptian "aggression along the Suez Canal in the form of artillery shelling, sniping, mining and raid attempts" "represent an advanced stage of Egypt's premeditated war against Israel."

The Israeli raid was followed by a sharp exchange of Israeli and Egyptian tank and artillery fire across the Suez Canal Apr. 30. According to Israeli accounts, the Egyptians started the firing, which ranged along a 60-mile front from

El Qantara to Port Tewfiq. 6 Israelis were killed; 3 were civilians working on fortifications.

Nasser warned Israel May 1 that further raids against the UAR could result in Egyptian retaliatory air strikes against civilian targets. Nasser asserted that the Israeli commando strike had failed because the Egyptian high command had been preparing for it since Apr. 27 and civilian volunteer defenders and anti-aircraft units were on the alert. He also said that the Egyptian commando strikes against Israeli positions on the east bank of the Suez Canal had largely attained their objectives. Described as "reconnaissance in depth," the raids had started Apr. 19, continued for several nights and then stopped. Scores of Israeli soldiers had been killed or wounded in the raids, he said.

UN Secy. Gen. U Thant was reported May 1 to have warned Israel and Egypt in letters sent Apr. 21 that the UN observers could not "be maintained indefinitely" along the Canal if they continued to be "subjected to unnecessary or excessive risks in the performance of their duties." In a report to the UN Security Council May 2, Thant said he was "increasingly concerned about recent developments which threaten the effectiveness of the [UN] observation of the cease-fire in the Suez Canal sector." Thant expressed particular concern over the serious wounding Apr. 22 of Capt. Joseph Young, a UN observer. Young was injured when his car struck an antitank mine in the Israeli sector. Thant said that Young was evacuated by an Israeli helicopter after the Egyptians refused to assure safe conduct for him. The Egyptians had fired at an ambulance summoned to evacuate Young.

Thant said that Lt. Gen. Odd Bull, commander of the UN observers, had proposed the establishment of "safe perimeters" around UN observation posts in the Suez sector. They "should be clearly marked and should be free of any manned or unmanned firing positions of any military personnel and equipment," Bull suggested. A report submitted by Bull May 2 claimed that Israeli forces had fired at a UN observation post the previous day during fighting with Egyptian forces across the Canal.

Israeli Defense Min. Dayan warned May 12 that continued Arab commando attacks against Israel and the Egyptian shelling of the east bank of the Suez Canal might prompt Israel to take the offensive. Asserting that Israel's patience was being tried, Dayan said: "we cannot win in defensive positions, but that does not mean that we will remain defensive." He boasted that Israeli forces could capture Amman and Damascus, yet he said it was not a matter of taking area but of holding the line. He said that since the June 1967 war Arab guerrillas had killed 70 Israeli soldiers and civilians in the occupied areas while suffering 400 fatalities themselves. Although the guerrillas had not succeeded in disrupting Israeli life or loosening Israel's grip on the Arab areas, they had become a powerful factor in the Arab world, he said.

(Israeli Foreign Min. Abba Eban charged May 12 that Jews in Arab lands, particularly in Egypt, Syria and Iraq, were "being ceaselessly persecuted by the authorities of those countries who regard them as hostages." Urging that they be permitted to emigrate, Eban said that "many Jews were languishing in prison under bad conditions for no crime except that they are Jews.")

Egypt & Israel Stage Commando Raids

Egyptian commandos raided Israeli positions on the east bank of the Suez Canal south of El Qantara June 23, 1969. A Jerusalem communiqué said that the attackers had been repulsed with 3 Egyptians killed and several wounded. The Israelis said their forces suffered no casualties. They denied an Egyptian claim that 18 Israelis had been killed and that a tank, armored car and other equipment had been destroyed. According to Cairo's account, Egyptian commandos attacked

2 Israeli positions on the Canal's east bank—one opposite the UAR base at El Ballah, south of El Qantara, and another nearby. The report said that the attackers, after finding that the Israelis had fled the 2d position, blew up emplacements and a fuel depot and then withdrew.

The Israeli military command announced June 30 that Israeli commandos had landed that day in the Nile Valley at Sohag and had sabotaged the electric power line between Cairo and the Aswan Dam. It was the 3d time in 9 months that Israeli commandos had penetrated the Nile Valley. The announcement said the contingent had returned safely, but it did not say how the commandos had reached their target 125 miles from the Red Sea. The raid was confirmed by photos made public July 1 by Israeli defense officials.

Israeli and Egyptian aircraft had clashed over the Suez Canal June 24, following a raid by Egyptian commandos into the Sinai Peninsula for the 3d night in succession. The Egyptian military command claimed that an Israeli plane was shot down in the air fight and that 12 Israelis had been killed by the commando assault. Israeli jet fighters again clashed with Egyptian MiGs over the Gulf of Suez June 26. Military spokesmen in Tel Aviv said that one Egyptian plane had been shot down and a 2d jet hit and "probably destroyed." An announcement in Cairo said that 2 Israeli jets had been shot down but that all Egyptian planes had returned safely.

Israeli Defense Min. Dayan warned June 26 that Egypt might resume war. Speaking in Tel Aviv, Dayan said that "activation of the Egyptian army is now taking place along the Suez Canal, south of the Canal, at the Gulf of Suez and northward along the Mediterranean." Predicting that the situation along the cease-fire lines would worsen, Dayan said he would not hesitate to call up reserve forces "in order to to fill security requirements and for training in preparation for the possibility of a new war."

Premier Golda Meir warned June 30 that Israel would

retaliate for Arab violations of cease-fire agreements. Speaking in the Israeli Knesset, Mrs. Meir said that Israel's policy of rapid and severe retaliation was intended for "self-defense and deterrence." Mrs. Meir also indicated that the talks under way on the Middle East by the Big 4 powers had provoked added Arab violence. "The big powers' intervention is being construed by the Arab states as acquiescence with their refusal to open negotiations with Israel," she said. She added that Israel would no longer interfere with the repair work on the Ghor Canal in the Jordan Valley. Israeli forces had been repeatedly sniping at repair crews on the Canal.

UAR Reservoir Hit, UNTSO Aide Killed

Clashes occurred on both sides of the Suez Canal between Egyptian and Israeli forces in July and August 1969. Israeli air strikes July 22 and Israeli artillery attacks heavily damaged the major source of drinking water for Egyptian cities in the Suez Isthmus from Ismailia to Suez. An officer on the Truce Supervision Organization (UNTSO) was killed during fighting July 27.

UN Secy. Gen. U Thant said July 31 that the death of Maj. Bo Roland Plane of Sweden while on duty near Port Tewfiq represented "a dramatic symptom of the breakdown of the cease-fire" that could result in "the utmost seriousness for the peace of the world." Thant expressed his concern in releasing the UNTSO report on Plane's death. It said he had been killed at his post by the explosion of an artillery shell that had been fired "from an area occupied by Israeli forces." Citing the constant danger faced by the UN observers, Thant noted that between June 1 and July 29 there had been 74 instances of firing by Egypt at or near observer posts and 15 instances by Israel.

An Israeli spokesman acknowledged that an Israeli shell had fallen short of Egyptian military positions near the Port

Tewfiq observation post July 27. But the spokesman criticized Thant for not stating in his report that Egypt had openly disavowed the cease-fire. In a letter received July 28 by Lt. Gen. Odd Bull, UNTSO chief of staff, Israeli Defense Min. Moshe Dayan expressed "deep sorrow" for Maj. Plane's death.

Gen. Bull reported July 29 that he had temporarily abandoned 2 of the 18 UN observation posts along the Suez Canal because the shelters were inadequate to cope with the "increasing danger."

The Palestinian Arab guerrilla group Al Fatah charged July 29 that it considered the UN observers enemies and would treat them as such. The commando group demanded the withdrawal of the observers from the Suez Canal and other areas on the ground that they were shielding Israel from the attacking Arabs who sought to recover their lost lands.

The UN Aug. 8 reported the temporary closing of a truce observation post 10 miles south of Port Said. The post was abandoned after serious damage to an access road by Israeli planes and orders by the Egyptians that the UN observers should not use the highway.

An Israeli military spokesman Aug. 8 confirmed reports that Israeli air and artillery attacks had heavily damaged a fresh-water canal that supplied drinking water to Egyptian cities and Egyptian troops along the Suez Canal. The conduit extended from the Nile River to Ismailia and all points north of it to Port Said. In an initial report on the incident, the *N.Y. Times* had said Aug. 7 that as a result of damage to the conduit, 7 tankers were transporting water to Port Said daily.

Pres. Nasser had alluded to attacks on the water canal in a speech July 23. He said "something strange" had happened at El Tina, just below Port Said. Referring to Israeli air strikes in the area the previous day, Nasser said there were no military targets there that justified such attacks. "Why then should the enemy strike at sand?" he asked.

Israeli & Egyptian Commandos Strike

Israeli commandos July 2, 1969 struck across the Suez Canal at Egyptian coastal positions near Ras Issaran. An Israeli military spokesman said that the commandos had killed 13 Egyptian soldiers and taken one prisoner. (Cairo claimed that 3 Egyptians had been killed and the others were wounded or missing.)   Muhammad H. el-Zayyat, Egypt's chief spokesman, scorned the commando attacks as futile. He declared that the raids were psychologically helping Egypt by sharpening "a fighting mood among the otherwise easygoing Egyptian people."

Israel claimed July 2 that its jets had shot down 4 Egyptians MiG-21s in clashes over Egyptian territory west of the Canal that day.   All of the Israeli planes were said to have returned safely.   Cairo said that 2 Israeli Mirage jets were downed in the dogfight.   Israel and Egypt also exchanged heavy artillery and mortar fire during the night along the Suez Canal.   The most intensive fire was in the El Qantara and Port Suez areas.

The next round of fighting began with an Israeli commando attack July 19 on an Egyptian artillery stronghold, Green Island, in the Gulf of Suez.   Reporting on the Green Island attack, Israeli authorities said that an Israeli force (apparently helicopter-borne) had seized the Egyptian fortress for an hour and destroyed antiaircraft and other installations. More than 25 of the island's 50 to 70 defenders were killed and dozens wounded, the Israelis said.   Israel admitted 6 were killed and 9 wounded in the assault.   A Cairo communiqué on the attack said that 30 Israelis had been killed or wounded, 2 landing craft sunk and a jet fighter shot down while flying cover for 2 rescue helicopters.   The Israelis were thrown back after hand-to-hand fighting on the island's beach, the Cairo report said.   (Cairo was reported July 21 to have sent 2 letters of complaint to the UN Security Council accusing Israel of "aggressive acts" in the Canal area.   One message referred to the Green Island fighting. The other charged that Israeli planes had bombed civilian areas in Port Said and Port Fuad.)

A military spokesman in Cairo reported Aug. 12 that Egyptian commandos had crossed the Canal the 3 previous nights and clashed with Israeli troops on the east bank. 2 Israelis were killed along the Canal Aug. 18. One died when an explosive charge blew up between the Firdan Bridge and Ismailia. It was believed the charge had been placed by Egyptian commandos the previous night. The other Israeli was killed by sniper fire near El Qantara.

Israeli Planes Hit Canal Targets

Israeli jets bombed and strafed Egyptian military installations on the west bank of the Canal during a 4-hour battle along the waterway from El Qantara to Port Said July 20, 1969. The raids were the first Israeli air strikes against Egypt since the 1967 war. A report from Jerusalem said that the Israeli planes had struck at Egyptian ground-to-air missile bases, antiaircraft positions and artillery installations between El Qantara and Port Said. Port Said itself was hit in the attack.

Cairo said that Egyptian ground gunners and pilots had downed 19 Israeli planes in the July 20 clashes. Israel said it had lost 2 aircraft while downing 5 Egyptian jets, including 2 MiG-17s and one MiG-21. The pilots of the Israeli planes were said to have parachuted safely into Israeli-held territory. The Egyptian statement also said that in response to the Israeli air strike against Egyptian military installations along the Suez Canal, UAR planes had bombed Israeli radar stations and antiaircraft missile sites in the Sinai Peninsula.

Nasser discussed the fighting with the Egyptian cabinet July 21. He was reported to have praised the Egyptian commanders for the "great results" achieved by their troops in the battle. Egyptian officials said that their forces had scored a victory and had dealt a "heavy blow" to Israel.

Cairo had reported finding the wreckage of 3 Israeli planes downed July 20. Foreign newsmen on a government-sponsored trip to the Canal July 21 to inspect the damage there and the wreckage of the Israeli planes were turned back on the outskirts of Cairo following reports of Israeli artillery bombardment of the Port Suez area. An Israeli army official acknowledged light shelling in the area, but he said that it had not started until after Cairo announced the newsmen's trip had been called off.

The Egyptian military command had announced July 6 that Egyptian fighters had shot down an Israeli Mirage that day over the Sinai Peninsula. Described as a reconnaissance mission, the Egyptian flight reportedly was the first over the Israeli-held peninsula since the 1967 war. Israeli military spokesmen denied the Egyptian claim.

Israel reported that its planes had again bombed Egyptian positions between El Qantara and Port Said July 22. The aerial assault was said to have been carried out in retaliation for UAR shelling of Israeli positions on the east bank. The Tel Aviv communiqué said that the air strike had silenced the Egyptian guns and that the planes had returned safely. Denying that Egyptian artillery positions had been hit, a Cairo military spokesman said Israeli jets flying over Port Said and El Tina were forced to flee by antiaircraft fire. The Egyptian military command said also that 6 civilians had been wounded by Israeli shelling of Port Suez and Port Tewfiq.

Israeli jets struck Egyptian targets along the Canal Aug. 13 and 17. The Aug. 13 strike was in response to the Egyptian shelling of Israeli positions at Ras Masla, 8 miles south of Port Tewfiq. 13 Israeli soldiers were wounded, 4 of them seriously, in the shelling.

Israel reported that one of its jets was downed by Egyptian groundfire during a 20-minute air strike against UAR positions 12 miles west of the Suez Canal Aug. 19. Cairo said that 3 Israeli jets were downed in the day's operations. The Israeli pilot parachuted and was captured by the Egyptians, according to a Jerusalem communiqué. Israel appealed to the International Committee of the Red Cross to negotiate his release. (The plane was the 3d Israeli jet acknowledged by Jerusalem as lost on the Egyptian front since the 1967 war. Egyptian plane losses reportedly totaled 27.) A Cairo communiqué said that the 3 Israeli jets had been downed by groundfire during a raid on positions in the southern sector of the Canal. According to the report, one of the aircraft fell in Egyptian territory, one in the Gulf of Suez and the 3d in the Israeli-held Sinai Peninsula.

An Israeli spokesman had said Aug. 10 that air strikes on Egyptian positions along the Canal had resulted in a decrease in combat activity along the waterway and had reduced the number of Israeli casualties in past days. The activity had reached an intense level early in July and again after mid-July; commando raids by Israeli forces had precipitated both series of clashes.

Soviet Military Men Advise Egyptians

In an address to the Israeli Labor Party convention Aug. 4, 1969, Defense Min. Dayan had disclosed that Soviet military experts were advising Egyptian forces on attacks against Israeli positions along the Canal. He said: "To my regret there has recently been some [Soviet] operational advice. If in the past they distributed arms and told the Egyptians how to use them, Soviet experts now tell them what to do." Israel, he said, would reject similar assistance if offered by another power. "We prefer getting the weapons and doing the fighting ourselves." Dayan described the intensified fighting as "the battle for the battle of the Canal." He said the Egyptians were attempting to soften up Israeli positions on the east bank in preparation for a large-scale invasion across the Canal. A possible major Egyptian crossing depended on the outcome of the "battle for the battle," he said. He disclosed that Israeli casualties on all fronts since the 1967 war totaled 2,100, including about 400 deaths. Israeli losses in the 1967 war were 3,336, including 778 dead.

Commenting on Dayan's claim that Soviet experts were planning Egyptian raids, an Egyptian source said: "It is no secret that we have been buying all sorts of modern, up-to-date weapons from the Soviet Union, weapons about which we know little or nothing at all. It is only logical, therefore, that we need Soviet instructors."

(The Egyptian Military Intelligence Department had announced July 6 that it had arrested a 4-member espionage ring working for Israel. The group, allegedly led by an Egyptian-born West German citizen, reportedly had acquired secret maps of the Suez Canal for Israel. The other members included a German and 2 Egyptians. The 4 were arrested in Cairo July 2.)

Upsurge in Canal Fighting

Israeli jets Sept. 10-16, 1969 pounded Egyptian positions on the western side of the Gulf of Suez, just south of the Canal, where Israeli commandos had carried out a damaging amphibious armored strike Sept. 9, 1969. The upsurge in aerial activity was marked Sept. 11 by one of the fiercest air clashes since the June 1967 war. Israel claimed the downing of 11 Egyptian planes in the Sept. 11 encounters, and Cairo said its forces had destroyed 6 Israeli aircraft.

Further details of Israel's commando raid Sept. 9 against Egyptian positions on the Gulf of Suez were released Sept. 10 by Israel. The follow-up account indicated that the Egyptian death toll had been considerably higher than the 100 to 150 first estimated. Eli Landau, a correspondent for the Israeli newspaper *Maariv*, who had accompanied the attackers, said that the entire Egyptian garrison had been virtually slaughtered, that every structure, vehicle and installation had been destroyed or put out of action. Landau said that the Egyptians had put up "increasing opposition" as the Israelis "approached their main target areas at Ras Abu Darag and Ras Zafarana, in the southernmost part" of their sweep. But this resistance soon crumbled.

(The Israeli government Sept. 10 lifted the accreditation of Anthony Hatch, CBS news correspondent in Jerusalem, for telephoning a report on the commando raid 2 hours before the official announcement and without submitting it to government censorship. On the basis of Hatch's report, the CBS network had erroneously described the raid as an Israeli invasion of Egypt.)

An Egyptian account Sept. 10 of the Israeli commando strike said that its purpose was to lure Egyptians into thinning out their forces. "But we did not fall into this trap, maintaining our strength where we judged it to be important," the statement said. The Israel attack had been directed only at minor coast-guard installations, and the Egyptians suffered no fatalities, according to Cairo's report.

The accelerated Israeli air strikes represented a new phase in military strategy in the fighting along the Canal front. The Israelis sought to neutralize superior Egyptian ground strength along the waterway and to frustrate Cairo's avowed "war of attrition" against Israel by striking at Egyptian forces elsewhere. An Israeli senior officer said Sept. 12 that one purpose of the new strategy was to force Egypt to "stop for breath," and maintaining the pressure "makes them stop for breath longer." Thus far, he said, the Egyptians were "not yet out of breath, but a little short of breath."

Defense Min. Dayan said Sept. 13 that the purpose of the Israeli air offensive was to "deter the Egyptians from taking any action whatsoever" and to remind Nasser that the Suez Canal was not the only front, "that his front is wide open" in the Gulf-of-Suez area. Maj. Gen. Chaim Herzog, former chief of military intelligence, said Sept. 13 that the Israeli air strikes served to show that the "front line with Egypt is not necessarily the Suez Canal but the whole of Egypt."

Israel, he said, was determined to counter Nasser's "policy," which Herzog described as one of "war of attrition within the narrow geographical framework of the Canal and to attempt to isolate this battlefield from the rest of Egypt." *Among the Sept. 10-16 air clashes:*

• Israeli jets Sept. 10 bombed Egyptian vehicles at Ras Abu Darag and Ras Zafarana, 2 of the targets struck by the Israeli commandos along the gulf coast the previous day.

• According to Jerusalem's account of the Sept. 11 clashes: Israeli fighter-bombers and ground units downed 11 Egyptian jets, while one Israeli jet was missing after the all-day aerial battles along both sides of the Canal. The Israeli pilot was seen parachuting into Egyptian territory. Egypt had committed 60 to 70 planes to the day's operations, while "we had dozens." The day's action was precipitated by an Egyptian air strike across the northern end of the Canal, and Israeli planes then took to the air. 8 of Egyptian planes lost had been downed in aerial combat.

An Egyptian communiqué on the Sept. 11 clashes said: Egyptian pilots had carried out 3 principal raids against Israeli installations in the Sinai Peninsula, downing 6 Israeli aircraft. Egyptian losses totaled 2 planes. The Egyptian planes in the first raid struck Israeli missile sites, antiaircraft guns, artillery batteries, infantry positions and radar sites deep inside Sinai. The 2d attack was centered on an Israeli naval base at Cape Mitla on the eastern shore of the Gulf of Suez. In the 3d raid, Egyptian planes pounded antiaircraft batteries, munitions dumps and supply depots in the northern Sinai. Military vehicles were hit, and Israeli soldiers in them were killed. Egyptian aircraft repelled an Israeli attack on Egyptian positions east and south of Port Said, shooting down 2 of the attackers.

The wreckage of one of the downed Israeli planes was displayed Sept. 12 to 30 correspondents in the Nile Delta, 8 miles southeast of El Simbillawen. The pilot had bailed out and was captured, the Egyptians said.

• Israeli jets Sept. 13 again attacked the Ras Abu Darag area. An Egyptian communiqué acknowledged that Israeli planes had flown over the eastern side of the Gulf of Suez, but it made no mention of the attack.

• Israeli authorities Sept. 14 reported a 50-minute air strike against UAR positions at Ras Ghareb and Ras Zafarana. Cairo said the Israeli jets had been forced to flee after they attempted to raid these positions.

• Israeli planes struck twice Sept. 16 at Egyptian targets in the gulf area of Bir Udayib within 20 miles of Port Suez. An Israeli official indicated the attack may have been in response to Egyptian artillery attacks across the canal. An Egyptian military spokesman said that

Egyptian ground fire that day had driven off a number of Israeli planes that had attempted to attack military posts at Ein el Sokhna and Ras Zafarana.

The Israeli army reported Oct. 28 that its troops had conducted 3 commando raids against Egyptian Canal positions the previous week, killing 6 Egyptian soldiers and capturing an undisclosed number of civilian workers. 2 of the attacks were along the Gulf of Suez. The 3d and deepest penetration was reported to be 100 miles southwest of the nearest Israeli base at Sharm El-Sheik.

Israeli Air Strikes Destroy UAR Missile Sites

A high-ranking Israeli military officer said Nov. 10, 1969 that all Egyptian ground-to-air missile sites along the Suez Canal had been destroyed by the intensive Israeli air strikes underway since September. He said that a number of Egyptian radar stations had also been destroyed or damaged in the raids and that Egyptian artillery and mortar positions had "taken a serious beating" in a 250-mile area extending from Port Said on the Mediterranean to the Red Sea.

The Israeli report of the destruction of Egyptian missile sites and radar stations was taken as a reaction to Egyptian claims of successful ground and sea attacks against Israeli positions along the Canal and in the Sinai Peninsula. Israeli Defense Min. Dayan Nov. 8 discounted the effectiveness of these forays. He said 3 Egyptian ambushes conducted Nov. 5–6 "could not undermine Israel's basic strength along the Canal front." Dayan conceded that there were gaps between Israeli positions that could be penetrated by Egyptian commandos. But he said that "we will find an answer to these raids."

Both sides provided widely divergent accounts of an Egyptian commando raid across the Canal Nov. 5. Cairo said that its forces, in a rare daylight assault, had attacked an Israeli armored patrol near El Shatt in the southern Canal region, had killed 9 soldiers and captured a 10th. Israel reported that 2 of its soldiers had been killed, 2 wounded and one captured by an Egyptian force that crossed the waterway 6 miles north of Port Tewfiq. In response to the Egyptian foray, Israeli planes bombed targets in the same area of the Canal's western bank. The Egyptians said the commando strike was in reprisal for the low-level flight of an Israeli Mirage jet across Cairo Nov. 4. The plane, flying at supersonic speed, presumably on a photographic mission, had created a sonic boom that shattered windows throughout the city.

Egyptian commando units of 30 men each carried out 2 separate strikes against Israeli positions 60 miles apart along the Canal Nov. 6. The first assault, launched 5 miles north of El Shatt, was directed against a lightly-armed Israeli patrol. But a Jerusalem communiqué said that the patrol was covered by a tank unit whose counterfire resulted in the killing of one commando and the capture of another. An Israeli account of the 2d Egyptian thrust, in the El-Kaff region, 5 miles north of El Qantara in the northern Canal sector, said the commando force had planted mines and ambushed an Israeli patrol digging them up. 5 Israelis were wounded in the skirmish that followed.

Cairo reported that the Egyptian navy earlier Nov. 8 had shelled an Israeli command center and other installations in the northern Sinai coastal region of Romani and Pelusium. The report said that command facilities, ammunition dumps and fuel depots had been destroyed. The ships came under Israeli air attack but were undamaged, according to the Egyptian communiqué.

Israeli authorities said that the Egyptian naval attack was directed against "installations on the western part of the El Arish-Qantara road" but caused neither damage nor casualties. 2 newsmen—a Briton and an Israeli—were taken to the target area Nov. 9 and reported that none of the Israeli positions had been damaged.

Israel & Egypt Trade Blows on Canal

Cairo reported that Egyptian commandos had crossed the Suez Canal Dec. 6 and 14, 1969 to attack Israeli positions. The report said that in the first assault, 250 Egyptian soldiers crossed the waterway in the northern sector, "forcing the enemy to retreat 5 kilometers [3 miles]" and destroying "all Israeli fortified positions before withdrawing" 24 hours later. An Israeli military spokesman denied that a commando raid had occurred. In the Dec. 14 attack, Egyptian commandos carried out a daylight mission against Israeli positions on the east bank of the Canal, killing 5 members of an Israeli patrol and capturing a captain, Cairo announced. Israeli officials Dec. 15 confirmed the capture of the officer.

Fighting along the Canal Dec. 16–28 was marked by intense Israeli air strikes against Egyptian targets and commando raids across the waterway by forces of both sides. Tel Aviv reported that Israeli forces Dec. 17 had repulsed 2 Egyptian commando crossings on the east bank of the Canal opposite El Ballah, north of Ismailia, killing 2 Egyptians and forcing the other raiders to flee before they could reach Israeli positions. Cairo said that the commandos had killed the entire garrison of an Israeli fort and that 3 members of the attacking force had been slain.

An Egyptian naval base came under attack Dec. 22, Israel reported, when Israeli commandos crossed the Red Sea and fired mortar shells at Safaga, 60 miles south of the entrance to the Gulf of Suez. Egypt denied that the raid had taken place.

The heaviest Israeli assault, a combined air and commando raid, was carried out Dec. 25 against an Egyptian naval post at Ras Ghareb, a coastal outpost on the Gulf of Suez, 115 miles south of Port Suez. According to Israeli accounts, demolition squads caused widespread destruction to the base and 4 prisoners were captured. Cairo acknowl-

edged the raid, reporting 2 Egyptian soldiers killed and 4
missing.

The most intense Israeli air strikes were carried out Dec.
25 and 26. The Dec. 25 raid, lasting more than 8 hours,
were the heaviest since the 1967 war. The Israelis said that
their planes destroyed Egyptian missile targets throughout a
10-mile-wide zone in the central and southern sectors of the
Canal. Egypt said its ground fire had downed 4 Israeli planes,
but Israel denied the loss of any aircraft. The Dec. 26 air
assaults were concentrated on Egyptian artillery and antiaircraft batteries in the southern sector of the Canal, especially around Port Suez, according to an Israeli communiqué.
The Israelis said that all their planes had returned from the
3½-hour raid, but Egypt said that one was downed.

Arabs Resist Israeli Rule of Gaza

Cairo had largely prevented the Arabs of the Gaza Strip,
most of whom were Palestinian refugees, from moving across
the Sinai Peninsula into Egypt after Israel had captured the
Gaza Strip in the June 1967 war. Many of these Arabs—
especially the younger ones—became increasingly radicalized
and showed growing hostility toward the Israeli occupation
administration. The situation was described in a general way
by Don Peretz (director of the North African studies program
at the State University of New York at Binghamton) in the
Jan. 1970 issue of the American quarterly *Foreign Affairs:*

Egypt . . . [had] kept most of the Palestinians under its jurisdiction
penned up in the tiny Gaza enclave, which was governed as though it
were still a separate country rather than part of the UAR. . . .
    After the 1967 fiasco, Palestinians were disillusioned with nearly
all the established leadership, organizations and governments. . . .
Wherever there were large concentrations of Palestinians, diverse
new groups emerged, led by a younger generation unfettered by the
political and social commitments of its elders. . . .
    . . . By far their greatest emphasis was on military or paramilitary
activity aimed at Israel. Disillusioned with failures of conventional
tactics against Israel and with Arab government fiascos, most of the
new groups drew inspiration from guerrilla techniques and activities

modeled on those of Algeria, North Vietnam and Latin American revolutionaries. The objective was no longer that of Arab governments such as the UAR or Jordan–to achieve Israel's withdrawal from the occupied territories and to circumscribe and delimit its frontiers–but to obliterate completely the Jewish state.

(Yasir Arafat, leader of the Arab guerrilla Al Fatah movement, was elected Feb. 3 as chairman of the newly-formed 11-man executive committee of the Palestine Liberation Organization [PLO]. In a statement made after his election at a PLO meeting in Cairo, Arafat pledged to intensify the "armed revolution in all parts of our Palestinian territory to make of it a war of liberation." "We reject all political settlements," Arafat added.)

Large-scale disorderly protests against the Israeli occupying forces in the Gaza Strip began erupting early in Feb. 1969.

Arab students staged riotous demonstrations in the city of Gaza Feb. 2–3. The violence was precipitated by the sentencing Feb. 2 of 3 Arab girls as members of a terrorist group in the Gaza Strip. One received a 3-year jail sentence; the 2 others drew terms of 2 years each for serving as messengers for terrorist bands. Israeli authorities released the 3 girls Feb. 3 on the condition that they end their connections with the guerrillas. About 2,000 to 3,000 Arab girls, protesting the sentences, poured out of 3 high schools Feb. 2 and rampaged through the streets of Gaza, blocked traffic and hurled stones, injuring several persons, including an Israeli woman soldier. Israeli troops, armed with night-sticks, drove the rioting girls back to their schools. More than 90 were injured and nearly half of them required hospitalization.

Tensions in Gaza were further heightened Feb. 3 when a grenade, hurled by an unknown assailant into a crowded square, killed 2 Arab boys (aged 9 and 16) and wounded 10 others. Israeli soldiers had clashed earlier in the day with Arab schoolboys demonstrating in the city.

UN Secy. Gen. U Thant received a note Feb. 3 from Egyptian Foreign Min. Mahmoud Riad protesting "Israel's barbarous acts against Gaza civilians, particularly women and children."

Israeli Premier Levi Eshkol was reported in mid-Feb. 1969 to have told an American journalist that Israel was in no position to repatriate Arab refugees (such as those thronging the Gaza Strip). Eshkol also said that Israel could not withdraw from such occupied Arab territories merely on the basis of (a) an Arab declaration of nonbelligerence and (b) recognition of Israel's territorial integrity together with (c) the prospect of renewed UN policing of a demilitarized zone along Israel's borders. Israel had to have a peace treaty with the Arabs; it "cannot live as a nation" without such a pact, Eshkol told Arnaud de Borchgrave, senior editor of *Newsweek* magazine.

Israel opposed the establishment of a separate Arab Palestinian state, Eshkol said. "Palestinian ties and connections should be with Jordan; they have the same customs, same religion, same language." The interview, granted so that Eshkol could reply to statements made by Egyptian Pres. Nasser in a similar interview, appeared in the magazine's Feb. 17 issue, which went on sale in Israel Feb. 10. Eshkol also said: "We don't want any part of the settled area of the West Bank–Nablus, Jenin, and so on. What we say is that the Jordan River must become a security border for Israel with all that implies. Our army shall be stationed only on the strip along that border." As for the Golan Heights and former Jordanian Jerusalem, "we will quite simply never give them up." Israel was in no position to take back Arab refugees because of its limited size and water supply. Since Arab leaders were using the refugees as "a convenient political football" and as "pawns," their return "would be a time bomb for Israel." Israel was ready to pay compensation for the resettlement of the refugees in such countries as Jordan, Lebanon, Syria, Egypt and Iraq, which had living space and water.

An Israeli military court ruled Apr. 13 that captured

Arab guerrillas could not be considered prisoners of war under the Geneva conventions. Another Israeli military court in the Gaza Strip Apr. 13 sentenced an 18-year-old girl to 20 years in prison. This was the stiffest penalty imposed on a woman since the war. The girl had been found guilty of throwing grenades at an Israeli patrol vehicle and injuring 4 soldiers. About 35 Arab residents of the Gaza Strip, many of them women, were injured May 15 by grenades and other explosive devices believed to have been thrown into market areas by Arab terrorists. (Since the 1967 war, hundreds of residents of Arab areas in Israel or Israeli-occupied territory had been injured by terrorist bombs.) Israeli security forces rounded up about 30 suspects. Israeli forces May 27 arrested 10 members of an Arab guerrilla group, the Popular Front for the Liberation of Palestine, accused of terrorizing Gaza Strip residents suspected of collaborating with the Israelis. The arrests followed the shooting May 26 of an Arab member of Israel's Gaza border police. An Israeli lieutenant was killed June 15 when a terrorist tossed a grenade at his patrol vehicle in the city of Gaza. 2 grenades thrown at Israeli vehicles in Gaza June 16 and 20 missed their marks and exploded among groups of Arab civilians. One Arab was killed and 21 others were injured in the first incident; another Arab was killed and 16 wounded in the 2d.

A 4-member committee of the UN Human Rights Commission visited Lebanon, Syria, Jordan and Egypt Aug. 11–24, 1969 and investigated alleged violations of human rights in Israeli-occupied Arab lands. The investigating committee had been formed under a Mar. 3 Human Rights Commission resolution that had condemned Israeli rule in the former Arab sectors. Members of the committee were Ibrahim Boye of Senegal, Chairman Felix Ermacora of Austria, N. N. Jha of India and Branimir Jankovic of Yugoslavia.

Witnesses at the Aug. 11 committee hearing in Beirut charged that Israeli authorities had tortured and executed civilians in occupied areas of the UAR and Jordan. Refugees from the Sinai Peninsula told the committee in Cairo Aug. 12 that Israeli soldiers had employed violence and repression to force them to abandon their homes and flee across the Suez Canal. An Israeli Defense Ministry spokesman Aug. 11 denied the allegations made that day in Beirut. Israel had refused to cooperate with the probe and barred the investigators from the occupied areas.

The report of a 6-country UN investigating team, issued Feb. 16, 1970, said that the Israelis had allegedly tortured Arab prisoners in Gaza. The panel also heard witnesses claim that Israeli forces "had occasionally ill-treated and killed civilians without provocation." The investigation was conducted in New York, Geneva, Beirut, Damascus, Amman and Cairo. Israel refused to cooperate with the group and barred it from all its territories. The UN unit's members were from Austria, India, Peru, Senegal, Tanzania and Yugoslavia.

A charge of torture of Arab prisoners in Israel and in Israeli-occupied Arab territories was contained in a report issued Apr. 1, 1970 by Amnesty International (AI), a private human rights organization based in London. Israel denied the allegations, and the U.S. section of the group dissociated itself from the report. AI's report was based on interrogation of a number of Arabs formerly imprisoned or held for investigation by the Israelis. It cited 4 specific cases of alleged brutality. AI said that the publication of its document had been delayed for a year while it pressed Israel to agree to a commission of inquiry to look further into the charges. The Israeli government Apr. 1 denounced the findings, charging that AI was "spreading unfounded and unchecked allegations, having their origin in a campaign of atrocity propaganda carried on by the Arab states and their supporters."

Israeli government leaders had announced Aug. 3, 1969 that Israel would retain the Gaza Strip, the Golan Heights and a major part of the eastern and southern Sinai Peninsula–the areas captured from the Arabs in June 1967. The statement did not specify the future disposition of the occupied West Bank of the Jordan River but it said the river would remain the "eastern security border" or one "not to be crossed by foreign armies." The declaration was in the form of a security and defense plank, drawn up by the ruling Labor Party's platform committee in preparation for national elections. The statement, presented at a Labor Party convention, was drafted by a 5-member group, including Foreign Min. Abba Eban, Defense Min. Dayan and Yisrael Galili, minister without portfolio. The decision on the occupied areas had first been desclosed in a government broadcast a few hours before the party convention opened. It said: "The Golan Heights shall remain under our rule and freedom of navigation from Eilat southward shall be guaranteed by the independent forces of Israel, which shall rule in the region of the Straits [of Tiran]. This region, Merhav Shlomo, will be linked contiguously with Israel commensurate with security functions and in view of possible attacks in the furture."The Merhav Shlomo (Region of Solomon) was a military administrative region of the entire southern sector of the Sinai Peninsula. It included the area south of an east-west line that cut across the peninsula north of Mount Sinai to a point in the region of Abu Rodeis on the eastern coast of the Gulf of Suez. The statement on the Gaza Strip was the first formal Israeli declaration that the area would be retained. The late Premier Levi Eshkol, who had died Feb. 26, 1969, had said that the strip jutted into Israel "like a sword in our stomach."

Israeli troops killed 12 Palestinian commandos in the Gaza Strip Nov. 29–Dec. 1, 1971. Of the dead guerrillas, 6 were slain during a search of the Burej refugee camp Dec. 1. Gaza Mayor Rashad Shawa disclosed Dec. 3 that Israeli authorities had released 300–400 Arabs held in administrative detention as guerrilla suspects.

Arab Summit in Rabat

A summit meeting of representatives of Egypt and 13 other Arab countries, held in Rabat, Morocco Dec. 21–23, 1969, ended in a dispute over the refusal by Saudi Arabia and Kuwait to increase financial assistance for strengthening Arab forces in their conflict with Israel. The conference was followed by a high-level meeting of the leaders of Egypt, Sudan and Libya in Tripoli, Libya Dec. 25–27 to map further coordinated action against Israel.

Pres. Nasser walked out of the summit meeting's final working session Dec. 23 after rebuking Saudi Arabian King Faisal and Kuwaiti ruler Sheik Sabah al-Salem al-Sabah for their rejection of other Arab states' demands for more war funds. Egyptian War Min. Muhammad Fawzi had prepared specific requests for weapons and troops and had submitted the requests in a report at the Dec. 22 meeting. All the attending countries, with the exception of Saudi Arabia and Kuwait, had agreed to supply men, weapons or money as proposed in the report. The 2 dissenting rulers were said to have explained that they lacked the money for modern weapons.

The delegates of Syria, Iraq and Southern Yemen, angered by the Saudi Arabian and Kuwaiti decision, boycotted the conference's closing ceremony, although Nasser returned to the gathering to attend. The meeting then hastily adjourned without the issuance of a communiqué. Moroccan King Hassan II explained that the secret nature of the discussions and decisions were the reason for the lack of a joint statement. Nasser said Dec. 25 that "we decided not to issue any communiqué that could have given unrealistic hopes to the peoples of the Arab nation." But he said that the conference had "achieved some positive results."

Also taking part in the Rabat conference was the Palestine Liberation Organization, represented by Yasir Arafat, chairman of the commando group's executive committee.

The leaders who stayed away were Presidents Ahmed Hassan al-Bakr of Iraq, Nureddin al-Attassi of Syria and Habib Bourguiba of Tunisia.

A communiqué issued Dec. 27 at the end of the Tripoli talks said that Nasser, the Libyan ruler, Col. Mouammar el-Qaddafi, and the Sudanese ruler, Maj. Gen. Gafaar al-Nimeiri, had agreed, to hold regular meetings every 4 months to coordinate measures against Israel in the military, political and economic spheres. Special committees were to be established in these fields. Stressing the need for greater Arab solidarity, the communiqué said that the Tripoli talks had expanded the Arab western front against Israel, which henceforth extended from Tripoli through Cairo to Khartoum. The Middle East News Agency in Cairo reported Dec. 27 that Libya would be included in the "front line" nations of Egypt, Syria, Jordan, Iraq and Sudan in future meetings to map plans for the struggle against Israel.

Nasser declared during a visit to Benghazi, Libya, Dec. 29, that the Arab lands seized by Israel in the 1967 war "can only be returned by force." He accused the U.S. of supporting Israeli efforts to annex more Arab territory.

French Arms to Libya Bolster Egypt

French Defense Min. Michael Debré announced Jan. 21, 1970 that France had agreed to sell Libya 100 jets, twice the number originally confirmed Jan. 9. It was widely charged that the planes, for which Libya was said to have insufficient pilots, would add to Egypt's strength, one way or another. In a report to the Defense Committee of the National Assembly, Debré said that during the next 4 years France would deliver to Libya 30 Mirage-3-E interceptors and 20 reconnaissance trainer planes, in addition to the 50 Mirage-5 ground attack planes initially reported. A French government spokesman said Jan. 26 that the figure was "closer to 110 than 100." The government spokesman explained that the figures cited by Debré were approximate and that the actual number was, therefore, slightly more than the 100 originally reported in the press.

In exchange for the aircraft, Libya had agreed to end its support of rebels in neighboring Chad, a former French colony, Debré said. France reportedly had a force of 2,600 to 3,000 men assisting the Chad government against the insurgents. Assailing critics who had argued that Libya would turn the planes over to Egypt for use against Israel, Debré charged that the "Anglo-Saxons"–Britain and the U.S.–had tried to sell planes to Libya but failed. "The Anglo-Saxons fear above all that France will take their economic markets," he said. Noting that the Soviet Union also had offered to sell weapons to Libya, Debré asked, "Why should it be more immoral to deal with France?" He confirmed that despite the French arms embargo against the principal belligerents in the Middle East, Israel had been getting, by official "selectivity," some French weapons and spare parts for Mirages previously received.

The U.S. State Department reported Jan. 21 that State Secy. William P. Rogers had summoned French Amb. Charles Lucet to protest that the French-Libyan arms deal "could disturb the arms balance in the Middle East." The department expressed displeasure with France's failure to consult Washington about the arms transaction. The French Foreign Ministry retorted Jan. 22 that Paris had "no obligation to inform anybody, but in the course of exchanges of views, we did in fact inform the United States" about the negotiations with Libya.

The French press Jan. 22 was virtually unanimous in condemning the French government's actions. The arms deal also provoked criticism from the political opposition, including Maurice Faure, president of the Radical Socialist Party, Sen. Jean Lecanuet and the Socialist Party.

The Israeli government Jan. 22 accused France of "aggravating the situation in the Middle East." Israeli Foreign Min.

Abba Eban had told the Knesset Jan. 14 that "France has become, with the Soviet Union, the most active element in upsetting the balance of security and peace in the Middle East." He disclosed that French Foreign Min. Maurice Schumann had informed Israeli Amb. Walter Eytan in Oct. 1969 that if Israel relinquished its claim to 50 French Mirages (paid for by Israel but not delivered because of the French embargo), France would not sell them to Israel's enemies, "near or far." Israel's "answer is to look to the United States for equipment and loans and to increase our self-sufficiency," Eban said. (The Belgian Foreign Ministry confirmed Jan. 15 that an Israeli ship had left the Belgian port of Zeebrugge Jan. 13 carrying a cargo of U.S. weapons and military equipment, surplus material that had been used by American forces in West Germany. The ministry said that Belgian authorities had been asked by U.S. and French officials to permit the transit and loading of the arms.)

A *N.Y. Times* dispatch from Washington Jan. 23 said that an Egyptian agent, Fathi el-Dib, had initiated the Libyan-French arms transaction in Oct. 1969 and that Egyptian officers with Libyan passports were members of the Libyan mission involved in the start of negotiations the following month. Dib was said to have pressed the Libyan government for more than 2 years to negotiate the purchase of the Mirages. His purpose, it was reported, was to enable Egypt to bypass France's arms embargo after Cairo had tried unsuccessfully to buy the planes from France. Defense Min. Debré and some of his top aides were said to have been aware that some of the Egyptians in the arms talks in November were carrying Libyan passports but that French Foreign Ministry officials involved in the actual talks were not informed about it. The French government and the Libyan embassy in Paris Jan. 24 denied the *Times* report.

U.S. government officials confirmed Mar. 19 that under an agreement concluded in May 1969, the U.S. was committed to sell Libya 8 Northrup F-5 Freedom fighter jets.

164 EGYPT & NASSER: 1967-72

The planes, due for delivery in 1971-3, were in addition to 10 jets already sent to Libya under an agreement signed in 1967. The transaction was disclosed after Adlai E. Stevenson 3d, the Illinois state treasurer and Democratic nominee for U.S. Senator, criticized the Nixon Administration Mar. 19 for arranging the deal while taking issue with France for doing the very same thing. The Administration "owes the nation an explanation," Stevenson said. Stevenson said he had learned of the U.S.-Libyan accord from a trade magazine while researching the Middle East question.

A State Department official said that American military aid to Libya was "under review." Other officials said the proposed shipment of the 8 planes was being reassessed in view of internal developments in Libya, including ouster of King Idris in Sept. 1969.

Greek officials disclosed Jan. 31 that the Greek Air Force Academy had graduated some 120 Libyan pilots over the past 4 years. They reported that 112 Libyans were currently being trained at the Greek school. The spokesmen said that the agreement for the training of Libyans dated from 1965. Libyans were also enrolled in the Greek Naval Cadet School.

Israeli Aerial Offensive

Penetrating deep into the Nile Delta, Sinai Peninsula-based Israeli jets bombed Egyptian military centers in the vicinity of Cairo Jan. 7, 13, 16 and 18, 1970. Among the targets struck Jan. 13 were an army base south of El Khanka (reportedly a major supply depot for the Egyptian air force), about 9 miles southeast of Cairo, and Tel el-Kabir, 25 miles northeast of the capital. The latter base had previously been hit Jan. 7 at the start of Israel's stepped-up aerial offensive against the Egyptian interior. Egyptian authorities acknowledged the attack on El Khanka but said that the Israeli raiders were driven off by Egyptian planes and antiaircraft defenses.

A Tel Aviv communiqué said that Israeli jets Jan. 7 had bombed 3 Egyptian military camps within 25 miles of Cairo. The raids were the closest to the Egyptian capital since the 1967 war. The targets were at Dahshur on the western bank of the Nile River, 18 miles south of Cairo, Inchass el-Raml, 18 miles northeast of the city, and Tel el-Kabir, 25 miles to the northeast. The raids were scored Jan. 14 by Ahmed Esmat Abdel Meguid, chief spokesman for the Egyptian govern-ment, as a futile Israeli attempt to achieve "political and psychological effects." (Tel Aviv had claimed the destruction of 2 Egyptian MiG-21s Jan. 4 during an attempted intercep-tion of an Israeli air strike across the northern sector of the Suez Canal, 20 miles inside Egypt. Cairo said that the at-tackers were driven off during an attempted bombing of Egyptian positions near El Qantara and that one Israeli plane was downed. Israel said that all its planes returned safely.)

Israeli jets Jan. 16 bombed Egyptian army camps and other military targets along the highway linking Port Suez and Cairo, flying to within 40 miles of the capital. A radar station at Bir Odeib, 20 miles south of Port Suez, was re-ported destroyed. Israeli authorities acknowledged the loss of one plane but denied Egyptian claims that 2 other jets had been downed. Israeli jets Jan. 18 bombed the Huckstep mili-tary camp, 12 miles east of Cairo, and a weapons depot at Gebel Hof, 16 miles south of the capital. Huckstep was only 5 miles from Almaza Airport, the international airfield east of Cairo. Egyptian authorities said that Israeli rockets fired at the base missed their target.

Israeli Premier Golda Meir said Jan. 16 that the latest aerial offensive against Egypt served "to impede [Cairo's] preparations for another war." Lt. Gen. Haim Bar-Lev, chief of staff, had said that the strikes had effectively halted sus-tained Egyptian artillery bombardments in the Suez Canal area, which had started in Mar. 1969.

Israel reported that its ground-to-air missiles Jan. 10 had destroyed 2 Egyptian fighter-bombers raiding an Israeli installation near Ras Sudr, 25 miles south of Port Suez. According to a Cairo communiqué, the Egyptian planes destroyed the Israeli missile installation and returned safely to their bases.

Egypt said Jan. 18 that one Israeli jet had been shot down and another damaged in the day's action along the Canal. Other Israeli planes ranged along the Canal sector, striking at El Qantara West and Port Suez.

An Israeli air strike took place Jan. 23 on Egyptian military targets in the vicinity of Cairo. The targets hit were a military camp 2 miles north of the industrial city of Helwan, 15 miles south of Cairo, and the Huckstep Camp, 12 miles east of the capital.

Israel's aerial offensive was explained further in public statements by 3 Israeli leaders. In a *N.Y. Times* interview Feb. 6, Premier Meir said that "we're not bombing the interior" of Egypt to force Nassar "to make peace." The purpose of the air strikes, she said, was "to make it well known to him and to the people of Egypt that either it's quiet on both sides or there's bombing on both sides." Soviet notes to the Western powers indicated that Nasser "is not happy, the war has been brought home to him," Mrs. Meir said. "He can't fool his people anymore" when "they hear planes right near Cairo."

Defense Min. Dayan had said Jan. 28 that the object of the raids in the Cairo area was to relieve Egyptian pressure along the Canal. This strategy already had succeeded and Israeli casualties on the Suez front had dropped since the onset of Israel's latest air offensive, Dayan said.

Yitzhak Rabin, Israeli ambassador to the U.S., said in Washington Jan. 30 that the Israeli raids on the outskirts of Cairo were not aimed at bringing down Nasser. He said their purpose was to convince Cairo's leaders they should curtail their ground and air attacks across the Suez Canal and possibly to convince them of the need to agree to the reimposition of the June 1967 cease-fire. Another aim of the Israeli jet strikes, Rabin said, was to make clear to the Egyptian people that if their leaders were unable to protect Cairo, "how can they think of mounting a complicated military operation against Israel?"

(Cairo claimed that its planes Jan. 23 had carried out an attack deep inside Israeli-held territory, bombing the Sinai Peninsula town of El Arish, 85 miles east of the Suez Canal. Israel said that only a single Egyptian plane had flown over El Arish, dropping 11 bombs, injuring 2 Arab residents and damaging some buildings.)

Commandos Active

Israeli commandos were reported Jan. 3, 1970 to have captured and airlifted to their lines a 7-ton Soviet-built radar installation in use by the Egyptians. The Israelis performed the feat during an attack Dec. 25, 1969 on an Egyptian coastal position at Ras Ghareb on the Gulf of Suez. After discovering the radar installation at the site, they dismantled it and airlifted it back to Israeli-occupied Sinai in 2 freight-carrying helicopters. The Israelis had made no mention of the seizure of the equipment in their initial report of the commando strike. Maj. Gen. Haim Herzog, former chief of Israeli army intelligence, described the radar as the Soviet P-12 type, designed to detect low-flying planes. He said it had a range of 188 miles. The Israelis had captured a P-12 system in the 1967 war, but it was burnt out, according to Herzog.

The capture of the P-12 system took place during an intensification of Israeli attacks on Egypt's interior. This intensification was said to have prompted the Egyptian government to tighten discipline in the armed forces and to spur civilian morale. It was reported Jan. 23 that severe punishment had been meted out to the officers involved in the Israeli capture of the radar system. 4 Egyptian army officers were said to have been executed by firing squad and up to 12 others had been given long prison terms for alleged laxity. Some of them were said to have fled from the radar site when the Israeli commandos landed.

In the fiercest fighting since the 1967 war, Israeli helicopter-borne troops had landed Jan. 22 on the Egyptian
island of Shadwan, at the entrance to the Gulf of Suez, and
neutralized the island as a military base before withdrawing
the following day. Israel said the 10-mile long Red Sea island,
which protected an Egyptian naval base at Safaga, 50 miles
south along the Egyptian coast, had been used to spy on
Israeli air and naval activities. The Israelis said that during the
30-hour operation, about 70 Egyptians were killed and 62
taken prisoner and that 3 Israelis were slain in 3 hours of
fierce hand-to-hand fighting. All Egyptian military installations were destroyed and all equipment, including a British-
built radar station, was airlifted back to Israel, according to
the Israeli report. A Jerusalem communiqué said the enemy
fatalities included 40 crew members of 3 torpedo boats sunk
Jan. 22 during attempts to relieve the beleaguered island
garrison. Israeli jets sank 2 of the vessels 10 miles south of
Shadwan, while a 3d was hit and sunk by Israeli guns on the
island. Cairo estimated that 50 attackers were killed or
wounded and acknowledged Egyptian losses at 80 killed,
wounded or missing. An Israeli military spokesman had said
Jan. 22 that the raid on Shadwan must be considered "within
the context of current military operations taking place as a
result of Egypt's decision to renounce the ceasefire" that
ended the 1967 war.

An apparent Egyptian attempt to resupply Shadwan by
sea was thwarted Jan. 25 when Israeli jets attacked and
disabled what a Jerusalem report described as a 120-ton
"auxiliary ship" used to carry men and supplies for the
Egyptian navy. Israel denied Cairo's contention that the ship
was a civilian freighter operating near the Red Sea port of
Hurghada. Cairo said the attack off Shadwan wounded 6
Egyptian crewmen.

Commenting on Israel's stepped-up drive against Egypt's
interior, Defense Min. Dayan had said Jan. 24 that "all of
Egypt is the field of battle." The offensive was aimed at

halting or at least diminishing Egypt's avowed tactic of carrying on a "half-war" of attrition against Israel, Dayan said.

An Israeli commando attack Jan. 17 had penetrated to within 36 miles of Cairo. It was the closest ground attack to the Egyptian capital. A Jerusalem report said the attackers slashed into "the center of the rear echelon" of Egypt's Suez Canal defense line. An Israeli spokesman said "it can be assumed that parts of Cairo and military installations along the Suez City-Cairo road were blacked out and deprived of telephone communications." Cairo denied the Israeli assertion.

Egyptian commandos had also acted during this period. Israel reported that its forces Jan. 5 had repelled an Egyptian commando raid on its positions near Port Tewfiq, at the southern end of the Suez Canal, killing at least 9 of the raiders. Cairo reported that Egyptian commandos the night of Jan. 25 had crossed the Canal and destroyed Israeli radar stations 20 miles inside the Sinai Peninsula. Israel scoffed at the claim as "pure imagination."

Cairo reported that an Egyptian infantry company Feb. 11 crossed the canal opposite El Shaluffa, in the southern sector, occupied an Israeli fortified position and later ambushed an armored column. At least 20 Israeli soldiers were killed or wounded, 2 were captured and 3 armored cars were destroyed, according to the Cairo report. Israeli authorities did not mention the attack.

Egyptian Civilian Factory & School Bombed

70 Egyptian civilian workers were killed and up to 98 were reported wounded in an Israeli air raid Feb. 12, 1970 on a scrap metal processing factory at Abu Zabal, 17 miles northeast of Cairo. Egypt said that 2 U.S.-made Phantom jets had carried out the strike. Israeli authorities explained that one of several attacking planes had dropped its bombs outside the intended military target area "as a result of a tech-

nical error" during a bombing mission aimed at destroying
Egyptian air force equipment at El Khanka, 3½ miles to the
northeast.

Israeli Defense Min. Dayan informed Gen. Odd Bull, chief
of the UN observer force, that among the bombs dropped
was a 1,000-pound bomb timed to explode after 24 hours.
Following Bull's transmission of the Israeli warning to the
Egyptians, UAR army engineers searched the factory rubble
and defused 3 unexploded time bombs. (Other Israeli planes
Feb. 12 bombed Egyptian military positions at Jebel
Aweibed, about 25 miles west of the Suez Canal, the site of a
radar station on the main road from Suez city to Cairo, an
Egyptian army camp and other military targets in the central
sector of the Canal Zone.)

The U.S. government castigated Israel for the attack. A
statement issued by State Undersecy. Elliot L. Richardson,
however, said that "neither can we disregard the tragic loss of
life and injury to civilians resulting from renewed attacks by
[Arab] terrorists against civilian passengers traveling on international air transports far from the area of conflict." He
referred to an incident involving Israeli airline passengers in
Munich, West Germany Feb. 10. Richardson appealed "to
both sides to adhere to the cease-fire resolutions of the UN
Security Council" and urged the major powers to press
efforts to reestablish the truce and limit arms deliveries to the
Middle East.

Thousands of Egyptians shouted for revenge against Israel
for the air strike as Pres. Nasser drove in an open car Feb. 13
from prayers at Al Azhar Mosque to his palace in Cairo. An
estimated half million persons thronged the streets in what
Cairo radio called "a massive demonstration of solidarity and
faith in the leadership" of the country. Accompanying Nasser
were Col. Mouammar el-Qaddafi, premier of Libya, and Maj.
Gen. Gaafar al-Nimeiry, premier of Sudan. Both men were in
Cairo to discuss with Nasser the implementation of their

3-state alliance agreed to Jan. 13. Nasser said Feb. 14 that he was seeking Soviet MiG-23 fighter planes and Russian technological aid to intercept Israeli jets attacking Egypt.

Egypt charged that 2 Israeli jets had bombed an elementary school Apr. 8 at Bahr el-Bakar, about 15 miles from the Suez Canal, killing 30 children and wounding 36. Israeli Defense Min. Dayan insisted, however, that a military target had been struck. If school children had been killed, he said, it was because the Egyptians had irresponsibly "set aside a floor or some rooms in a military structure for civilian purposes such as a school." Dayan said that aerial photos taken before and after the raid showed a fortified building with trenches around it and camouflaged vehicles nearby.

The Israeli account disagreed with the Egyptians about the location of the raid. The Israelis placed the site 23 miles from the Canal and said that this site was the only target struck by Israeli planes Apr. 8. Foreign newpapermen in Cairo were taken to a hospital in El Husseiniya, 10 to 15 miles west of Bahr el-Bakar, to see victims of the raid. Egyptian authorities, however, rejected reporters' request to go to Bahr el-Bakar because of darkness and bad roads. The correspondents again were refused permission to visit the area the following day.

The U.S. State Department said Apr. 8 that if the reports of the raid were "confirmed, this tragic incident would be another deplorable and saddening consequence of the continuing disregard of the UN Security Council cease-fire resolutions." Egypt charged Apr. 8 that U.S. military aid to Israel made the attack possible. The accusation was delivered by UN Amb. Muhammad H. el-Zayyat to UN Undersecy. Ralph Bunche. Zayyat also submitted a protest to UN Secy. Gen. U Thant. The Egyptian government Apr. 9 denounced the U.S. State Department's statement on the raid as one of cynical indifference.

Among previous Israeli-Egyptian air clashes:

• Egyptian planes carried out a series of low-level, hit-and-run raids against Israeli positions along the Suez Canal Feb. 13. Israel claimed that one of 6 Egyptian planes was shot down by ground fire. After a 3-day lull, Israeli jets Feb. 15 attacked Egyptian positions along the Canal, bombing artillery positions.

• Israeli jets carried out 3 raids Apr. 13, hitting Egyptian targets in the Nile Delta and along the Canal. The Israeli reports said among the centers struck were El Manzala in the north, 20 miles from the Canal, and near the industrial city of Helwan, south of Cairo.

• Israel reported the downing of an Egyptian jet Apr. 18 during widespread UAR air strikes along the Canal. 2 other Egyptian planes were struck by Hawk missiles. 3 Israeli soldiers were killed and 8 wounded in the attacks.

• Egyptian planes Apr. 21 ranged east of the Canal to strike at Israeli positions in the Sinai Peninsula near the Mediterranean coast. Cairo conceded the loss of one plane, but said that its fighter-bombers had scored direct hits on the targets causing "heavy losses" in Israeli troops and equipment. Israel said its air force shot down one of the Egyptian raiders. It said that the attack took place 15 miles east of the waterway.

• Egyptian planes attacked Israeli targets along the entire 100-mile length of the Canal Apr. 28. Israel claimed that its interceptors shot down 2 Sukhoi-7 fighter-bombers, but Cairo said all its planes returned safely. According to Israeli estimates, Egyptian plane losses since the 1967 war totaled 91.

USSR & Red China Voice Support for UAR

Soviet Premier Aleksei N. Kosygin hinted in a letter delivered to U.S. Pres. Nixon Jan. 31, 1970 that the USSR would increase its supply of planes and other military equipment to Egypt if the U.S. did not refrain from delivering arms to Israel. Kosygin sent similar notes to French Pres. Georges Pompidou and British Prime Min. Harold Wilson Feb. 2.

Communist Chinese support of the Arabs in their struggle against Israel was pledged in a letter handed to Egyptian Amb. Salah el-Abid by Premier Chou En-lai in Peking Feb. 1. The message, addressed to Pres. Nasser, said "the Chinese people will forever remain the most reliable friend of the UAR, Palestine and other Arab countries." It denounced Israeli attacks on Arab targets, contending that they had been made possible with American support. Chou also denounced

Pres. Nixon for a statement Jan. 25 that the U.S. was considering new military supplies for Israel.

Kosygin had argued that Washington should be held responsible for the deteriorating situation in the Middle East because of its sale of jets to Israel and its failure to get the Israelis to stop their air strikes against the Arab states. In a reply to Kosygin delivered Feb. 4, Nixon urged the adoption of a 3-point proposal aimed at alleviating the crisis. It called for (a) encouragement of the Arabs and Israelis to observe the ceasefire that had ended the 1967 war, (b) a limitation of arms deliveries to the Middle East and (c) a more positive Soviet response to the peace formulas advanced by the U.S. in October and December 1969.

Kosygin's views were reflected in the Soviet unofficial government newspaper *Izvestia* Feb. 6. It suggested that the Big 4 powers and other nations "take the most urgent measures . . . to put an end to the military escalation of Israel against the UAR and other Arab states." The newspaper charged that "Israel is openly balancing on the brink of a big war, and the situation is fraught with extremely serious consequences." Western diplomats said the *Izvestia* article was repeating the "gist" of Kosygin's note to the U.S., Britain and France.

(Nasser had warned Feb. 4 that if the U.S. sold Israel the 50 Phantom jets it had requested, Egypt would call on the Soviet Union to supply it with more arms. Moscow, he said, "will have to give us more arms to be able to retaliate." Nasser conceded that the Israelis had air superiority, but he said the Arabs' problem was not lack of planes. "We have more planes than pilots," he declared, "the Israelis have 2 pilots for every plane; so the Israelis have air security and air supremacy.")

Yasir Arafat, head of Al Fatah, the guerrilla organization, visited Moscow Feb. 10–20 and then spent 10 days in China and North Vietnam. His hosts in Moscow were functionaries of the "Soviet Afro-Asian Solidarity Committee." The committee, at the end of Arafat's stay issued a statement in which it indorsed the Palestinian Arab cause and denounced U.S. "imperialism" and Israeli "aggression."

Arafat told a correspondent of the Cairo daily *Al-Ahram* Apr. 5 that Chinese Premier Chou had said during his visit to China that "China backs the Palestinian guerrillas with no limits and to the very end." (Arafat also told *Al-Ahram* that there were only 6,000 guns among the 32,000 guerrillas based in Jordan.)

Egypt Receives Soviet SAM-3 Missiles

The arrival of Soviet-made SAM-3 (surface to air) antiaircraft missiles in Egypt, accompanied by an estimated 1,500 Soviet soldiers to operate them, was reported by the *N.Y. Times* Mar. 19, 1970. Quoting reliable diplomatic sources in Cairo, the dispatch said: The Soviet equipment was being installed at Alexandria, at an air base west of Cairo and elsewhere in the UAR. Soviet soldiers had been observed driving trucks carrying missiles on a highway linking Cairo with Alexandria. The SAM-3s were designed to cope with low-flying Israeli planes attacking Egyptian targets. They were to supplement the Soviet-supplied SAM-2 missiles, which were effective against high-flying planes but not against low-flying aircraft. Egyptian newspapers Mar. 20 confirmed the shipment of the SAM-3 missiles by quoting the *Times'* report.

Israeli Defense Min. Moshe Dayan indicated Mar. 20 that Israel would attempt to neutralize the new missiles despite the risk to Soviet troops manning them. Calling the new equipment "the first stage of Sovietization of the Egyptian war machine," Dayan said: "I hope we succeed in preventing the stationing of the new missiles in areas vital to our military hold on the Suez Canal Zone and to the effectiveness of our air operations of deeper penetration."

U.S. State Secy. William P. Rogers, referring at a press conference Mar. 23 to reports of the Soviet shipment of

SAM-3s to Egypt, pointed out that they were "defensive weapons, and all we can do is assume that they are there for defensive purposes." Rogers said: The U.S. would postpone a decision on Israel's request to purchase 125 jets because it regarded Israel's air capacity "sufficient to meet its needs for the time being." The U.S. had agreed, however, to give Israel about $100 million in short-term credit and to study its longer-range financial needs. Israel had expressed "disappointment and concern" over the delay of the sale of the planes it had requested in Sept. 1969.

Pres. Nixon, Rogers said, "has instructed that close watch be kept on the military balance in the Middle East." Washington would provide Israel with "additional as well as replacement aircraft promptly if the situation requires," Rogers pledged. (Officials explained that this meant the U.S. would respond immediately with more military aid to Israel if the Soviet Union granted offensive weapons to Egypt or if Israel was otherwise threatened.)

The decision to defer the sale of jets to Israel had been indicated by Nixon at a news conference Mar. 21. The U.S., he said, "intends to continue to watch the Mideast situation to see whether further shipments of arms or personnel to the Middle East does tip the balance in a way that it would be necessary for us to provide" Israel with additional military aid "so that they would not be in an inferior position."

The Israeli response to Rogers' announcement was made Mar. 23 by Foreign Min. Abba Eban. He said that Israel's "vital needs for self-defense are not met" in the secretary's statement. "A policy of deterrence should insure that the prospective aggressor be convinced that no interruption will occur in the reinforcement of the defender," Eban declared. He said that the new missiles being installed by the Russians were designed "to serve the Egyptians as an umbrella, under whose shelter they plan to intensify their continued attacks across the cease-fire lines."

Soviet Pilots Downed by Israel Over Canal

9 Egyptian Mig-21s shot down by Israeli jets over the Suez Canal Mar. 25 and 27, 1970 were piloted by Soviet fliers, it was reported in a *Washington Post* dispatch from Beirut Apr. 1. There had been periodic reports of Russians flying Egyptian planes, but this was believed to be the first known instance of Soviet military personnel involved in combat in the Middle East. The *Post* said that the downed planes apparently were defending the newly-installed Soviet-made SAM-3 surface-to-air missiles.

In an interview published May 20 in the West German newspaper *Die Welt*, Nasser confirmed that Soviet pilots were flying armed Egyptian planes and were "training our own pilots." Nasser was quoted as saying that the Russians could have encountered Israeli planes.

Commenting on the *Post* account, U.S. State Secy. Rogers said Apr. 2 that the Nixon Administration had "no evidence whatsoever" that Soviet pilots had been flying combat missions for the Egyptians.

A *N.Y. Times* report from Cairo Apr. 1 had told of an increasing number of Soviet military personnel in Egypt. The newspaper quoted sources as saying that at least 5,000 Russians—and possibly as many as 10,000—were in the country. About 80 Soviet pilots were said to have arrived ready for possible direct action against Israeli aerial strikes. Some Soviet soldiers were said to have been observed Mar. 29 on the western shore of the Nile River, 15 miles south of Cairo. They were traveling in an Egyptian army truck and were wearing Egyptian army fatigue uniforms. The *Times* said that many of the Soviet military personnel were specialists in the operation of the newly installed SAM-3s. The antiaircraft missiles were said to have been installed near Alexandria, at a military air base west of Cairo used by Soviet planes, at Helwan, around the Aswan High Dam and elsewhere in the

Nile Valley and Delta, but not in the vicinity of the Suez Canal.

Israeli Deputy Premier Yigal Allon had said Mar. 28 that the Israeli air attacks across the Suez Canal were aimed at destroying the Egyptian air-defense system in the area. Allon stressed the need of "going along not only with smashing of the existing antiaircraft systems and other military installations, but also preventing them from rehabilitating the old one." Allon said that 1,500 Soviet military experts had arrived in Egypt and that this was evidence that Moscow was not interested in any mutual arms reduction in the region.

According to Israeli intelligence reports disclosed Apr. 28, the new pattern of Soviet air operations had first been detected Apr. 18 when 8 Soviet-operated MiG fighters pursued 2 Israeli reconnaissance planes, although no fire was exchanged. Since then the Israelis were reported to have largely avoided provocative flights beyond the Suez Canal region, and the Russian pilots, in turn, were said to have stayed away from the Canal sector. The Israelis were said to have intercepted messages of Russian-speaking pilots since Apr. 18 and to have transmitted intelligence reports to Washington. The Soviet Union's new phase of aerial operations was accompanied by an increase in Egyptian attacks on Israeli positions in the Sinai Peninsula, causing a sharp rise in Israeli casualties.

A U.S. State Department statement on the Israeli reports said Apr. 29 that the U.S. "regards this as a serious development and potentially dangerous." The White House voiced apprehension and noted that Pres. Nixon's Mar. 23 decision to defer the sale of 125 jets to Israel had been only an "interim decision," subject to the continuing assessment of "the military balance in the Middle East." Nixon had said at the time that the Israeli request would be filled "promptly if the situation requires."

The State Department and White House statements followed a report Apr. 28 that Israeli Premier Golda Meir had sent Nixon expressions of concern. Mrs. Meir said: "We do not want to hit Russian pilots, or Syrian pilots, or any other pilots, but we have no choice."

The Israeli government Apr. 29 officially confirmed previous reports that Soviet pilots were flying operational missions in support of the Egyptian air force. According to Kol Israel (the Voice of Israel):

> In the past few days it has become clear beyond any doubt that Soviet pilots are now taking part in operational missions from military installations under Soviet control in Egypt. However, so far the operational activities of the Soviet pilots have not reached the cease-fire line and the pilots have not been involved in battles in this area.
>
> In a statement published this morning the Israeli government stresses the gravity of this development in Soviet involvement in the Middle East which allows the Egyptians to step up their aggression against Israel. The government has informed world political circles of the dangerous implications of this development.
>
> The escalation of Soviet involvement in Egypt, the government statement says, should perturb not only Israel but all freedom-loving countries. The government statement notes the various stages of Soviet government policy of identification with Egypt, including the supply of Soviet arms in massive quantities to the Egyptian army, identification with Abdel Nasser's declaration last year regarding repudiation of the cease-fire line, and support of Egypt in its rejection of Israel's appeal to renew the cease-fire without time limitation and conditions.
>
> Soviet policy is also expressed in the wild anti-Israel propaganda campaign emanating from the Soviet Union during the past few months—a campaign which reached its peak with the installation of SA-3 missiles operated by Russians in Egypt.
>
> The government statement also says that Israel will continue to defend itself against any attack which violates the cease-fire and is aimed at renewing the war in the region. . . .

Reflecting American alarm over the situation, Pres. Nixon Apr. 29 ordered an "immediate and full evaluation" of the reports. Jacob D. Beam, U.S. ambassador to Moscow, called on Soviet officials May 1 to express Washington's deep concern.

Israeli Foreign Min. Abba Eban said Apr. 30 that the use of Soviet pilots in the UAR was "an almost revolutionary change" in the military situation and required immediate

U.S. military assistance to Israel to offset it. Eban charged there was an "integrated Soviet-Egyptian design" to break the 1967 cease-fire. The Soviet Communist Party newspaper *Pravda* assailed Eban May 1 for blaming the USSR for rising tensions in the Middle East. Israel, *Pravda* said, was "ready for any tricks to continue to receive military aid from the United States in increasing quantity."

The Soviet Union Apr. 30 had dismissed the Israeli allegations as "stupidities." Egyptian denials Apr. 29 had asserted that the Israeli charges were designed to discredit a current Egyptian air and ground offensive along the Suez Canal.

Nasser charged May 1 that the Israeli reports of Soviet military aid to Egypt were a pretext to extract more jet planes from the U.S. In view of this, Nasser warned Washington that compliance with the Israeli request would have "dangerous consequences" for American interests in the Arab world for decades to come. Nasser insisted that the USSR "is not helping us to launch aggression. The Soviet Union is helping us to liberate our occupied lands."

Eban conferred with U.S. officials in Washington May 20–22 on Israel's request to buy 25 Phantom and 100 Skyhawk jet planes. He stressed that the increased Soviet commitment to the Egyptian air force posed a threat to Israel's security. He met with State Department officials and State Secy. Rogers May 21 and with Pres. Nixon May 21 and 22. Eban said at a news conference May 21 that he had not received a positive response to Israel's call for the additional planes, "nor has there been a negative response, so we are still waiting." White House Press Secy. Ronald Ziegler said that the Nixon Administration was still awaiting a "full and immediate" intelligence assessment of the significance of Soviet military intervention in Egypt before acting on Israel's request. (The State Department had confirmed May 19 that the U.S. was providing Israel with bombs as part of a continuing military assistance program.)

Premier Golda Meir charged May 26 that the Middle East

had been "flung into a new dimension of tension" as a result of the installation of Soviet SAM-3 missiles in Egypt and the participation of Soviet pilots in operational missions over the UAR. Speaking in the Knesset, Mrs. Meir asserted that these developments jeopardized Israel's security and were "dragging the region into an escalation of warfare and killing." She warned that any American delay in selling Israel the additional planes "is liable to injure our interests and be interpreted by our enemies as encouragement of their aggression, and by the Soviet Union as condonation of its intensified involvement." Mrs. Meir said that in the past 3 years Moscow had supplied Egypt, Syria and Iraq with 2,000 tanks and 800 fighter planes at a cost of $3½ billion.

Soviet Premier Aleksei N. Kosygin had acknowledged May 20 that the USSR was providing Arab countries with "extensive aid," but he said its only purpose was to enable them to "successfully defend their legitimate national rights." Kosygin emphasized that the Soviet Union was "consistently working to have the earliest political settlement in the Middle East." Kosygin accused Israel of thwarting such efforts. His remarks were described as a reply to a message he had received May 7 from the chiefs of state of Iran, Turkey and Pakistan after a meeting that they had held in Ankara. Their statement appealed to all powers to "insure the undelayed withdrawal of Israeli armed forces from territories occupied by them in June 1967."

The USSR reiterated May 21 that its aid to Egypt was solely for defense and posed no threat to Israel. "The consolidation of the United Arab Republic's defense is directed first of all at dampening the aggressor's eagerness to launch barbaric raids against civilian objectives in Arab countries and to commit evil acts against the peaceful Arab population," the Soviet press agency Tass said.

The June 1 issue of *Newsweek* magazine carried a detailed report of Soviet military involvement in Egypt. The article reported that: The Russians had installed 22 SAM-3 missile sites near Alexandria, Baltim, Cairo, the Aswan Dam and the Cairo West area. An additional 23 sites were under construction and another 17 were planned, including some near the Suez Canal. Israeli forces had captured 4 Russian advisers along with the Russian-made missile site seized on the Gulf of Suez Dec. 25, 1969. The Russians were later released through the Rumanian embassy in Jerusalem. Israeli attacks on other SAM-2 missile sites in 1969 had resulted in the killing of 12 Russian advisers and the wounding of 29.

U.S. officials said June 21 that Soviet pilots were flying fewer sorties over Egypt since May 14 and that current flights were restricted to training missions. An apparently contradictory report by foreign intelligence in Washington June 24 said that the Russian pilots were flying combat missions south of the Canal and had challenged Israeli jets that crossed the Gulf of Suez on reconnaissance and surveillance missions. The sources reported, however, that the Israeli pilots were under orders not to engage the Russians unless they entered the Canal cease-fire zone.

Commandos Cross Canal

Egypt claimed credit for 7 commando raids in 35 days on positions in Israeli-occupied parts of the country during April and May 1970. A military spokesman in Cairo Apr. 26 said that 35 Israeli soldiers had been killed or wounded in one of 2 Egyptian crossings of the Suez Canal that day. The first raid, involving 200 Egyptian troops, was said to have wiped out an Israeli infantry platoon, to have destroyed several Israeli tanks and trucks at El Shatt and to have suffered only light casulaties. An Israeli spokesman called the Egyptian statement a "fable." He said Israeli casualties were 5 men wounded in an ambush of an Israeli motorized patrol, and he asserted that Israeli forces had sunk a boat with 8 Egyptian soldiers aboard in the 2d incident.

Cairo asserted that 600 Egyptian troops had crossed the Suez Canal along a 15-mile front Apr. 29 and inflicted heavy damage on Israeli positions. (The attack was said to be part of an intensified drive, launched by forces Apr. 18, consisting of Egyptian sustained air and artillery attacks along the waterway and deep inside the Sinai Peninsula. The Cairo report said a UAR batallion, striking between El Ballah and Ismailia, had killed or wounded 10 Israeli defenders, destroyed 3 Israeli tanks and several armored vehicles and shot down an Israeli jet in a related raid. It was described as the largest engagement between Israeli and Egyptian forces since the 1967 war. The assault followed a report of a daytime raid in which an Egyptian unit had ambushed an Israeli armored patrol south of the Bitter Lakes, destroying 3 Israeli half-tracks and killing their occupants. An Israeli version of the Apr. 29 commando crossing said the raid was thrown back after a 12-hour battle. 4 Egyptian landing boats were sunk. 2 Israeli soldiers were killed in artillery fire, which continued until daybreak.

An Egyptian commando crossing 20 miles across the Gulf of Suez May 3, the first by sea in several months, was reported by Cairo to have destroyed Israeli installations at El Tor. The target was near the southern end of the Sinai Peninsula.

Israel reported that an Egyptian commando raid across the Canal May 19 had been repulsed and 7 raiders killed after a 3-hour fight in which there were no Israeli casualties. According to the Egyptians, the raiders had inflicted heavy casualties on an Israeli armored unit near Shallufa near the Canal's southern end.

2 Egyptian commando units crossed the Canal in rubber boats during the daylight hours of May 30 and surprised and ambushed a convoy of Israeli soldiers south of Port Fuad. Egyptian sources said that 16 Israelis were killed and 2 captured. Israeli authorities acknowledge 15 soldiers killed, 8 wounded and 2 missing. The Cairo daily *Al-Ahram* described the engagement as "heralding a new stage in the confrontation with Israel."

A 2,575-ton "Z"-class Egyptian destroyer and a Soviet-built missile boat were sunk by Israeli planes May 16 in the Red Sea naval base of Ras Banas north of Sudan. Israeli bombers flew 650 miles round-trip in the raid, in which 2 Israeli planes were said by Egyptian authorities to have been downed. But an Israeli spokesman said that all aircraft had returned safely from the raid, which reportedly was a reprisal for 2 incidents—(1) the sinking off the Sinai coast late May 13 of an Israeli fishing vessel and the killing of 2 of its crew of 4 by an Egyptian missile boat, and (2) the death of an Israeli harbor worker May 15 from an explosive charge in a wreck on which he was working in the port of Eilat. The spokesman asserted that Egyptian frogmen had placed the charge.

Israel reported July 6 that Soviet missile experts were involved in the downing of 3 Israeli planes in the vicinity of the 3 Canal in the past 6 days. Cairo denied the report, and the U.S. questioned Israeli claims of Soviet offensive air operations.

Gen. Haim Bar-Lev, Israeli chief of staff, said that the 3 Israeli planes had been lost to improved SAM-2 missiles, whose crews included Russian personnel. He said Israeli planes had damaged 7 of the 12 batteries installed thus far. Israeli aircraft had been fired at for the first time by at least 2 batteries of SAM-3 missiles manned by Soviet crews, but they missed their targets, according to Bar-Lev. He said that the 12 batteries had been installed near the canal June 29, were sighted by Israeli pilots June 30 and came under their attack that day. 2 of the 3 Israeli planes were lost June 30 and the 3d was downed July 5. The missile system, Bar-Lev said, was established in a strip starting 15 miles west of the Canal and extending up to 17 miles farther west. It covered a 45-mile stretch between the Cairo-Ismailia and Cairo-Port Suez roads. Bar-Lev said that the Russians were operating the SAM-3s and that they had final authority in the firing of the SAM-2s.

The positioning of the new missile system was within the

20-mile limit regarded as vital by Israel for the defense of its air and ground positions on the east bank of the Canal. Bar-Lev said that the purpose of the joint Egyptian-Soviet operations was "first, to drive us from our freedom of air operations along the Canal, and 2d, to enable the Egyptians to concentrate and intensify their offensive ability along the Canal." The Israeli general conceded that the new missile system had upset the balance of power along the Canal, but he said that the missiles had not "turned it totally upside down."

The semi-official Cairo newspaper *Al-Ahram* July 6 denied that the missile sites responsible for the downing of the 3 Israeli planes were operated by Soviet personnel. The newspaper asserted that the charge was "a mere attempt to justify the high Israeli losses along the Canal. Israel is raising a political furor while knowning that only Egyptian military personnel are operating the air defense system."

Israeli commandos reported killing at least 20 Egyptian soldiers in 2 raids across the Suez Canal and the Gulf of Suez June 12. A number of other Egyptians were believed killed and buried within demolished bunkers. 4 Israelis were killed and 15 were wounded in the Canal operation, a Jerusalem spokesman said. The attack on the Egyptian side of the Canal was directed at a line of bunkers and fortified positions 1½ miles north of El Qantara. The raiders presumably crossed in boats. The target in the Gulf of Suez strike was described as a guard station 9 miles north of Ras Gharib. A spokesman said that the Israeli force, apparently landing by helicopter, had destroyed the station and suffered no casualties.

Cairo reported June 12 that Egyptian forces had smashed 2 Israeli attempts that day to cross the Canal and said that the Israelis had lost 25 dead or wounded in the 2 operations. One attempted strike was made north of El Tina and the other, 2 hours later, at El Cap. All Israeli boats involved in the latter mission were sunk by Egyptian fire, according to the Cairo report.

Israel reported that its commandos had crossed the Gulf of Suez June 23 and killed at least 10 Egyptians at an army center at Bir Araida, 45 miles inland. Cairo said that at least 20 Israelis had been killed or wounded in the assault.

Israeli Planes Hit SAMs & Other Targets

Israeli planes pounded Egyptian installations along the Suez Canal beginning May 31, 1970 in a drive to prevent the reestablishment of antiaircraft missle sites. The Israeli aircraft June 2 carried out 4 sorties lasting 7 hours. UAR officials reported the downing of one of the raiders, but Israel denied any losses.

Israel reported that 3 Egyptian MiG-21s had been downed within 3 minutes in a dogfight over the northern sector of the Suez Canal June 3. Cairo that claimed its planes had shot down 2 Israeli Mirages and damaged 2 others in an engagement west of the Canal. In what was described as the longest and most intense foray of the week, Israeli planes June 5 bombed Egyptian positions for 11 hours. (The day was the 3d anniversary of the beginning of the June 1967 war.)

Jerusalem authorities reported June 7 that the Israeli raids of the previous week had completely severed all land connections with Port Said at the northern terminus of the Canal. As a result, the city was running short of food and water.

Israeli planes June 21 began their 4th consecutive week of intensive raids on Egyptian positions along the Suez Canal and continued them through June 27. In Israeli air strikes the previous week, Cairo reported that 15 Egyptian soldiers were killed June 17. The Kuwaiti armed forces reported that 16 of its soldiers were killed by Israeli attacks along the canal the same day. The Egyptian newspaper *Al-Ahram* reported June 18 that Israeli jets the previous day had dropped late-model American bombs on Egyptian targets. The report said that they ranged from 1,000-pound bombs to antipersonnel and incendiary weapons.

Cairo reported July 5 that 11 Israeli planes had been either shot down or hit over the Canal by Egyptian anti-aircraft during the past 5 days. 2 were downed July 5 and their 2 pilots captured. 2 others had been shot down June 30 and 3 of the 4 crewmen taken prisoner, according to the Cairo report.

U.S. officials in Washington said July 6 that their information indicated that the Soviet SAM-3 missiles had not been installed within the 20-mile belt along the Canal. These officials conceded the Soviet expansion of the Egyptian missile defense system, which included SAM-2s, SAM-3s, radar-controlled antiaircraft guns and Soviet pilots. But they said that there were no operational SAM-3s within 25 miles of the Canal and that the few SAM-2s located 15 to 18 miles from the waterway had been there for some time. The American officials reported no evidence that the Soviets had introduced a new missile in Egypt known as the Ganef. It had first been reported July 3 that the weapon had arrived in the UAR. (As first displayed in the 1964 May Day parade in Moscow, it was a winged 30-foot rocket carried on a tracked twin-launcher vehicle.)

Cairo reported that Egyptian antiaircraft fire had hit an Israeli Skyhawk fighter-bomber July 7 during a raid on Egyptian positions in the central sector of the Canal. Israel denied that any of its jets had been hit.

The destruction of 3 Egyptian MiG-21s in a brief but intense dogfight over the waterway July 10 was reported by an Israeli military spokesman. Cairo said all its planes had returned safely from clashes with Israeli jets over the Canal that day. The statement said that 2 Israeli jets were hit.

A spokesman in Tel Aviv reported that Israeli jets had pounded Egyptian positions in 2 separate attacks in the southern sector of the Canal July 11. A military official in

Cairo said that Egyptian air defenses had driven off 10 Israeli aircraft that had tried to raid the southern sector.

Israel acknowledged the loss of a jet in the resumption of its bombing of Soviet-Egyptian missile batteries in the central sector of the Canal July 18. The report said that the designated targets had been hit. Cairo said the downed plane was a Phantom, reportedly the 5th Phantom Israel had lost since the acquisition of the U.S.-made plane in 1969. The Israeli air strike was directed at the SAM-2 and SAM-3 missile batteries about 20 miles from the Canal's western bank; it was the first Israeli penetration of this zone since July 7. Cairo said that one of the pilots in the downed Israeli jet had been captured and the other killed.

Egypt reported that its ground defenses had shot down one of 24 Israeli Skyhawk planes raiding the southern end of the Canal July 20. But Israel said that all its planes had returned safely from the attack. Israeli planes again raided SAM-2 missile sites and other targets in the southern and central sectors of the Canal July 21. 2 Israeli jets were reported downed by Egyptians missiles in the central sector.

WORLD DIPLOMATIC FRONT (Jan. 1969-Sept. 1970)

Big-4 Envoys Confer at UN

France disclosed Jan. 17, 1969 that it had proposed a meeting of the Big 4 ambassadors to the UN Security Council to discuss ways of "establishing a just and lasting peace in the Middle East." Several such meetings were ultimately held during the first half of 1969, but nothing tangible came of them.

The French plan, submitted to the U.S., Britain and the USSR, said the purpose of the talks would be to "open the road to a settlement" in which the Arabs and the Israelis would be "intimately associated." The immediate purpose of the discussions, to be held in cooperation with UN Secy. Gen. U Thant, would be to "define the conditions" in which the Nov. 22, 1967 Security Council resolution could be implemented. (The resolution called for an end to Arab belligerency against Israel and Israeli withdrawal from Arab territories.) Roger Vaurs, French Foreign Ministry spokesman who disclosed the proposal, made it clear that Paris had no intention of having the Big 4 impose a settlement.

The Soviet Union Jan. 21 announced acceptance of the French proposal.

The new U.S. Administration of Pres. Richard M. Nixon announced its agreement "in principle" Feb. 5. A State Department statement, issued after State Secy. William Rogers had met with French Amb. Charles Lucet, said that Washington's support of Paris' plan was conditional on the holding of such formal talks "within the framework of the [UN] Security Council" and on the assumption that the meetings would serve as an aid to the Middle East peace efforts of UN Special Envoy Gunnar V. Jarring. Jarring, who returned to New York from Moscow Jan. 27, had held separate meetings with the Big 4 representatives. It was disclosed that he had held secret talks with Israeli Foreign Min. Abba Eban in Zurich, Switzerland Jan. 14–15.

The Big 4 representatives at the UN began preliminary consultations Feb. 5 and 6 to determine whether conditions existed for formal discussions on a Middle East peace settlement. U.S. Amb. Charles W. Yost met Feb. 5 with Amb. Armand Berard of France. Yost then held separate talks Feb. 6 with Yakov Malik, the Soviet Union's chief delegate, and with Sir Leslie Glass, Britain's acting permanent representative, and Malik and Berard conferred. UN Secy. Gen. U Thant Feb. 7 lauded the preliminary discussions as "an auspicious beginning" toward permanent peace in the Middle East.

Meanwhile, Egyptian Pres. Gamal Abdel Nasser received a note from Pres. Nixon Feb. 5. The message was in reply to a letter Nasser had sent Jan. 5 congratulating Nixon on his election and suggesting, by implication, that his administration follow a new course in the Middle East. Although the contents of his response was not disclosed, diplomatic sources said Nixon had made no specific proposals but had stressed in general terms the need for renewed peace efforts in the Middle East.

Nixon said at a news conference Feb. 6 that the U.S. was pursuing a "new policy" in the Middle East and was "assuming the initiative" there. The principle objective of U.S. policy, Nixon asserted, was to give "all-out support" to Jarring's peace initiatives. Nixon said at his news conference Mar. 14 after meeting with Israeli Foreign Min. Abba Eban, that "I would not like to leave the impression" that the U.S. and France were "completely together" on a common policy for the Middle East. "We are closer together than we were, but we still have a lot of yardage to cover."

Israel's continued opposition to a Big 4 solution to the Middle East impasse had been made clear in meetings Abba Eban held with U.S. officials in Washington Mar. 12–14 and in a statement made Mar. 18 by Mrs. Golda Meir, at her first news conference as premier. Eban had several talks with State Secy. Rogers and met Mar. 14 with Pres. Nixon. Eban conferred with Amb. Yost at the UN Mar. 17 and again with Rogers Mar. 20. Speaking to a National Press Club gathering in Washington Mar. 14, Eban warned of the "complexity and peril" of big-power guarantees for the Middle East. He was particularly critical of France and the Soviet Union, asserting that "the unbalanced attitude of some of the great powers rules them out as guarantors." Israel, Eban said, insisted on these "4 principles" for a peace settlement: (a) ". . . No movement from the cease-fire situation except to peace—in its full political and juridical sense"; (b) "the peace must have treaty form so as directly to engage the interest and honor of the Arab states and Israel"; (c) "there must be an opportunity to negotiate secure and agreed boundaries"; (d) there must be an integral peace, not a piecemeal or phased process: it is only when agreement is concluded that implementation can begin."

In her statement Mar. 18 Mrs. Meir said that Israel would insist on direct negotiations with the Arab states. She said that Israel would oppose the imposition of a Big 4 settlement and the reintroduction of UN troops into the Middle East to patrol Israeli and Arab frontiers. "It was absolutely essential," Mrs. Meir said, "that in signing a peace settlement we must see to it that our borders are such that if at any time the Arabs want to attack they will not be able to do it from a point of natural superiority of borders." She referred to Israel's natural borders as the Golan Heights and Sharm el-Sheik, overlooking the Strait of Tiran, both captured by Israel in 1967. As for Israel's relations with Washington, Mrs. Meir said "there are differences in our views and approach, but it is far too early to come to any conclusions as to the extent of differences between the United States government and ourselves."

The U.S. proposed Mar. 24 that the bilateral talks it had been holding in the past several weeks with Britain, France and the USSR to seek a peaceful solution in the Middle East be expanded into a full-fledged Big 4 conference. Amb.-to-

UN Yost made the suggestion at meetings with the UN delegates of the Soviet Union (Yakov Malik), France (Armand Berard) and Britain (Lord Caradon). Yost then forwarded the proposal to Secy. Gen. U Thant. Yost had made a similar suggestion to the USSR and France 3 weeks previously, urging them to join in a statement supporting the peace efforts of UN Envoy Jarring. But France and the Soviet Union had rejected the idea on the ground that it did not advance the implementation of the Security Council's Nov. 22, 1967 resolution, which had prescribed general terms for a peace settlement in the Middle East.

The U.S. State Department said Mar. 25 that Yost's meetings with Malik "appear . . . likely to lead to a meeting of the 4 permanent members of the Security Council soon." The department also disclosed that in the past day or 2 the U.S. had circulated at the UN a series of "talking points" that could be the basis of future Big 4 discussions.

The Israeli government Mar. 30 formally rejected any Big 4 proposals on the Middle East that were contrary to Israel's vital interests, rights and security. The statement, issued after a cabinet meeting, detailed Israel's own position on a peace settlement. The statement said:

Israel would not accept "any settlement and any procedure that is not agreed upon by the governments concerned," Israel and the Arab states. "Israel entirely opposes the plan to convene the representatives of states that lie outside the Middle East [the U.S., France, Britain and USSR] in order to prepare recommendations concerning the region. Such a procedure undermines the responsibility devolving on the states of the region to attain peace among themselves." Israel deplored Egyptian Pres. Nasser's statement Mar. 27 that "the Arab states will not recognize Israel, will not conduct negotiations with her, will not make peace with her but will continue to perpetrate aggressive acts against her." Israel's policy would continue to be guided by parliamentary decisions reaffirmed by the new government of Premier Golda Meir.

"Israel will make constant efforts to achieve a durable peace with her neighbors, a peace to be based upon peace treaties to be achieved in direct negotiations between the parts.

"The agreed, secure and recognized boundaries will be laid down in the peace treaties. The peace treaties will provide for cooperation and mutual aid, the solution by peaceful means of all problems at issue, and abstention from all aggression, direct or indirect.

"Israel will maintain her readiness to conduct negotiations—without prior conditions from any side—with any of the neighboring states for the purpose of concluding peace treaties.

"In the absence of peace treaties, Israel will continue to maintain in full the situations as determined by the cease-fire and will consolidate her position in accordance with the vital needs of her security and development."

The cabinet statement was made after the receipt of a detailed report from Foreign Min. Eban on his Mar. 12–20 meetings with Pres. Nixon and other American officials. (A spokesman for Eban Mar. 26 had denied a *N.Y. Times* report from Washington Mar. 24 that the foreign minister had met secretly with Jordanian King Hussein in London in Sept. 1968 and in Jan. 1969.)

The Big 4 representatives to the UN opened formal joint discussions in New York Apr. 3. A 2d conference was held Apr. 8. Progress on substantive issues was reported after both meetings. The first meeting was held at the residence of Armand Berard of France and was attended by Charles W. Yost of the U.S., Lord Caradon of Britain and Yakov A. Malik of the USSR. A communiqué issued after 4 hours of talks said: "The 4 powers are agreed that the situation in the Middle East is serious and urgent and must not be permitted to jeopardize international peace and security. They have straightaway entered into a discussion on matters of substance and have started defining areas of agreement." The communiqué promised that "active consultations will continue" and indicated that Israel and the Arab states would be apprised of progress. It expressed full support for the peace efforts of UN envoy Jarring.

Just before the issuance of the Big 4 statement, Yosef Tekoah, Israeli representative to the UN, had said that "nothing good can come of the talks" because anything approved by France and the Soviet Union would be "inimical to Israel's vital interests." Tekoah charged that Big 4 intervention in the Middle East had already toughened an "Arab intransigence" that was reflected in Pres. Nasser's recent war-like pronouncements and an increase in Egypt's acts of aggression."

No communiqué was issued after the 2d Big 4 meeting, held Apr. 8 at the Soviet mission to the UN, but Lord Caradon said progress had been made.

U.S. objectives in the Big 4 discussions were stressed by State Secy. Rogers at his news conference in Washington Apr. 7. He said the major powers were seeking an agreement "on a certain general formula" and would use the "force of public opinion" to get Israel and the Arab states to approve. "If the world community should agree on a certain general formula for the settlement of the Middle East, then I think the governments in that area would want to think long and hard before they turned it down," he declared. The Nixon Administration supported UN guarantees for a Middle East settlement that "would be more satisfactory, more lasting than the previous ones," he said. Rogers called on the Arab states to recognize Israel's right to exist. He regretted Israel's strong objections to Big 4 involvement in seeking peace, but he insisted that eventually "there will have to be some direct negotiations" between Israel and the Arab states as demanded by Israel but refused by the Arabs.

Jordanian King Hussein held separate meetings with UN representatives of the Big 4 at UN headquarters in New York Apr. 14. The 4 representatives then held their 3d joint meeting on the Middle East. After several additional meetings, the conferences of the Big-4 envoys were adjourned July 1 sending projected U.S.-Soviet bilateral talks in Moscow.

UN Secy. Gen. U Thant had announced in Geneva May 1 that Gunnar Jarring, his special envoy to the Middle East, would not resume his mediation efforts for awhile. Jarring had flown to Geneva Apr. 30 to confer with Thant. In announcing a postponement of his peace moves, Thant said that Jarring had told him that "for the moment there is not anything he can do by going to New York" or by taking any other initiatives.

Hussein Offers New Arab Peace Plan

King Hussein of Jordan Apr. 11, 1969 proposed a 6-point peace plan to settle the Arab countries' dispute with Israel. Hussein's plan contained the first public pledge by an Arab leader that Israeli ships would be permitted to use the Suez Canal if other settlement terms were met. The king's proposal was made in a speech to the National Press Club in Washington, D.C., where he had been since Apr. 8 for talks with Pres. Nixon and other U.S. officials.

Hussein, saying that he spoke with the "personal authority" of Pres. Nasser of Egypt, proposed: "(1) The end of all belligerency; (2) respect for and acknowledgment of the sovereignty, territorial integrity and political independence of all states in the area; (3) recognition of the rights of all to live in peace within secure and recognized boundaries, free from threats or acts of war; (4) guarantees for all the freedom of navigation through the Gulf of Aqaba and the Suez Canal; (5) guaranteeing the territorial inviolability of all states in the area through whatever measures necessary, including the establishment of demilitarized zones; (6) accepting a just settlement of the refugee problem."

The 6-point plan consisted essentially of the same elements as the UN Security Council's Nov. 22, 1967 resolution outlining general peace terms. In exchange for the guarantees cited, Hussein demanded that Israeli forces withdraw "from all territories occupied in the June 1967 war. The challenge that these principles present is that Israel may have peace or territory—but she can never have both."

Hussein said that his 6th point, dealing with the plight of the Arab refugees, was the "crux" of a settlement. Once the refugees' "rights have been restored—by Israel's acceptance of their right to repatriation or compensation—then the final step toward peace will not be far off," he said. But the king warned that until the refugees were granted their rights, he "would not stop" Arab commando attacks on Israel from Jordanian territory. "I am not willing to be responsible for the security of the forces of occupation," he declared. "It is the intolerable situation that produces the commandos, not the commandos who provoke the situation." There was no policy conflict between Jordan and the commandos, he insisted. "There is no difference in my aim in seeking a peaceful settlement and their aim in a settlement by conflict."

The status of Jerusalem was another essential element of an eventual peace, Hussein said. "We cannot envision any settlement that does not include the return of the Arab part of the city of Jerusalem to us with all our holy places." As for Israeli demands for direct talks with the Arabs, he said there was "no basis" for such negotiations because Israel had not yet accepted the Security Council's Nov. 22 resolution, which had been approved by Jordan and Egypt. (Israeli officials, calling Hussein's charge a distortion, noted that Foreign Min. Abba Eban had announced Oct. 8, 1968 that Israel accepted the resolution and was prepared "to negotiate agreements on all the principles mentioned therein.")

A joint U.S.-Jordanian statement was issued Apr. 10, based on Hussein's talks Apr. 8–10 with Pres. Nixon, State Secy. William P. Rogers and other Administration officials. It said: "The principal topic of discussion was the common United States and Jordanian desire for a just and durable peace in the Middle East." Hussein "explained that the explosive nature of the situation in the Middle East is caused by the occupation of Jordanian and other Arab territories, and expressed his conviction that peace can only be achieved by early withdrawal of the forces of occupation in the context" of the Nov. 22 Security Council resolution, the statement said. The U.S. "called attention to the government of Jordan and reaffirmed the statement made by Secy. Rogers on this point and on other points before the Senate Foreign Relations Committee on March 27." The U.S. and Jordan reaffirmed their support of the peace efforts of Gunnar Jarring. The U.S. "reaffirmed its support for the political independence and territorial integrity" of Jordan.

Pres. Nixon exchanged views on the Middle East with Dr. Mahmoud Fawzi of the UAR at a White House meeting Apr. 11, Fawzi, a special assistant to Pres. Nasser, outlined Cairo's terms for peace. Nixon said the U.S. favored an improvement of relations with Cairo, severed in June 1967. Officials said that in his previous days of talks with Rogers and other Administration leaders, Fawzi had confirmed that Hussein's peace proposal was an "Arab offer to Israel."

But the Cairo newspaper *Al-Ahram* Apr. 12 took issue with Hussein's statement linking a peace settlement to the opening of the Suez Canal to Israeli shipping. The newspaper, which was said to reflect Nasser's views, recalled Nasser's previous declarations that the Canal would never be opened to Israeli use until the Palestine refugee problem was settled. The issue of Israeli shipping rights in the Canal, *Al-Ahram* said, "bears no relation to the 1967 war or the liquidation of its consequences," that is, Israeli withdrawal from Arab territories captured in that war.

Israel spurned King Hussein's 6-point peace plan and expressed further opposition to the Big 4 meetings on the Middle East. Israeli officials Apr. 11 described Hussein's proposal as an exercise in propaganda that contained nothing new. They said the plan was designed to divert attention from the need for direct Arab-Israeli talks.

Israeli Premier Golda Meir asserted Apr. 12 that Hussein was not interested in genuine peace. "If King Hussein genuinely wished to have peace, he would have little difficulty in getting it," she said. Mrs. Meir repeated Israeli demands for direct Arab-Israeli negotiations. Mrs. Meir contended that the current Big 4 talks at the UN favored the Arabs because, "while Moscow as well as de Gaulle and his government—I do not say the French people—are pro-Arab—the United States and Great Britain, though friends of Israel, are equally friends of the Arabs and take into account Arab interests."

Yosef Tekoah, Israeli representative to the UN, said Apr. 10 that he had told Secy. Gen. U Thant that day that the Big 4 talks had paralyzed the peace efforts of UN envoy Jarring. Tekoah also argued that the discussions of the U.S., France, Britain and the Soviet Union had resulted in a hardening of the Arab position and had led the Arabs to increase their military activities against Israel. (Tekoah met with Thant ostensibly to deliver a letter of complaint on the presence of Iraqi troops in Syria, a situation confirmed by Iraq but denied by Damascus.)

A counterstatement delivered by Thant held that the Big 4 talks, which he had encouraged, were designed to reinforce Jarring's mission and not to hinder it. Thant's statement was said to have been provoked principally by a report published by the *Jerusalem Post* Apr. 10 that Jarring had ended his Middle East mission and had resumed his duties as Swedish ambassador to the USSR. The report had been broadcast by U.S. radio stations. Thant denied that Jarring was "giving up, even temporarily, his mission in the Middle East, or that his efforts are being suspended." Thant explained that a point had been reached in Jarring's "efforts in which it appears that there is no further move that he might make at the moment which would be helpful and thus it is advisable to take some time to assess the situation and await new developments."

Israeli Foreign Min. Abba Eban said Apr. 13 that the Big 4 talks were an "unfortunate duplication" of Jarring's activities and that his "peace mission consequently has been virtually paralyzed." Eban predicted that the talks would fail because peace could be achieved only through direct negotiations between the belligerents. Eban expressed doubts that the U.S. had modified its Middle East policy since his talks with American leaders in Washington in March. "Sufficient agreement and harmony" existed between the U.S. and Israel despite their differences on certain specific points, Eban said.

Israeli Premier Meir May 5 reiterated her government's demands for Arab-Israeli peace treaties to replace the cease-fire agreements that had ended the June 1967 war. She described King Hussein's 6-point peace plan as "nothing but an Arab interpretation of the Security Council resolution" of Nov. 1967. In a major address to the Knesset, Mrs. Meir declared that "the only situation that can replace the cease-fire is permanent peace, namely, the final and declared liquidation of the Arab-Israeli conflict." Peace, she said, "must be expressed in signed peace treaties between Israel and each of the neighboring states." Alluding to Big 4 efforts to find a settlement, Mrs. Meir said that "the governments of the region, and not external factors, are responsible for working out and drafting the peace treaties." The pacts must include "agreed, secure and recognized boundaries" and must "annul claims of belligerency, blockades, interference with free navigation" or encouragement of guerrilla attacks against Israel, she said. In a demand not hitherto publicly voiced by Israel, Mrs. Meir insisted that no signatory state "sign a treaty with any other state aimed against its neighbor which is a cosignatory to the peace treaty." (Taking note of Mrs. Meir's statement, the Knesset by 58–5 vote upheld the government's handling of the dispute with the Arabs.)

Soviet Bloc Warns Arabs of War Danger

Czechoslovakia warned Egypt, Syria and Iraq Apr. 14, 1969 against any moves that would precipitate a Middle East war. The warning, delivered verbally by Czechoslovak ambassadors in the 3 Arab capitals, was said to have been drawn up in close coordination with the Soviet Union. Moscow was said to have indicated to Prague that a deterioration of the Middle East situation could adversely affect East-West contacts and reduce chances for a Soviet arms agreement with the U.S. Czechoslovakia, a heavy supplier of arms to the Arab nations, was said to have decided to reduce its shipments of military equipment to those countries and to bar any further arms contracts with them.

The operations and political position of Al Fatah came in for implied criticism Apr. 14 by the newspaper *Sovetskaya Rossiya*, a publication of the Soviet Communist Party's Central Committee. It said that "the liquidation of Israel," as demanded by Al Fatah, "is not realistic." The newspaper expressed "mixed feelings of sympathy" for the Arab guerrillas but "some doubts about their methods of struggle."

The Soviet Communist Party organ *Pravda* May 9 criticized Arab extremists for "whipping up nationalistic and revenge-seeking moods in the people and army with the aim of pushing Egypt on an adventurist course . . . as a result of . . . [which], by their calculations, the existing régime would not survive." These elements, the newspaper charged, "actually help the Israeli invaders to frustrate a political settlement . . . and continue their [Israel's] attempt to overthrow progressive Arab regimes." *Pravda* asserted that "imperialists and reactionary propaganda, lately joined by voices from Peking, . . . give the just cause of the Arabs such a color that would deprive it of its social content and thereby sidetrack it from the revolutionary struggle of our time." *Pravda* reiterated the Soviet view that the Middle East dispute was not a conflict between the Arabs and Israelis as such but was a confrontation "between forces of imperialism and the Arab national liberation movement." It assailed a "well-known Cairo journalist" for writing in the Egyptian newspaper *Al-Ahram* that the Arab resistance movement must be waged "outside politics, outside the social struggle." *Pravda* apparently was referring to *Al-Ahram* editor Muhammad Hassanein Heykal, a close confidant of UAR Pres. Nasser.

Heykal June 5 predicted a "very hot and explosive" winter in which the Arabs would try to oust the Israelis from occupied Arab lands. The Arabs "will not have to observe a 3d anniversary of June 5, 1967, the start of the 6-day war," Heykal wrote.

UAR & Israel React to de Gaulle's Departure

Egypt expressed praise for Charles de Gaulle, 78, who resigned as president of France Apr. 28, 1969 after his government's proposals for Senate and regional reforms were rejected by a national referendum held the previous day. In a statement issued Apr. 28 by Muhammad H. el-Zayyat, the chief government spokesman, the UAR described de Gaulle as "a man who lived by his principles" and "should be a shining example for statesmen everywhere."

Israelis, embittered by de Gaulle's shift from a pro-Israel policy to strong support of the Arab cause, expressed satisfaction with the general's resignation, although there was no official comment from the government. A leading newspaper, *Maariv*, said Apr. 28: "The world, including Israel, has been saved from the obstinacy of a stubborn, vindictive and vengeful man."

The possibility of a reversal of the de Gaulle policy by the new administration in Paris evoked strong reaction among Arab states. Newspapers in Beirut and Cairo June 29 and 30 expressed concern that a reversal could end French-Arab friendship, especially in the economic sphere. French Premier Jacques Chaban-Delmas had said June 28 that the government of Pres. Georges Pompidou might reconsider supplying arms to Israel if other nations continued to provide arms to Arab countries. Chaban-Delmas said that Pompidou regarded the French embargo on arms deliveries to Israel, imposed June 5, 1967, as an "example" to be followed by other nations in their relations with Middle East countries. "If this example is not followed," he said, "it's obvious that the French government must reconsider its position." (*Le Monde* of Paris reported June 28 that de Gaulle had viewed the embargo as a "punitive measure" against Israel, which he considered an "aggressor state," rather than an embargo intended to reduce arms deliveries to all Middle East states.) Paris sources reported that France had resumed the supply of some spare parts to Israel.

UAR Spurns U.S. Peace Plan

The Soviet Union reportedly received a negative response from Egypt towards mid-June 1969 when it consulted with Nasser on a plan for peace in the Middle East proposed by the U.S. May 26. The resultant Soviet reply June 17 was described by U.S. officials June 20 as a "disappointment."

Neither the U.S. proposal nor the Soviet response was made public, but the plan was said to have contained these general principles: Any peace settlement must be in the form of a single package, not in separate phases; the agreement must be "contractual" among Israel and the Arab states, not imposed by outside countries; future boundaries between Israel and its Arab neighbors must be agreed on by the parties themselves, not defined by the Big 4 powers; these frontiers should not "reflect the weight of conquest," that is, Israel must withdraw from territories it had captured in 1967.

Soviet Foreign Min. Andrei Gromyko reportedly sounded out Egypt on the American proposal in talks with Nasser and other UAR officials in Cairo June 10–13. A joint communiqué issued June 13 said that a settlement of the Middle East dispute could be achieved only by acceptance of "all parts and provisions" of the UN Security Council's Nov. 22, 1967 peace resolution. The statement attributed the Middle East crisis to Israel's "expansion policy" and demanded that Israel withdraw from all Arab territories.

Muhammad Hassanein Heykal, editor of the Egyptian newspaper *Al-Ahram*, reported June 20 that Nasser had told Gromyko that Cairo would not hold direct negotiations with Israel, that Israel must relinquish all Arab areas it had captured in 1967 and that no peace settlement would be made at the expense of the Arab refugees. Heykal said that Gromyko had delivered to Nasser a letter in which Soviet leaders reported receiving Washington's May 26 peace message. He quoted Gromyko as telling Nasser that the U.S. proposal reflected the interests only of Israel and that the

USSR wanted "to consult with you" before submitting a counterproposal. Gromyko told Nasser that the Soviet Union would halt its lateral talks with the U.S. on the Middle East if Nasser made such a request, Heykal said. But Nasser was said to have replied that Egypt would not object to the continuation of these discussions as long as it was understood that the UAR would not alter its demand for an Israeli withdrawal or its refusal to hold direct talks with Israel.

The U.S. and the Soviet Union resumed bilateral talks on the Middle East June 2 after a 6-week recess. The meeting, held in Washington by State Secy. William P. Rogers and Amb. Anatoly Dobrynin, made little progress in the bilateral search for a solution to the Arab-Israeli conflict. Rogers reportedly told Dobrynin that the U.S. took a serious view of increased Soviet military aid to Egypt.

Moscow charged June 6 that the resumption of the talks was being used by some quarters in the U.S. to bring pressure on the USSR to withdraw its military personnel from the UAR. The Soviet statement said that some American newspapers "even threaten the immediate delivery of 125 Phantom and Skyhawk fighter bombers to Israel if the USSR does not make concessions to the American side during the contacts." The statement hinted that Washington's compliance with the Israeli request for the aircraft would probably lead to more Soviet aid to the Arab states.

Resolutions introduced in the U.S. Senate and House of Representatives June 2 urged diplomatic action to bring about a halt to increased Soviet military assistance to Cairo. Rogers had received a plea from 73 Senators June 1 for prompt agreement to Israel's standing request to buy the 125 planes. The appeal, contained in a letter to the State Department, said "such action will serve as a significant element of a credible response to the reckless Soviet escalation of the Middle East conflict."

Libya warned the U.S. June 2 that a sale of the jets to Israel "may be the final break" in U.S.-Arab relations.

Deputy Premier Abdul Salam Jallud said that "there is no reason for America to give Israel more planes, because if America wants Israel to keep the [Arab] occupied territories, then Israel has enough power to do so."

Soviet Foreign Minister Gromyko, in a wide-ranging foreign policy address before the Supreme Soviet in Moscow July 10, called for friendly relations with the U.S. and expressed concern over Communist China. Gromyko said the Mideast conflict should be resolved "on the basis of withdrawal of Israeli troops from occupied areas and simultaneous recognition of the right of all Middle-Eastern states, including Israel, to independent national existence."

Joseph J. Sisco, U.S. Assistant State Secretary for Near Eastern and South Asian affairs, discussed the Middle East situation with Soviet officials in Moscow July 14–17. Little progress was reported in efforts to resolve U.S. and Soviet differences and to draw up a joint proposal to settle the Arab-Israeli problem. The only substantial achievement of the 4-day meeting was an agreement to continue the bilateral talks begun in April in Washington by Sisco and Soviet Amb. Anatoly F. Dobrynin. After leaving Moscow, Sisco went to Stockholm to inform UN envoy Gunnar Jarring of his talks with the Soviet leaders. Prior to arriving in the Soviet capital July 12, Sisco had delivered to British and French officials in London and Paris the U.S. reply to the Soviet peace proposal of June 17, which, in turn, was Moscow's answer to the Washington plan of May 26. The State Department had said June 26 that the Soviet counterproposal represented progress but lacked what the U.S. considered the basic prerequisites for a lasting peace in the Middle East.

Egypt said July 18 that a political solution of the Arab-Israeli dispute was possible and that the Arabs' resort to arms was unavoidable. Writing in *Al-Ahram*, Muhammad Heykal said that even Arabs who favored a political solution found themselves "face to face with the inevitability of armed struggle." A peaceful solution "is not available," Heykal said, "regardless of all that the big powers and their super-powers have done or are still doing."

Foreign Relations

The UAR initiated or took part in 3 diplomatic moves in midsummer 1969.

Cairo sent a delegation to a consultative conference of 51 nonaligned countries held in Belgrade, Yugoslavia July 8–12 to "exchange views on the role of the policy of nonalignment in the present-day world, especially regarding peace, independence and development." 12 other North African and Mid-eastern countries also sent representatives. All sessions but the opening one were closed to outsiders and the press.

After a long procedural debate, the Belgrade conferees July 8 approved a request from the Palestine Liberation Organization (PLO) to present its views. Algerian Amb.-to-Yugoslavia Tayeb Boulharouf insisted July 9 that all "liberation movements" be invited to any summit conference of nonaligned countries, since nonalignment signified "not merely a moral and political force" but "an active policy that should assist all movements combatting imperialism."

PLO delegation chairman Khaled Yasharuti said July 10 that the PLO was "determined to bear the brunt of the burden" of reconquering his homeland for the Palestinian Arabs but would welcome any assistance from nonaligned countries. He accused Israel of "acts of genocide" against the Palestinian Arabs. When asked after the session whether he was aware of a report that UAR Pres. Nasser regarded the recognition of Israel as possible, Yasharuti replied that the PLO had "nothing to do" with any statement by any Arab leader. He outlined as his movement's goal the establishment of an independent Palestinian Arab state guaranteeing all religious rights, including those of Jews who had lived in the Holy Land before the creation of Israel, which he termed "not a legal state."

The Belgrade conference's final communiqué reaffirmed the basic principles of nonalignment enunciated in Belgrade in 1961 and in Cairo in 1964. On the subject of the Middle East, the conference also "reaffirmed the Cairo resolution of 1964, in which the heads of state and government of the non-aligned countries, in conformity with the UN Charter, in-dorsed the full restoration of the rights of the Arab people of Palestine to their usurped homeland." The conference's par-ticipants "declared full support to the Arab people of Pales-tine in their struggle for liberation from colonialism and racism and for the recovery of their inalienable rights." They reasserted "the inadmissibility of the acquisition of territory by war" and urged "the withdrawal of foreign troops from all Arab territories occupied since June 5, 1967, in accordance with the resolution of the UN Security Council of Nov. 22, 1967."

Dr. Muhammad el-Zayyat, chief Egyptian government spokesman, confirmed in Cairo July 9 that the UAR had de-cided to extend diplomatic recognition to East Germany. Zayyat said, however, that the decision was not taken to affect relations adversely with West Germany. "Our relations with East Germany," he said, "are completely separate from those with West Germany." (Egypt had severed diplomatic relations with West Germany May 13, 1965 over Bonn's rec-ognition of Israel.)

(Conrad Ahlers, West German government deputy spokes-man, said in Bonn July 9: "There is information that the Soviet Union had made further weapons deliveries to Egypt dependent on the recognition of East Berlin." West German Foreign Min. Willy Brandt July 10 accused the East German government of accepting "disgusting anti-Semitism" by its formal recognition of the UAR.)

Egypt Aug. 23 announced the recall of its ambassador to Rumania in retaliation for Bucharest's agreement Aug. 13 to raise diplomatic relations with Israel to the ambassadorial level. Cairo charged that Rumania's action represented "a consolidation of Zionist aggression and encouragement of Israeli expansionism." (In another reprisal move, Sudan had ordered Rumania Aug. 20 to close its embassy in Khartoum.)

Pro-Nasser Coup in Libya

A group of pro-Nasser military officers seized power in Libya Sept. 1, 1969. They ousted the regime of Muhammad Idris Al Mahdi as-Sanusi, king of Libya, and announced that the oil-rich North African country had become the Libyan Arab Republic. The victorious cabal adopted the Arab nationalist slogan of "Socialism, Unity and Freedom" for Libya. Arab nationalist states granted immediate recognition to the new regime. Col. Saaduddin Abu Shweirib, a onetime student of the Army Command & General Staff School at Fort Leavenworth, Kan. and defense chief of the new regime, sent to Egypt's Pres. Nasser a message supporting anti-Zionist principles. In its first policy statement, the new regime announced Sept. 2 that it would follow an Arab nationalist policy and would seek to cooperate with nonaligned nations. It promised to respect existing agreements with other nations and to protect the lives and property of foreigners.

Rebellious troops had executed the coup by reportedly moving into Tripoli, the western capital, in the early morning hours and securing government and military installations. A Revolutionary Command Council (RCC) was established and an around-the-clock curfew imposed. The new regime Sept. 1 announced the dissolution of parliament and all other constitutional bodies, closed all airports and seaports and cut external phone and telegraph communications. Several persons, including the army chief of staff and the security chief, were arrested, but most reports termed the coup bloodless. Reports Sept. 4 that troops and tanks were occupying Benghazi and that Libyan air force planes were patrolling oil installations indicated possible opposition from desert chieftains said to be loyal to King Idris. The Libyan radio broadcast messages of support from labor and student groups, Libyan ambassadors stationed in foreign countries, and military and political leaders. Demonstrations supporting the new regime took place Sept. 4 and 5 during the temporary lifting of the curfew. The RCC announced Sept. 7 that it had decreed a general amnesty for all political prisoners. It announced an end to restricted travel within the country and the opening of key ports Sept. 8.

King Idris, 79, who had been in Turkey receiving medical treatment, was reportedly surprised by news of the coup. Idris' nephew and heir, Crown Prince Al-Hasan Rida as-Sanusi, 40, announced over Tripoli radio Sept. 1 that he had abdicated voluntarily and had renounced all power. Later reports said the prince had been placed under arrest.

U.S. recognition was officially extended Sept. 6 by the State Department. Some observers contended that the delivery by the U.S. of the first consignment of F-4 Phantom fighter jets to Israel Sept. 5 had hastened recognition. They held that the U.S. Administration had adopted the policy of prompt recognition as an expedient to assuage militant Arabs. Commanders at Wheelus Air Force Base near Tripoli, center for bomber training for U.S. NATO troops, and at Britain's El Adem and Tobruk bases had ceased operations Sept. 3 on request of the RCC.

King Idris, who had left for Greece Sept. 2, cabled Egypt's Pres. Nasser a request that Nasser intervene with the RCC for the safety of his adopted daughter, Suleimah. He said in the cable: "We assure your excellency that all rumors about our intention to return to Libya are untrue." Idris' secretary announced in Athens Sept. 7 that the king was "ready to abdicate his throne if asked." (A statement carried on Tripoli Radio Sept. 7 said that Idris' daughter and other members of his household were well and not under arrest.)

The editor of the Cairo newspaper *Al-Ahram*, Muhammad Hassanein Heikal, who was in Libya Sept. 1-3, reported that the RCC chairman, who wished to remain anonymous for awhile, was "in his 20s" and that his colleagues were "all be-tween 20 and 30 years old." An interview with the chairman carried by Cairo's semiofficial Middle East News Agency quoted him as saying the régime would follow a policy of "pan-Arab and pan-Islamic brotherhood and solidarity." (The London *Times* said Sept. 2 that the coup leaders had enrolled in military academies with the intent of overthrow-ing the monarchy and had twice postponed the coup during 1969.) Heikal also reported Sept. 5 that the British had drawn up a contingency plan, dated July 27, 1964, outlining measures to resist internal disturbances in Libya. Heikal said the plan, which was signed by Lord Mountbatten and other military personnel, "came into Arab hands in 1965." *Al-Ahram*, reprinted the document, which said in part that Brit-ish troops could be used to combat internal disturbances that "coincide with or are part of open aggression by Egypt or anyone else."

A civilian Libyan prime minister and a cabinet were appointed Sept. 8. Mahmoud Soliman al-Maghreby, a lawyer and former union leader, was named prime minister and min-ister of finance, agriculture and agrarian reform. The cabinet included only 2 army officers.

Rabat Summit Conference

Leaders representing Egypt and 24 other Islamic coun-tries—both Arab and non-Arab—held a summit conference in Rabat, Morocco Sept. 22–25, 1969 to consider the conse-quences of a fire that had damaged part of Al Aksa Mosque in Jerusalem in August and to take up other aspects of the Arabs' dispute with Israel. (Israeli authorities had indicted a young Australian tourist Sept. 1 on charges of arson and the violation of holy places in connection with the fire. The mosque had reopened for prayer Sept. 19 after repair. An Israeli inquiry commission concluded Sept. 24 that an arson-ist had succeeded in setting the fire because of the negligence of Moslem guards.)

A declaration adopted by the conferees on the final day of the conference Sept. 25 turned aside Egypt's assertion that the mosque fire was a "premeditated act by Israel." It merely held Israel responsible as the occupying power. The declaration also: (a) called on the major powers to help obtain the "speedy withdrawal" of Israeli forces from occupied Arab territory; (b) gave "full support for the Palestinian people for restitution of their usurped rights and their struggle for national liberation"; (c) pledged that the Moslem countries would work for the implementation of UN resolutions that called for the withdrawal of Israeli forces from occupied territories; and (d) called for a meeting of Moslem foreign ministers at Jidda, Saudi Arabia in Mar. 1970 to organize a permanent Islamic secretariat. The conference ignored demands by Egypt and Sudan for military and economic support of the Palestinians and a proposal by Libya Sept. 23 that all Moslem countries sever diplomatic relations with Israel.

A delegation of the Palestine Liberation Organization (PLO), headed by its chairman, Yasir Arafat, had participated with observer status. The PLO delegation had been seated Sept. 23 on the insistence of Algeria's chief delegate, Pres. Houari Boumedienne. Iran and Turkey, which had diplomatic relations with Israel, had argued against the seating of the PLO on the ground that it did not constitute a government.

Syria and Iraq were among 10 Moslem countries that had refused invitations to attend. Syria based its boycott on the fact that it had no diplomatic relations with Morocco. An announcement in Baghdad Sept. 22 said Iraq would not attend because it could not be guaranteed 3 conditions: the drawing up of an agenda that would assure the summit's success; a preparatory meeting in New York of Islamic foreign ministers; and the attendance of a PLO delegation.

Islamic countries attending the conference were (names in parentheses are those of delegation chiefs) Afghanistan (Premier Nour Ahmed Entemadi), Algeria (Pres. Houari

Boumedienne), Chad, Egypt (Anwar el-Sadat for Pres. Nasser, ill with influenza), Guinea, Indonesia, Iran (Shah Muhammad Riza Pahlevi), Jordan (King Hussein), Kuwait (Emir Sabah al-Salem al-Sabah), Lebanon, Libya, Malaysia (Prime Min. Tunku Abdul Rahman), Mali, Mauritania (Pres. Mokhtar Ould Daddah), Morocco (King Hassan II, the host), Niger, Pakistan (Pres. Muhammad Yahya Khan), Saudi Arabia (King Faisal), Senegal, Somalia (Pres. Abdel Rashid Schermarke), South Yemen, Sudan, Tunisia, Turkey (Foreign Min. Ihsan Sabri Caglayangil) and Yemen (Pres. Abdul Rahman al-Iryany). The gathering represented about 450 million of the world's 650 million Moslems.

At a news conference reviewing the meeting, King Hassan Sept. 26 assailed the Arab extremists among the anti-Israeli guerrilla forces as "wild and harebrained" and said that they did not serve "the Palestinian cause, the Arab cause or the Moslem cause." He said Morocco supported only those anti-Israeli elements "who fight at the United Nations, who fight to convince states of their cause and their right."

UAR Command Shift

Pres. Nasser replaced 2 top military commanders Sept. 18, 1969, and the government announced Sept. 20 the removal of former Vice Pres. Aly Sabry from a top post in the Arab Socialist Union, the UAR's only legal political party. Sources in Beirut, Lebanon speculated that these major shifts of men ideologically aligned with the Soviet Union were aimed at foiling a Soviet-directed conspiracy to overthrow Nasser. The reports of a plot received further weight by the disclosure Sept. 17 that Nasser was ill with acute influenza and had canceled all engagements and a scheduled trip to the USSR. But the semi-official newspaper *Al-Ahram* Sept. 21 denied reports of a plot.

In a command shift, Lt. Gen. Muhammad Sadek, chief of military intelligence since 1966, replaced Lt. Gen. Ahmed

Ismail as chief of staff, and naval Col. Mahmoud Fahmi
Abdul Rahman was appointed commander of Egypt's naval
forces, succeeding Capt. Fuad Zikry. *Al-Ahram* explained
Sept. 19 that the appointments were designed to "push
forward militant youthful elements" into command positions. Government sources denied that the changes were connected with Israel's Sept. 9 commando attack across the Gulf
of Suez.

Sabry was removed as secretary of the Arab Socialist
Union's Organizing Committee and replaced by Interior Min.
Sharawi Muhammad Gomaa. He was permitted to remain a
member of the party's executive committee. *Al-Ahram* said
Sept. 21 that Sabry had been demoted because of his return
from a private trip to Moscow in July with "personal effects
beyond the limit permitted into Egypt." He handed in his
resignation following a government inquiry.

Al-Ahram Sept. 21 denounced the reports of an anti-
government plot as "psychological warfare" by U.S. intelligence. Alluding to the reports, published by the Beirut newspaper *Al Jarida*, *Al-Ahram* assailed "certain shady newspapers
in the Arab area" as well as Western dailies for linking the
command shift, Sabry's demotion and the dismissal of about
30 journalists to the alleged plot. The command shift, the
newspaper said, was dictated by "the exigencies of war," not
politics. The dismissal of the Cairo newsmen, who were said
to have been sympathetic to the left-wing views of Sabry,
were motivated not by politics but by inefficiencies that
caused a decline in the circulation of Cairo's newspapers, *Al-
Ahram* said. Among those dismissed was Amin el-Alem,
managing editor of *Al-Akhbar*.

Big 4 Resume Talks; UAR Rejects Rhodes Formula

The Big 4 powers agreed Sept. 20, 1969 to resume joint
UN ambassadorial talks on the Middle East. The discussions
had been suspended July 1 to await the outcome of bilateral
talks between the U.S. and the Soviet Union.

The agreement to reopen the Big 4 parley was announced after a meeting of UN Secy. Gen. U Thant with U.S. State Secy. William P. Rogers, Soviet Foreign Min. Andrei Gromyko, French Foreign Min. Maurice Schumann and British Foreign Secy. Michael Stewart. A joint statement said the ministers had "agreed that a durable peace should be established in the Middle East" and had "reaffirmed that all states in the Middle East have an inalienable right to exist as independent and sovereign states." The Big 4 agreement followed a statement by Thant Sept. 12 that there was "need for even more sustained and concentrated effort on the part of the 4 permanent members [of the UN Security Council] in the months ahead to save the situation."

Rogers and Gromyko conferred at UN headquarters Sept. 26. Their discussions had been preceded by lower-level talks held Sept. 18 by Soviet Amb. Anatoly Dobrynin and U.S. Assistant State Secy. Joseph Sisco.

After conferring with State Secy. Rogers Sept. 24, Egyptian Foreign Min. Mahmoud Riad was quoted as saying that direct Arab negotiations with Israel were possible if Israel withdrew from Arab occupied territories and "renounces expansionism." The Egyptian government Sept. 25 denied the Riad statement, saying that his remarks had been misinterpreted as part of a campaign aimed at "spreading confusion" about Cairo's stand on a Middle East solution. A government spokesman insisted that the UAR would never agree to direct talks with Israel.

Riad conceded Sept. 25 that Israel and the Arab states were currently engaged in indirect "Rhodes-type" negotiations. (This was a reference to the armistice talks both sides had held on the Mediterranean island of Rhodes in 1948–9.) But Riad emphasized that direct talks with Israel would amount to "surrender" as long as Israeli forces occupied Arab territories. Riad insisted that the Rhodes discussions were indirect, having been conducted through the mediation of Dr. Ralph Bunche, currently UN undersecretary general. According to Israel's interpretation, the Rhodes negotiations had constituted direct discussions between the disputing parties. Riad described Gunnar Jarring, Thant's mediator in the Middle East, as "the new Dr. Bunche," who was "in a better position than . . . Bunche because he has a Security Council resolution to work with. All he has to do is to see that" Israel complied with the resolution by withdrawing from Arab areas, Riad said. Although he insisted on "full withdrawal" by Israel, Riad denied that Cairo regarded this as a "precondition" for negotiating a settlement. The Security Council's Nov. 22, 1967 resolution, he noted, "contains several points, withdrawal among them. It's a package deal and we want all of it implemented."

The Egyptian newspaper *Al-Ahram* asserted Oct. 11 that Riad's remarks on the "Rhodes formula" had been subjected to "deliberate gross distortions aimed at undermining the position of the United Arab Republic." The newspaper said that Cairo "does not believe in the possibility of conducting direct or indirect negotiations with Israel either on the basis of the Rhodes formula or any other formula."

The Higher Executive Committee of Egypt's ruling Arab Socialist Union held a public meeting Oct. 11 and charged that Israel and its supporters had brought up the Rhodes formula to create distrust between Egypt and its Arab neighbors. One speaker, Anwar Sadat, said that the UAR's position remained "No recognition of Israel, no peace treaty and no negotiations."

Al-Ahram reported Oct. 12 that Riad, during his UN consultations in September, had rejected a proposal that he and Jordanian Foreign Min. Abdel Rifai meet with Israeli Foreign Min. Abba Eban in New York in November to facilitate the efforts of UN envoy Jarring to enforce the 1967 UN Security Council resolution on the Middle East. *Al-Ahram* said Riad informed Jarring that "the attempt to raise the issue of the Rhodes formula is to undermine the main objective of your mission in the Middle East." Cairo accepted the 1967 resolution and the Jarring mission, but it refused "to discuss the details relating to procedure" of the resolution's implementation, "which do not concern the heart of the matter," Riad was reported to have told Jarring.

Jarring concluded his mediation efforts at UN headquarters in New York Oct. 8 and departed to resume his duties as Swedish ambassador to Moscow. A spokesman for Secy. Gen. U Thant said Jarring's departure did not mean that his mediation efforts were suspended. "While in Moscow, Amb. Jarring will continue to keep closely in touch with developments and intends to resume his active efforts at an appropriate time," the spokesman said.

U Thant warned Oct. 28 that "we may be witnessing in the Middle East something like the early stages of a new 100 years' war." He said that if UN members continued to defy Security Council resolutions on peace," we shall have taken a very dangerous step backwards toward anarchy."

UAR, Israel & USSR Rebuff U.S. Plan

A U.S. Mideastern peace plan, proposed Oct. 28, 1969, failed to enlist the interest of either Egypt or Israel and subsequently drew a verbal rejection from the Soviet leadership, which at first had seemed favorably disposed toward it. According to a dispatch from Washington Nov. 5, U.S. diplomats indicated that Washington and Moscow, engaged in peace discussions at the U.N. since February, were close to agreement on proposals that would be submitted to the Arab states and Israel for negotiations.

Nasser, spurning political "half-solutions," declared Nov. 6 that the Arab states had "no other alternative" but "to go along a road covered with blood" to recover Arab territories occupied by Israel. He said: "The liberation should be for all Arab lands. And foremost among these are Jerusalem, the West Bank [of the Jordan], the Gaza Strip and the Golan Heights." Speaking to the Egyptian National Assembly in Cairo, he charged that the U.S. "actually has assumed the position of our enemy," Israel, while "our friend is the Soviet Union." He repeated the Arab charge that the U.S. was arming Israel and that Americans were fighting "from behind guns and from aircraft that carry the [Israeli] Star of David."

Referring to Arab guerrillas attacking Israel, Nasser asserted that the "Palestinian commandos are here to stay until the Palestinian nation is established." This was Nasser's first reference to a Palestine nation. Nasser also said: "The countries in direct confrontation with Israel bear special responsibility. But the wide expanse of the Arab world and the vast Arab potentialities are the main support of this first line."

Israeli Foreign Min. Abba Eban said Nov. 6 that Nasser's speech "once more revealed his true aspirations to eliminate Israel's independence and existence."

U.S. State Secy. Rogers Nov. 7 called Nasser's speech "a setback to efforts to find a peaceful solution" for the Middle East. He said Nasser was "mistaken in describing the United States as an enemy of Egypt," and he denied Nasser's charges that the U.S. was involved in Israeli military actions against Egypt.

The Egyptian newspaper *Al-Ahram* Nov. 9 took issue with "American interpretations" that Nasser had "rejected peace." Nasser had "clarified that it was Israel that had rejected" the UN Security Council's 1967 resolution on peace, "while Egypt accepted it," the newspaper said. *Al-Ahram* indicated that Cairo desired continued U.S. efforts to seek a peace formula despite initial negative Arab reaction to its proposals, which, the newspaper said, "did not advance anything that would be a basis for a just solution of the crisis."

At the Arab League's Joint Defense Council meeting, convened in Cairo to discuss the "mobilization of all Arab energies" for a war against Israel, Egyptian Foreign Min. Mahmoud Riad charged Nov. 8 that the latest U.S. peace plan "was even worse than previous proposals." (Cairo sources said that the U.S. plan, among other things, called for Israel to return the entire Sinai Peninsula to Egypt and for Israel and Jordan to negotiate together with Egypt over the future of the Israeli-occupied Gaza Strip.) Accusing the U.S. of attempting to divide the Arab people, Riad declared that the Gaza Strip was "Arab territory owned by the Palestinian people." He charged that the U.S. was not merely an "advocate" of Israel but had become an "accomplice." In a communiqué issued at the conclusion of the meeting Nov. 10, the Defense Council accused the U.S. of blocking efforts for a peaceful settlement and pledged full support to the Palestinian commandos. The Defense Council's meeting, the first since the June 1967 war, was attended by all Arab League members except Tunisia, which continued its boycott of the high-level talks.

U.S. State Secy. Rogers Dec. 9 called for Israeli withdrawal from occupied Arab territories in exchange for a binding peace agreement with the Arab states. The statement drew a negative response from Israel, the USSR and Egypt. It was the first U.S. disclosure of the U.S.' hitherto private Middle East peace formula submitted to the Soviet Union Oct. 28. Asserting that Washington's policy "is and will continue to be a balanced one," Rogers said: "To call for Israeli withdrawal without achieving agreement on peace would be partisan toward the Arabs. To call on the Arabs to accept peace without Israeli withdrawal would be partisan toward Israel. Therefore, our policy is to encourage the Arabs to accept a permanent peace based on a binding agreement and to urge the Israelis to withdraw from occupied territory when their territorial integrity is assured."

Rogers expressed opposition to Israel's absorption of the former Jordanian sector of Jerusalem. He proposed instead that the city be unified under an administration that "should take into account the interests of all its inhabitants and of the Jewish, Islamic and Christian communities. And there should be roles for both Israel and Jordan in the civic, eco-

nomic and religious life of the city." The other principal
elements of the plan:

- Israel and the UAR should commit themselves to a binding accord
"with all the specific obligations of peace spelled out. . . ."
- "The detailed provisions of peace relating to security safeguards on
the ground should be worked out between the parties" themselves.
These safeguards should apply to the Sharm el-Sheik area, the point
controlling access to the Gulf of Aqaba, the demilitarization of the
Sinai Peninsula and the "final arrangements in the Gaza Strip."

Rogers conceded that "peace rests with the parties to the
conflict," but he said that the U.S. and the other major powers could help by "stimulating the parties to talks."

An Israeli rebuke to Rogers' remarks was given Dec. 11 in
a cabinet statement that asserted that "negotiations to peace
must be free from prior conditions and external influences
and pressures." The cabinet warned that "the prospects for
peace will be seriously marred if states outside the region
continue to raise territorial prospects and suggestions on subjects that cannot promote peace and security."

Israeli Premier Golda Meir Dec. 12 accused the U.S. of
"moralizing" and took issue with Rogers for attempting to
equate Arab and Israeli intentions. Israel wanted peace while
the Arabs were "preparing for war," she said. But the U.S.
"put us both on the scales of justice so that . . . they
shouldn't appear to be favoring one nation over another."
Mrs. Meir added: "It was the Arab leaders who took their
people to war, and they must now declare their willingness
for peace. It will not help if the big powers say it for them."
(At his news conference Dec. 23, Rogers denied Mrs. Meir's
contention that the U.S. proposal was an appeasement of the
Arabs. He also took issue with the Israeli view that outside
powers should not make specific proposals that might prejudice either side's position in the projected peace talks. The
U.S., Rogers said, "has a right to make suggestions just as the
Soviet Union has a right to make suggestions.")

The Soviet Communist Party newspaper *Pravda* responded to Rogers' statement Dec. 14 by saying that despite

attempts to "erase from the Arabs' memory the facts of its complicity in the Israeli aggression," the U.S. had failed "to conceal the evident facts" of its support of Israel's "stubborn attempts to annex seized territories." The U.S. was still adhering to its "one-sided and obviously anti-Arab stand," the newspaper said.

Although the Egyptian government had not yet responded officially to Rogers' statement, *Al Goumhouria*, the newspaper of the Arab Socialist Union, the UAR's only political party, noted Dec. 11 that Cairo had rejected the American peace plan Nov. 6.

Soviet and Egyptian officials held a high-level conference in Moscow Dec. 10–12. A joint communiqué issued Dec. 12 listed these demands as "absolutely essential for a political settlement": "The withdrawal of Israeli troops from occupied Arab territories, elimination of other consequences of Israeli aggression, and the establishment of a lasting peace based on respect for the legitimate rights and interests of all Arab peoples, including the Arab people of Palestine." The statement said the USSR "will continue supporting the just cause of the Arab countries . . . and will continue struggling in and outside the United Nations for a political settlement."

The Egyptian delegation, led by Anwar el-Sadat, included War Min. Muhammad Fawzi and Foreign Min. Mahmoud Riad. The Soviet group was headed by Communist Party Chairman Leonid I. Brezhnev and Premier Aleksei N. Kosygin. In greeting the Egyptians Dec. 10, Kosygin had promised that Moscow would take "active measures to strengthen the defense potential" of the Arab nations in their conflict with Israel.

(U.S. Deputy Assistant Defense Secy. Robert Pranger had conferred with Riad in Cairo Nov. 29. His visit was the first to Egypt by a high U.S. official since Cairo had severed diplomatic relations with Washington during the June 1967 war. *Al-Ahram* said Riad had told Pranger that U.S. military aid to Israel was increasing the danger of new fighting with Israel.)

The U.S. State Department announced Dec. 23 that a Soviet answer that day to Washington's Oct. 28 proposal for the Middle East "indicated that it [the Kremlin] is not constructively responsive." The Soviet reply, delivered orally by Amb. Anatoly Dobrynin to State Secy. Rogers, was said to have represented a reversal of Moscow's previous acceptance of the "Rhodes formula" for indirect negotiations between Egypt and Israel. The *N.Y. Times* reported Jan. 12, 1970 that the Soviet reply criticized the U.S. proposal as having "a one-sided, pro-Israeli character" and made these 8 major objections:

• Against the proposal for an end to the Mid-Eastern war simultaneous with the registration in the UN of the final peace agreement of all of the principals (Israel, Egypt, Iraq, Jordan, Syria, etc.), the Kremlin advocated a *"de facto* cessation" when Israeli forces began withdrawing from occupied Arab territories and a *"de jure* cessation" as soon as the withdrawals were completed.
• Against the U.S. proposal of a 3-month withdrawal timetable, the Kremlin urged a 2-month schedule.
• Against the U.S. proposal that all territory evacuated by Israel be demilitarized, the Kremlin insisted that demilitarized zones be set up on both sides of Israel's borders.
• Against the U.S. proposal that both Egypt and Israel define and agree on their common border, the Kremlin maintained that any joint declaration would have to uphold as Egyptian territory the Sinai Peninsula's southern seaside point of Sharm el-Sheikh.
• Against the U.S. proposal that both the Strait of Tiran and the Gulf of Aqaba be proclaimed international waterways always free to navigation by all countries' ships, the Kremlin argued that free passage for all shipping would be sufficiently guaranteed if navigation rights questions "should be solved in conformity with generally agreed principles of international law."
• Against the U.S. proposal of guaranteed rights of passage through the Suez Canal to all countries' ships, the Kremlin held that Egypt was entitled to close the Canal to the ships of any country with which it considered itself at war.
• Against the U.S. proposal of talks between Egypt, Israel and Jordan, under UN envoy Gunnar Jarring's sponsorship, on the future of the Gaza Strip, the Kremlin held that the Strip was "Arab territory" and would have to revert to its pre-June 1967 status.
• Against the U.S. proposal that Palestinian Arab refugees be allowed the options of repatriation according to an agreed annual quota or re-

settlement outside Israel with compensation, the Kremlin demanded Israeli compliance with all past UN resolutions on the problem.

Radio Cairo Apr. 19, 1970 broadcast an interview in which Nasser was quoted as saying that "the so-called Rogers plan . . . attempts to help the enemy [Israel] to pressure us and to destroy Arab unity and Arab determination. . . . Washington encourages them [the Israelis] with arms and funds as well as false peace offers." Nasser said that "Israel is the U.S. advance base in Western Asia [the Middle East]. What involvement could be deeper than the U.S. involvement with Israel? On every occasion Washington has been repeating whatever Israel says. The U.S. notes to us repeat, like parrots, the words and phrases of [Israeli Premier Golda] Meir and [Foreign Min. Abba] Eban. The obvious truth is that the United States encourages Israel and orders us to enter negotiations with the aggressor without any guarantee of withdrawal. The United States wants to compensate Israel for its aggression. This is substantially the contents of the '10 commandments' presented by Rogers."

"I tell you I want peace in order to develop my country," Nasser declared in the interview. "The other fraternal Arab states also want peace. Believe me, we have knocked on every door in search of peace, but the answer from Israel and its Western partners has been war, war, war." Nasser charged that "Israel's policy is based on constant aggression, expansion, annexation and colonization. . . . Israel's founders never concealed their plan for a greater Israel to include the Suez Canal, the [Nile] Delta, Jordan, Lebanon, Syria, Iraq and the whole area between the Nile and the Euphrates." According to Nasser, Israeli Defense Min. "Moshe Dayan is boasting that his generation succeeded in achieving and extending the borders of 1948 and 1967. He is demanding that the coming generation, by conquest, complete the mission to achieve greater Israel. How can we negotiate a firm and permanent settlement of the borders with people who neither know nor recognize any border?"

Israel Seeks U.S. Arms

Israel's dependence on continued U.S. military and economic aid was emphasized by Israeli Premier Golda Meir at
a meeting with Pres. Nixon at the White House Sept. 25,
1969 at the start of a 2-day state visit to Washington.

Israel had been reported Aug. 6 to have asked the U.S.
to sell it more than 100 planes at an estimated cost of $150
million to maintain its air superiority over the Arab states.
The request, reportedly submitted in July by Israeli Amb.
Itzhak Rabin, called for the purchase of about 80 Skyhawk
A-4 fighter-bombers and about 25 F-4 supersonic Phantom
jets. The Nixon Administration had not yet responded to the
Israeli bid but had taken it under consideration, the report
said.

Under an agreement announced Dec. 27, 1968, Israel had
begun receiving 50 U.S. Phantoms in September. In addition,
Mrs. Meir reportedly was seeking about 80 A-4 Skyhawk jets,
another 25 Phantoms and ground-to-air missiles.

After the first day's conference, Presidential Press Secy.
Ronald L. Ziegler said that both leaders had dealt largely
with "the achievement of peace" in the Middle East and that
there was "no need at this time for an immediate decision"
on Israel's request for more arms. Ziegler said Mrs. Meir had
"emphasized to the President the importance of continued
military supplies from the United States and said that as long
as the present situation continues Israel would need additional equipment from time to time."

At the conclusion of their talks Sept. 26, Nixon said that
"we will not announce any decisions at this time." But he
said that his meeting with Mrs. Meir could produce "progress
toward solutions" of Middle East problems.

Mrs. Meir indicated later at the National Press Club in
Washington that Nixon had assured her of providing Israel
with continued arms shipments and economic assistance. She
said: "There has been a policy followed by the United States

of sensitivity to the balance of power in the Middle East. I have reason to believe it will be followed in the future."

In an interview Sept. 27, Mrs. Meir expressed skepticism over Big 4 efforts to achieve peace in the Middle East without the consent of the major parties concerned. She acknowledged that "there is a role for the 4 powers and the United Nations in this Arab-Israeli conflict. And the role is to get the parties together for negotiations for a peace agreement— period." But "the differences of opinion arise," Mrs. Meir said, "when the powers think that they have a role to play beyond that, or sometimes even instead of that."

Mrs. Meir returned to Israel Oct. 5 after completing a 10-day tour of the U.S. Commenting on her meeting with Nixon, Mrs. Meir had said in Los Angeles Oct. 2 that he had given her "no concrete, direct promise" of American arms. But she said she had found "the policy of the United States government . . . one of sensitivity" for Israel's problems. (The Israeli state radio had reported Sept. 29 that Mrs. Meir had asked Nixon for a billion dollars worth of economic assistance over the next 5 years. The aid was requested to balance an expected billion-dollar deficit during that period resulting from Israel's huge defense expenditures, the broadcast said.)

(Nixon had met Dec. 9, 1969 with a group of top American industrialists with oil and other interests in the Middle East to discuss "the political situation" there, the White House confirmed Dec. 21. The N.Y. Times reported that the businessmen had complained that the U.S. position in the region had deteriorated and that Soviet influence had increased proportionately, partially because of Washington's support of Israel. The men were said to have recommended that the U.S. improve its relations with the oil-producing states of the Middle East to prevent a loss of American standing in the region and to avert damage to U.S. oil interests in in the area. Among those participating in the White House talks were David Rockefeller, president of Chase Manhattan

Bank; ex-Treasury Secy. Robert B. Anderson, a director of Dresser Industries Co., which had oil interests in Kuwait and Libya; and John J. McCloy, ex-president of Chase Manhattan. (State Secy. Rogers defended the U.S.' Middle East policies at a meeting with 14 American Jewish leaders in Washington Dec. 22. A statement issued after the talks by a delegation of the Conference of Presidents of Major Jewish Organizations said that official American pronouncements lately had contributed "neither to the long-term interests of the United States nor to the security of Israel or the cause of peace in the Middle East.")

Heykal Explains Egyptian Policy

Al-Ahram's chief editor, Muhammad Hassanein Heykal, long known as a close confidant of Pres. Nasser, clarified Egyptian policy in a March 26, 1970 article. In his weekly "Frankly Speaking" article, Heykal discussed the Mideastern struggle:

Every major crisis in the world has 2 conflict levels: A local level among the apparent parties to the conflict and an international level among the major powers interested in the area of the conflict, in the events taking place in the area, in the results of the conflict, and in the effects of such results on the delicate scales of the question of peace and war in the world. We find this to be true in nearly all major crises throughout the world. The Middle East crisis has its local level between the Arabs and Israel and its international level between the Soviet Union and the United States. . . .

In every crisis the conflict on one level or another varies according to various reasons and circumstances. In some crises, the conflict remains on the local level and in others escalates to the international level, creating the danger of a clash between superpowers. . . .

In the Vietnam crisis, the conflict has remained on the local level for a long time for various reasons. The Vietnamese crisis has been affected by one political will comprised of North Vietnam and the NFLSV.* Coordination between these 2 has been comprehensive, thus facilitating movement in the military, diplomatic, and propaganda fields. It has also given the Vietnamese message strong penetration power.

---

*National Front for the Liberation of South Vietnam, the political arm of the Viet Cong.

The Arabs lack this advantage in the Middle East crisis. There are 14 states with differing conditions, tempers and commitments. In the Palestinian field, the center of the question, there are 24 or more resistance organizations, each with different conditions, tempers and commitments.
. . . Last week . . . we tried to take a microscopic look at the movement of power relations in the Middle East. We also tried to analyze . . . the mechanics of the conflict. . . . In this connection, we must review . . . a number of points . . . in order to build up and continue from there. (1) Because of the question of the Arab people's rights and security against the claims and ambitions of the Zionist movement, there is a struggle between the Arab nation and the Zionist movement. This struggle is basically reflected in the war between Egypt and Israel. Since the Middle East is the heart of the world and in view of its political, economic, and strategic importance, the Middle East conflict reflects itself on the 2 contemporary superpowers, the United States and the Soviet Union, particularly in view of Israel's special relationship to the United States and Egypt's close friendship with the Soviet Union. (2) Israel could not impose the peace that suits its interests despite its military victory in the June 1967 battles. Neither can the Arabs impose the peace that suits their interests because of their military defeat in the June battles.

At the same time the 2 superpowers . . . were forced to limit the scope of direct intervention in the crisis because direct intervention would lead to an armed clash between them which in turn could lead to a nuclear confrontation. Hence, . . . the Middle East crisis has entered a strange state: a vacuum in which it is lost between peace and war. This state has been dominating the Middle East crisis for over 2 years. The movement of power relations in the crisis, however, has not ceased, and the mechanics of the struggle have been causing actions and reactions. All this has led to strong pressures which in turn have pushed the crisis from its local level between Egypt and Israel to an international level between the Soviet Union and the United States.

We now find ourselves confronted with 2 questions: (1) How did the mechanics of the struggle in the crisis develop so that it pushed the crisis from the local to the international level? (2) What are the historical developments that further complicated the crisis and helped its move from the local to the international level?

As for the first question, the mechanics of the struggle—what happened—was as follows or something close to it: (1) In view of the area where the crisis is taking place and of the conditions, it is difficult . . . to leave it to be solved with the passage of years. As long as it exists, violent clashes will continue, and these clashes add new complications. Such complications are evident today in Egypt's refusal to accept a cease-fire and in Israel's insistence on carrying out raids deep in Egypt. These complictaions accumulate; that is, rather than easing the crisis they intensify it, and the intensification of the crisis means its repercussions become directly felt in the other level of the crisis, the international level. (2) With the continuation of the violent clashes on the local level, both parties—Egypt and Israel—will exhaust their stocks of arms. Both Egypt and Israel are not producers of the main weapons of the battle, such as planes, tanks, heavy artillery and other sophisticated equipment. This means both replace whatever arms they lose from the international party from which they obtain arms. This in turn leads to increasingly insistent demands at the international level. The fact that should be considered in this regard is this: Soviet arms in the hands of the Arabs and American arms in the hands of Israel at the front line places the reputation of both international powers in the balance. This is a matter of great importance to the big powers because the prestige of any big power is partly dependent on the effectiveness of its weapons, even in the hands of others. This and the belief in Arab rights are the reasons for the excellent efforts being exerted by the Soviet experts in training the Arabs to use Soviet arms. The prestige factor and Israel's role as a tool for American terrorism are the reasons for the unlimited American equipment and training opportunities which Israel has. (3) The Middle East is closely linked with the higher strategies of every big power at an international level. For this reason neither of the international parties involved in the Middle East crisis, the Soviet Union and the United States, can leave it for the other party or retreat before it. This, so far, does not mean that either party can suddenly shift from this position to direct confrontation with the other party. It means that the situation would become extremely critical because, despite all this, both are facing 2 forbidden risks which they must try to avoid: the risk of surrendering or retreating and the risk of becoming involved and clashing.

With regard to the 2d question on the historic developments which further complicated the crisis, here is what has happened, or some of it:

(1) The Libyan revolution . . . represents a serious move in the critical balance of power in the Middle East crisis. Before the revolution Libya freed itself from this control and added its strength to the Arab current, which is hostile to U.S. control. Before the revolution Libya was isolated from the Arab-Israeli conflict. With the revolution, Libya came to the forefront of the Arab struggle. Moreover, Libya has a 3,000-kilometer coastline on the southern Mediterranean and produces 150 million tons of oil a year. Moreover, Libya has an expansive depth behind the Western front with Israel. Adding to this the depth of the Sudanese airspace after the revolution, this would have a great effect on the dimensions of the conflict. (2) The meaning of the Libyan revolution is a clear signal of the danger threatening U.S. domination of the area. The United States thought after the June 1967 battles that the winds of change in the Arab world would blow against those quarters hostile to U.S. domination—quarters which have been leading the struggle against Israel. However, the Libyan revolution refuted this belief and emphasized that the winds of change are blowing in the other direction.

The meaning of these 2 factors—the Libyan revolution itself and its meaning—is that time is running out for the United States and therefore it is vital for the United States to support Israel more and to help intensify and expand Israel's attacks in order to liquidate the crisis if possible for the benefit of Israel and the United States.

Perhaps the Libyan revolution is the real cause for the apparent contradiction in U.S. policy. On one hand the United States is increasing its support for Israel to enable Israel to liquidate the situation quickly, even against "the Libyan revolution itself." On the other hand the United States is maneuvering to appear as if it wants to postpone delivery of the Phantoms in the hope that this would help water down the effect of the meaning of the Libyan revolution.

(3) Israel, in implementation of its plan to link itself with the United States, has been seeking to convince certain quarters in the United States that it can play a big role in wearing down the Soviet Union. American journalist Joseph Kraft, one of Israel's closest friends in Washington, has said: "Let us cool down our attempts to reach a peaceful solution to the Middle East crisis. Why should we work for a peaceful solution when it is in our interest to do the opposite? Let us give Israel all the arms it wants to strike Egypt. Russia will be compelled to continue helping Egypt. This will wear it down in the Middle East, just as the United States is being worn down by the Vietnam War in the Far East." (4) In this connection Israel has offered its services to the United States to influence Jews in Eastern Europe itself." . . . This clearly means Israel is a party to undercover plots by American organizations trying to attack the Soviet Union in its own territory or nearby.

Again this does not mean that, because of the Libyan revolution itself and its meaning, the United States can jump to a direct confrontation with the Soviet Union or that because of Israel's attempts against the Soviet Union in the Middle East and in Eastern Europe the Soviet Union can jump to a direct confrontation with the United States. It simply means that the situation between the 2 superpowers is growing more tense.

This is what we are witnessing today when we say that the Middle East crisis is proceeding along the course of a grave struggle—we mean this tension. It is tension created by the movement of power in the Middle East struggle, or the mechanics of the struggle; the tension created by complications arising from this movement; and over and above this are events which further increase the tension.

The 2 superpowers have been meeting in Helsinki to discuss the dangers of the nuclear weapons in their arsenals. Piled-up weapons could, through miscalculation, lead to an explosion; but piled-up tension is more dangerous than piled-up nuclear weapons—tension is liable to explode not from miscalculation but from a touch in the wrong place.

New U.S. Peace Proposal

The U.S. announced June 25, 1970, that it had advanced a new proposal to bring peace to the Middle East. The proposal ultimately led to a truce along the Suez Canal. In announcing Washington's fresh initiative to break the Israeli-Arab impasse, State Secy. William P. Rogers June 25 withheld details of the plan while all sides in the conflict took it under consideration. Described by Rogers in general terms, the plan in essence called for a 90-day cease-fire while UN envoy Gunnar Jarring resumed indirect peace talks with Egypt, Jordan, and Israel. It stressed the UN Security Council resolution of Nov. 22, 1967, providing for Israeli withdrawal from occupied Arab areas and Arab recognition of Israel's right to exist within secure boundaries.

The U.S. plan had been submitted June 19 to the Middle East countries involved in the conflict and to a number of European nations, including the USSR, Britain and France. The initial reaction from Israel and the Arab states was negative. Rogers said that the U.S. was "in the process of having further discussions" with the other governments in the hope that the start of peace talks would result.

Rogers did not mention Israel's long-standing request for the purchase of 125 American jets. But Washington was said to have assured the Israelis privately that they would be allowed to buy the aircraft if the proposed 3-month truce period failed to materialize. His refusal to discuss American military aid to Israel at this time, Rogers said, did not imply a change in U.S. policy. "Our policy vis-à-vis Israel remains constant. It has not changed. We believe that the sovereignty, independence and territorial integrity of Israel is very important for our national interest."

The completion of the latest U.S. assessment of the Middle East crisis, ordered by Pres. Nixon Apr. 29, had revealed "a new and very serious factor"—"the presence of Soviet personnel and military equipment" in Egypt, Rogers reported. Despite these new developments, Rogers said, "we are not inclined to think that Israel, at the moment, is unable to support itself militarily." Rogers expressed encouragement over earlier remarks by Pres. Nasser and Israeli Premier Golda Meir that their governments might be favorable toward a cease-fire.

But Nasser initially rebuffed the American proposal in an address at Benghazi, Libya June 25. Referring indirectly to the U.S. initiative, Nasser said: "There is talk about a plan for the evacuation of Israel from all Arab territories except for the Golan Heights of Syria, but I tell you . . . that evacuation from the Golan Heights must be first." Nasser's statement appeared to confirm reports that Washington's formula called for Israeli withdrawal from Egyptian and Jordanian territory but not the Golan Heights. The Arabs, Nasser asserted, refuse to compromise on the pullout of Israeli forces. "Withdrawal must be from the Golan Heights before Sinai. If we had wanted only withdrawal from the Sinai we could have agreed with the United States on this 2 years ago. But we have declared more than once that withdrawal must be from Jerusalem, the West Bank of Jordan, the Golan Heights and from Sinai later." Nasser announced that the Egyptian army had completed its training for an all out assault on the Israeli side of the Suez Canal. He said Egypt would soon receive "hundreds of new planes from the Soviet Union to offset Israeli air power.

Syria June 25 denounced the U.S. peace proposal as "a bloody, malicious declaration against the Arab world's future" that was aimed at "rescuing" Israel. Radio Damascus said the Arabs "were determined to wage the war of liberation until all Arab territory held by Israel was purged of the enemy."

The Palestinian Arab guerrilla organization, Al Fatah announced that the American plan showed that the Arab guerrillas would have to continue their "struggle" against Israel. Other Arab commando organizations also spurned the proposal.

One positive reaction came from Lebanon. Lebanese Information Min. Osman Dana lauded Rogers' silence on Israel's request for American planes. "This is a good initiative on the part of the U.S. not to give Israel military assistance," he said.

Israeli Premier Golda Meir indicated her government's rejection of the plan in a major speech in the Knesset June 29. She expressed opposition to a temporary or conditional ceasefire and total Israeli withdrawal from occupied Arab areas. A

temporary stop to the fighting would only permit Egypt to
facilitate the installation of Soviet SAM-3 missiles along the
Suez Canal "to prevent our air force from silencing Egyptian
artillery aimed at our positions, and enabling Egypt to attempt
to cross the Canal," Mrs. Meir predicted. She took issue with
the view that statements by Nasser appeared to be an encouraging step toward peace. Mrs. Meir recalled that Nasser had at-
tached 2 preconditions to any settlement: Israeli withdrawal
from occupied territories and "the restoration of the rights of
the Palestinian people in its homeland." These conditions, she
said, "rule out any settlement." Asserting that there was no
"substantial possibility" of peace at this time, Mrs. Meir said
Israel would continue to pursue its current policies and
methods. She reiterated "the absolute vital nature" of Israel's
request for the purchase of American planes.

Mrs. Meir June 22 had rejected the idea of a temporary
cease-fire broached by the Egyptian government June 17. "We
are not prepared to accept something which is not a cease-fire
as a cease-fire," she said. A resumption of the 1967 truce
should be without time limit and without conditions, Mrs.
Meir insisted. She reiterated Israel's demands for direct negotiations with the Arabs. Asserting that her country's borders
"cannot be identified" with the pre-1967 frontiers, Mrs. Meir
said Israel could not surrender all the Arab territories it occupied. She specifically singled out the Golan Heights as vital
to Israel's security. On the Soviet military role in Egypt, Mrs.
Meir warned that Israel would fight back if Russian pilots flew
combat missions near the Suez Canal. "Anybody who will
stand in the way of our self-defense, we won't run away from
him—no matter who he is." Mrs. Meir blamed the Soviet
Union "for preventing peace" in the Middle East and termed
its motives there "pure, simple imperialism."

The USSR June 26 had criticized the new U.S. formula.
The government newspaper *Izvestia* said that Washington's new
initiative constituted "further support of the Israeli military
with maneuvers intended to make the United States look like

a supporter of peaceful settlement" of the Middle East crisis.

The U.S.' growing concern over the Middle East crisis was reflected in a series of statements issued by the White House July 2–5. A White House official said in a briefing to newsmen July 2 that the U.S. wished to expel the Soviet military presence from Egypt. Press Secy. Ronald L. Ziegler said July 3 that "there were no plans to inject United States military personnel" into the Middle East since Washington preferred to resolve the impasse by political means. But Ziegler said that the Administration refused to foreclose this possibility, which would include providing Israel with U.S. advisers. A White House statement July 5, however, said such a course "is not even under consideration." Officials explained that the spate of White House statements on the Middle East was not designed to "frighten anybody with the thought of sending combat personnel or advisers" but to keep the public informed of the larger dimensions of the problem.

Pres. Nixon said at his news conference July 20 that his Administration was pressing for acceptance of its Middle East proposal. "We have not announced any sale of planes or delivery of planes to Israel at this time because we want to give that peace initiative every chance to succeed," Nixon said. He reiterated the need "to maintain a military balance of power [in the Middle East] so that no state in the area would be encouraged to launch an offensive against another state or be driven to launching a pre-emptive strike because of the fear of an offensive or buildup."

The President said that the U.S. wanted to avoid a confrontation with the Soviet Union in the Middle East but that the movement of Soviet military equipment and personnel in Egypt "increases the risks" of such a confrontation. Nixon sought to clarify a background statement in which White House foreign affairs adviser Henry Kissinger had said that the U.S. wanted to "expel" the Soviet military men from Egypt. The word was not meant to imply "the idea of using armed

force" to remove the Soviet military presence "but to negotiate the removal of these forces," he explained.

Soviet Peace Plan; Nasser in Moscow

The Soviet Union also advanced a new Middle East plan.
Its proposal was made at one of the regular meetings of representatives of the Big 4 in New York June 24, 1970. Although
details were not made public, Western sources at UN headquarters said July 1 that it called for a "formalized state of peace"
between Israel and the Arabs only after the "first stage" of Israeli withdrawal from Arab territories had been completed.
Western sources described the Soviet proposal as a "substantial
move forward" and a "positive contribution" toward peace.
The Soviet plan had preceded by one day the U.S. proposal
of a 90-day cease-fire.

Pres. Nasser and other Egyptian officials arrived in Moscow June 29 for a series of high-level talks with Soviet leaders
on the Middle East. The meetings stretched on for 18 days.

At a dinner given in Nasser's honor June 30, Nasser and
Soviet Pres. Nikolai Podgorny stressed the need for a peaceful solution. Nasser said: "Peace should be based not on violence, but on justice. Peace cannot be based on forcible occupation of territory, peace cannot be based on gross trampling
on the rights of people. . . . Only peace will . . . fully serve
the political and socioeconomic reconstruction of our countries."

Podgorny said that the Soviet Union favored "settling the
Middle East conflict on the basis of the well-known [Nov. 22,
1967] Security Council resolution, with due account for the
legitimate right and interests of all the peoples in the area."

Nasser conferred July 1 with Premier Aleksei N. Kosygin
and Communist Party Secy. Gen. Leonid I. Brezhnev. Nasser
resumed discussions with the Soviet leaders July 11. These
talks were followed by a conference July 12 between Foreign
Mins. Andrei A. Gromyko and Mahmoud Riad.

A joint Soviet-Egyptian communiqué was issued July 17. The statement stressed the need for a political solution of the Middle East crisis, branded Israel an aggressor, blamed the U.S. support of Israel for the impasse in the region and reaffirmed Soviet backing for the Arab cause. The communiqué said that "both sides confirmed their support for the efforts taken in the framework of the United Nations aimed at the achievement of a political settlement in the Middle East." It said Israel was solely responsible for "the continuing grave crisis situation" by its "aggression against the UAR and the other Arab states." "Israel would not have been able to persist in this aggressive and expansionist policy were it not for the continuing support it receives from the imperialist circles and specifically the United States," the communiqué charged. "The withdrawal of Israeli forces from all the occupied territories," the statement added, was the only way "a just and durable peace in the Middle East can be realized." According to the joint statement, Egypt and the Soviet Union planned to expand and strengthen their cooperation "in the political, economic and defense fields in the interests of the peoples of both states."

Israeli Foreign Min. Abba Eban said that the communiqué "contained neither surprise nor novelty." The USSR, he said, "wants no peace in the Middle East as is seen from this stress on the demand for a complete Israeli withdrawal from all areas occupied in the 1967 war."

The Soviet Union July 21 denied that it posed a threat to the existence of Israel. The Communist Party newspaper *Pravda* said that Moscow upheld the right of every Middle Eastern country—including Israel—to full independence. The newspaper said Soviet military aid to Egypt was not aimed at crushing Israel but was designed to bolster Egypt's defenses against Israeli attacks. *Pravda* criticized U.S. Pres. Nixon's July 1 statement that the Arab states sought to "push Israel into the sea." In making this remark, Nixon had "poured oil on the fire without any basis," *Pravda* said.

Eban Calls for Cairo Parley

Israeli Foreign Min. Abba Eban proposed July 13, 1970 that Israel and Egypt begin informal talks in an attempt to end the Middle East crisis. In a speech to the Knesset described by the Foreign Ministry as "a new initiative for peace," Eban said: "As a first step to break the deadlock why should not Egypt and Israel send authorized representatives to an agreed place in order to decide together, without prejudice to their respective positions and claims on the arrangements, the frameworks, the formulation or subjects and procedures for official negotiations." The foreign minister said these preliminary discussions "could prepare the ground for the conduct of effective and realistic negotiations."

Eban said Israel was "ready to accept the cease-fire as decided" by the UN Security Council resolution of June 1967. He said Israel was prepared to have UN envoy Gunnar Jarring "invite the parties to conduct negotiations on establishment of peace" on the basis of the Rhodes formula, used in Arab-Israeli negotiations in 1949. Eban discounted the Soviet Union's latest peace proposal, asserting it was aimed at maintaining tensions in the Middle East and at enabling the USSR to establish a military foothold in Africa."

Israeli Premier Golda Meir had disclosed June 30, in an interview published in the French news magazine *L'Express* July 12, that Israeli representatives had held secret talks with Arab representatives since the end of the 1967 war. Details of the contacts had not been made public at the request of the Arab representatives, Mrs. Meir said. She noted that the Israeli government had proposed secret negotiations with Egypt "5, 10, 20 times, and again 2 weeks ago" but had received no reply. Mrs. Meir said: "We've done everything" to achieve peace. "They tell me for example that Nasser cannot accept public negotiations. Well, we've proposed secret conversations . . . We never got the slightest response."

Cease-Fire Halts Egypto–Israeli Fighting

Israeli and Egyptian forces halted military operations along the Suez Canal Aug. 7, 1970, as the 90-day truce proposed by the U.S. went into effect. Although the cease-fire also applied to other Middle East battle fronts, fighting continued in the Jordanian, Syrian and Lebanese sectors as Palestinian commandos, who refused to recognize the truce agreement, carried out sporadic attacks against Israel. The text of the cease-fire/standstill agreement as accepted by Egypt and Israel:

(a) Israel and the United Arab Republic will observe a cease-fire effective at 2200 GMT Friday, Aug. 7;

(b) Both sides will stop all incursions and all firing on the ground and in the air across the cease-fire lines;

(c) Both sides will refrain from changing the military *status quo* within the zones extending 50 kilometers [31 miles] to the east and to the west of the cease-fire line. Neither side will introduce or construct any new military installations in these zones. Activities within the zones will be limited to the maintenance of existing installations at their present sites and positions and to the rotation and supply of forces presently within the zones.

(d) For the purpose of verifying observance of the cease-fire, each side will rely on its own national means, including reconnaissance aircraft which will be free to operate without interference up to 10 kilometers [6¼ miles] from the cease-fire line on its own side of the line.

(e) Each side may avail itself as appropriate of all United Nations machinery in reporting alleged violations to each other of the cease-fire and of the military standstill.

(f) Both sides will abide by the Geneva Convention of 1949 relative to the treatment of prisoners of war and will accept the assistance of the ICRC [International Committee of the Red Cross] in carrying out their obligations under that convention.

The halting of the Suez combat was accompanied by reactivation of the peace mission of UN Special Envoy Gunnar V. Jarring, as called for in the U.S. peace plan. Jarring held separate preliminary meetings Aug. 7–8 with the UN envoys of Israel, Egypt and Jordan to discuss a site, starting date and the level of state representation for substantive peace talks.

The Egyptian Foreign Ministry Aug. 7 published the text of (but furnished no date for) a message that Foreign Min.

Mahmoud Riad sent to U.S. State Secy. William Rogers through Donald C. Bergus, the U.S. representative in Cairo, Riad's message was in reply to Secy. Rogers' message of June 19 proposing a solution for the Middle East crisis. Riad said in his message:

I received your message dated 19 June 1970 in which you refer to the gravity of the situation and in which you say that our common interest necessitates that the United States preserve and strengthen friendly relations with all peoples and states of the area. You also expressed readiness to carry out your role in this respect, and you also asked others to act with you and seize this opportunity.

In your message you also spoke of more effective means to reach a settlement, suggesting that the sides begin working under Amb. Jarring's supervision to agree on the detailed steps necessary to implement Security Council resolution No. 242 issued on 22 Nov. 1967.

. . . We have always called for, as have all our friends—foremost the Soviet Union—the need to insure that Amb. Jarring succeeds in his mission of implementing the Security Council resolution. We and all our friends have exerted and are still exerting all efforts to achieve this.

The grave situation in the Middle East has been caused by Israel's aggression and its occupation of Arab territories. Israel's continued occupation and its persistence in committing aggression against the Arab people further aggravates the situation. Israel's withdrawal from all the Arab territories it occupied as a result of its 5 June 1967 aggression . . . is essential for achieving peace in the area. Liberation of the Arab territories is not only a natural right but also a national duty. This right is confirmed by the UN Charter to which we are all committed. It is also reinforced by the Security Council resolution which affirms the illegality of annexing land through war. The resolution also stresses the need to respect the territorial sovereignty and integrity of the area states . . .

I wish to assure you that the UAR has no expansionist aims, unlike Israel which seeks expansion and which seeks to annex Arab land. Its leaders have said that they waged their war for expansion and are up to this day continually making statements about their intention to annex the Arab territories to Israel.

It is also undoubtedly important that your statements about the U.S. desire to promote friendly relations with all the peoples and states of the region be materialized. We believe that this would help consolidate peace in the region. This could have been achieved had the United States really followed a balanced policy.

I am sure that you realize that the continued disregard for the rights of the Palestinian people, who were driven out of their homeland, could not possibly help the establishment of peace in the region. It is necessary that the just and legitimate rights of the Palestinian people be recognized in accordance with the UN resolutions so that peace may prevail in the Middle East.

When the Security Council unanimously passed its resolution on 22 Nov. 1967 it gave international society a chance to establish peace in the region, but Israel rejected the resolution and, as a result, the war continued until now. Therefore, it interested us when you said that the opportunity available now should be taken for the implementation of the Security Council resolution, which we have been calling for since Nov. 1967. . . .

. . . We still believe that peace can be achieved through the application of the solution approved by the Security Council on 22 Nov. 1967. Since Amb. Jarring began his mission in Dec. 1967, we have always been careful to explain that it is important for the disputing sides to declare, at the beginning, their acceptance of the Security Council resolution and their preparedness to implement all its provisions. . . . The UAR has notified Amb. Jarring, more than once and in more than one document, of its acceptance of the resolution and its preparedness to implement it. The UAR has also declared this officially before the UN General Assembly and seized every opportunity to declare its adherence to this stand.

The UAR has fully cooperated with Amb. Jarring and made every possible effort for his mission to succeed. Furthermore, I would like to point out that on 9 May 1968, I received from Dr. Jarring proposals similar to the proposals in your letter. I handed Dr. Jarring a letter on the same day expressing anew the UAR acceptance of the Security Council resolution, and, on Dr. Jarring's request, I have agreed to send the necessary instructions to the UAR permanent delegate to the United Nations in New York to meet with the personal representative of the UN Secretary General to resume the contacts in accordance with the Security Council resolution, for the purpose of its implementation. I have suggested in this letter that Dr. Jarring set up a timetable for implementing the resolution.

It was clear that in order to enable Dr. Jarring to carry out his mission, Israel had to declare its acceptance of and readiness to implement the Security Council resolution. However, this was not done; on the contrary, Israel refused to inform Amb. Jarring of readiness to implement the resolution. This forced Dr. Jarring to abandon his mission. It is evident, then, that Israel bears the responsibility for hampering Amb. Jarring's attempts to carry out his mission provided for in the Security Council resolution.

When France found that the situation was deteriorating and that Amb. Jarring was unable to complete his mission, it forwarded its resolution for meetings of the Big 4 representatives to work for implementation of the Security Council resolution and for helping the UN Secretary General's personal representative to carry out his mission. However, Israel continued its rejection and consequently obstructed the work of the Big 4 representatives.

As for the cease-fire resolution which the Security Council issued in June 1967, we have respected the resolution from the beginning.

However, Israel has at no time respected this resolution and has continued its acts of aggression in the Suez Canal area, raided the Suez Canal cities, and destroyed the industrial installations in these cities. With the issuance of the 22 Nov. 1967 UN Security Council resolution calling for a peaceful settlement, the cease-fire resolution became linked to implementation of the 22 Nov. 1967 resolution. We have explained this in our letters to the United Nations. However, Israel's refusal to implement Security Council resolution No. 242 led to the continuation of fighting and obstruction of a peaceful settlement. Therefore it is clear that for Jarring to resume his mission successfully Israel should announce without ambiguity its acceptance of the Security Council resolution and its preparedness to implement it.

We also believe that for Jarring to achieve quick progress in the first phase of his work the 4 powers should give him specific instructions in connection with implementation of the Security Council resolution provisions, and especially with regard to withdrawal and peace guarantees.

We are prepared to reemphasize to Amb. Jarring our preparedness to implement all provisions of the Security Council resolution and to appoint a representative to discuss with him implementation of this resolution.

In this respect, we are prepared to accept a cease-fire for a limited period of 3 months in accordance with your proposal, though we believe the correct procedure to start in this case is to begin drawing up a timetable for withdrawal of the Israeli forces from the occupied territories. This was where the earlier efforts of the representative of the Secretary General stopped because of the obstacles Israel placed before him by not agreeing to implement Security Council resolution No. 242. . . .

Pres. Nasser himself July 22 had publicly announced Egypt's acceptance of the U.S. plan. He broke the news in Cairo at the opening session of the national congress of the Arab Socialist Union (ASU), Egypt's sole legal political party, on the eve of the 18th anniversary of the overthrow of King Farouk. Nasser said that the government had decided to accept U.S. State Secy. Rogers' proposal of June 19 as a "final opportunity" for peace in the Middle East. Excerpts from his statement to the congress:

. . . I have told you about the points in the message of the U.S. Secretary of State: First point: A cease-fire between Egypt and Israel for 3 months. 2nd point: [UN envoy] Jarring resumes his mission. He will subsequently ask the states to implement the Security Council resolution fully and in all its parts by reaching agreement to establish a just and permanent peace based on recognition by all sides of the sovereignty and integrity of the territory and independence of every state. Then Israel's withdrawal from the territories occupied during the 1967 conflict in accordance with Security Council Resolution 242 [of Nov. 22, 1967]. . . .

The Egyptian foreign minister informed the U.S. Secretary of State that there was nothing new in the proposals and that they were all included in the Security Council resolution which the U.S.A. helped not to implement because U.S. policy was . . . aligned with Israel. The Egyptian foreign minister informed the U.S. . . . that we agreed to the U.S. proposals.

. . . This is now an opportunity. The U.S. President . . . [and other American leaders] everywhere are saying that Israel is endangered, Israel fights the Soviet Union, Israel seeks peace, and the Arabs only want war for the sake of war. It was inevitable for us to make a constructive reply and say that we had accepted all these points in 1967. This is a final opportunity. We inform the U.S. that we approved of its decision [plan] provided Jarring obtained his instructions and guidelines from the Big 4 states. . . .

We must look to the future to determine the U.S. position. We say that if the U.S.A. continues its policy . . . based on supplying Israel with large quantities of arms, then the situation will be grave. It will show that the U.S.A. did not want peace but wanted the Arab nation to fall under Israeli occupation and helped Israel to occupy the Arab nation's territories. . . .

The report on the July 22 meeting by the Cairo newspaper *Al-Ahram* contained the first purported text of the June 19 message from U.S. State Secy. Rogers to the Middle East belligerents. *Al-Ahram*'s report forced the State Department to release its official version of Roger's letter in Washington later that day. Comparison of the 2 versions showed them to differ on these 3 points:

(1) The U.S. version called for Israel's "withdrawal from occupied territories"; the *Al-Ahram* text said it called for an Israeli withdrawal from "the occupied territories," implying that all former Arab territory would have to be surrendered.

(2) The U.S. version said that after indirect Arab-Israeli talks had been held, it was likely that the 2 sides "will" find it necessary to meet directly; the UAR text substituted the word "may."

(3) The Washington version called on all parties to "strictly observe, effective July 1 until at least Oct. 1, the cease-fire resolutions of the Security Council." It also sum-

marized this as an initiative to bring "both Israel and the UAR [to] subscribe to a restoration of the cease-fire for at least a limited period." The *Al-Ahram* version added to this the words "3 months" in parentheses.

In a party declaration at the close of the congress July 26, Dr. Labib Shukair of the ASU's supreme executive committee said: "The congress believes that acceptance of the U.S. initiative . . . is an important political move in the annals of our continuing struggle to liberate our homeland. This move is of world-wide significance. . . . The ASU National Congress would like to explain to the world public, its parties and political organizations that we do not advocate war for the sake of war, as the Zionist propaganda and the forces supporting it attempt to mislead the world; we are seekers of right and of the liberation of a territory usurped by Israel. . . . "

Palestinian Arab guerilla organizations bitterly denounced Egypt for accepting the cease-fire. The Egyptian government Aug. 28 retaliated by suspending the broadcasts of these militants from Egyptian radio wave-lengths. A government spokesman explained the move: "UAR authorities have adopted a decision providing for suspension of broadcasts beamed by some Palestinian organizations on UAR radio wavelengths. This was decided following the stand adopted by some Palestinian organizations regarding Egypt's acceptance of the so-called U.S. initiative. The UAR explained its view on this matter at all levels . . . to all official and popular sectors of Arab opinion. These included contacts, explanations, and direct guarantees to the Palestinian organizations. Moreover, the UAR's adherence to principles is clear and is proved by its history, struggle, and sacrifices. It transpired through the contacts that the Palestinian organizations understood the UAR's policy and comprehended its intentions. However, this did not cause the desired effect. The excuse was that bidding among the Palestinian organizations pushed them to a stand opposite to what they want. . . . The UAR believes there are limits whereby every side must bear its responsibilities. The UAR placed its radios at the service of some Palestinian organizations to facilitate propaganda for the resistance. However, it is wrong to leave such means at the mercy of any local maneuverings in the power struggle among the Palestinian organizations. The UAR has supported and will always support the Palestinian resistance movement. It has placed and will always place all possible material, military and political resources at the movement's disposal. The UAR still considers that fundamentally the Palestinian resistance movement is the noblest feature of the Arab nation's reaction to the 1967 setback. The UAR's greatest wish is to see the resistance organizations succeed in establishing healthy relations permitting them to carry out their anticipated great role in a manner that makes them one of the vanguards of victory in the violent war waged by the Arab nation on many fronts to liberate the land and regain the rights."

Iraq and Syria, 2 of the 5 "confrontation countries" directly involved in hostilities with Israel, also rejected the U.S. cease-fire proposal. The Syrian government July 31 announced Syria's "firm rejection" of the U.S. plan; Radio Damascus July 26 had termed "absolute" and "unalterable" Syria's rejection of the UN Security Council resolution of Nov. 22, 1967. The Iraqi Revolutionary Command Council July 31 announced Iraq's "categorical rejection of all plans aimed at liquidating the cause of Palestine and the rights of the Palestinian people to return to their own land, particularly the latest American proposals."

(Egypt's relations with Syria and Iraq were strained by their divergent policies. Some incidents developed as a result of this. Radio Baghdad reported Aug. 20: "The Egyptian authorities this morning sealed off the Iraqi trade center in Cairo. Egyptian intelligence authorities had arrested Director of the center Dawud ar-Rawi and his assistant Ibrahim al-Husawi on 18 August. Another report says that the Egyptian intelligence authorities arrested, at the gate of the Iraqi embassy in Cairo, Salah Husayn, director of the Iraqi Airlines office in Cairo.

Husayn was entering the embassy gate when Egyptian intelligence men seized him, removed him from the embassy, assaulted him, put him in a civilian car and drove him to an unidentified destination. Egyptian police and intelligence men are being reinforced around the Iraqi embassy building in Cairo and the vehicles of diplomats and embassy employes are being prevented from entering the embassy compound. Egyptian intelligence authorities today arrested Faruq as-Samarrai, the new director of the Iraqi Center in Cairo. Samarrai arrived in Cairo 5 days ago to assume his post. His whereabouts are still unknown.")

Israel was the last of the combatants to announce its acceptance of the 3-month cease-fire. In her formal acceptance of the U.S. peace plan, Premier Golda Meir had told the Israeli Knesset Aug. 4 that her government's approval was unconditional. She asserted that her initial opposition had been overcome by assurances received from Pres. Nixon in the previous 2 weeks. She hinted at these assurances in saying "we have reason to assume that Israel will not find herself weaker if the Arabs decide to renew the war" after the cease-fire term expired.

Mrs. Meir's version of the American plan differed in some respects from the original proposal advanced by State Secy. Rogers. She said that the Arab-Israeli negotiations under UN envoy Jarring's auspices should be aimed at achieving "an agreed and binding contractual agreement between the parties." Rogers had not spelled out detailed plans for the negotiations in deference to the Arabs, who were opposed to direct negotiations with Israel. Israel insisted that the Arab governments be held responsible for the "prevention of all hostile acts" against Israel by Palestinian commandos operating on their territories. The U.S. did not press this point in its approach to Egypt and Jordan. Israeli troops would be withdrawn from Arab territories "to secure recognized and agreed boundaries in the peace agreements," Mrs. Meir said. The Rogers formula made reference only to "withdrawal from territories occupied in the 1967 conflict." The Arabs had insisted on Israeli withdrawals before negotiations.

The Israeli government had debated the U.S. proposal July 23–Aug. 4. The cabinet discussed the proposal for 5 hours July 26, reportedly with special attention to the question of conditions and cease-fire guarantees. Israel was known to be seeking U.S. assurances that the 3-month cease-fire would not be used by Egypt to bolster its defenses along the Suez Canal and that the negotiations to be attempted by Jarring would be without prior conditions on an Israeli withdrawal from Arab territories. (Joseph J. Sisco, U.S. assistant State Secretary for Near Eastern and South Asian affairs, had conferred with Israeli diplomats in Washington late July 23 in an effort to persuade them to accept the plan. Washington sources said the Israelis were urged to agree without imposing crippling conditions.)

Addressing the Foreign Press Association in Tel Aviv July 23, Foreign Min. Abba Eban rejected the U.S. plan's call for a limited cease-fire as a mandate for renewed aggression after 3 months. He advanced instead an Israeli peace plan that called for (a) an effective cease-fire superseded by peace treaties; (b) negotiation of all Arab-Israeli differences; (c) both sides to regard border and territorial questions as open until settled by negotiation; (d) an international conference on the refugee problem to work out a 5–year plan for the refugees' resettlement; and (e) an open border between Israel and Jordan.

2 Israeli cabinet ministers commented publicly July 24 on Nasser's response to the U.S. plan. Shimon Peres, minister without portfolio, asserted that Nasser had "turned everything upside down" by reading the plan as he saw fit and insisting that Israel accept all permanent provisions of UN Middle East resolutions in return for Egypt's assent to a 90-day cease-fire. Development Min. Haim Landau of the right-wing Gahal Party said the Egyptian move was calculated simply to lead to Israel's destruction.

Although Israel was regarded as having military superiority in the war of attrition with Egypt, an important–perhaps persuading–argument for a truce was its casualties. Military sources in Israel reported Aug. 10 that a total of 642 Israelis had been killed and 2,033 wounded in fighting with the Arabs between the 1967 war and the start of the 90-day truce. In the 1967 war itself, Israeli losses had totaled 803 killed and about 2,700 wounded.

The halt in fighting along the Canal was confirmed by official announcements Aug. 7 in Jerusalem, Cairo, Washington and at UN headquarters in New York. Premier Meir declared that she and her cabinet had decided to accept the truce "after we had reached the conviction that the cease-fire would become effective on conditions which would prevent its being abused." Israel, she pledged, "declares her complete readiness to maintain the cease-fire arrangements meticulously in all their provisions, on a basis of reciprocity." Mrs. Meir expressed hope that the truce would "be a first step toward peace." An Egyptian Foreign Ministry announcement said that Cairo's acceptance of the cease-fire rested on assurances of security for Egypt's Suez Canal front and other Arab sectors.

The time the cease-fire was to take effect–10 p.m. GMT Aug. 7–was first announced by U.S. State Secy. Rogers. In his statement, Rogers welcomed "this statesmanlike action taken by the leaders of the governments concerned. We hope this important decision will advance the prospects for a just and lasting peace in the Middle East." Pres. Nixon expressed hope that the cease-fire "will help move the Middle East conflict to a peaceful and enduring settlement."

UN Secy. Gen. U Thant called the cease-fire "an important step forward in the search for peace in the Middle East." He warned "that the road ahead is long, arduous and uncertain" but expressed hope that "a will for peace" would overcome "all obstacles." The U.S. peace initiative had received formal approval Aug. 5 from the UN representatives of the USSR, France and Britain at a meeting of the Big 4 in New York.

The mechanics of policing the truce along the Canal and the delineation of the truce zone were not officially disclosed. But it was reported that Israeli and Egyptian planes were conducting aerial reconnaissance of the zone and its military positions without actually crossing the waterway. The purpose of the flights was to make certain that the 2 sides honored a commitment barring military build-ups or offensive action within a zone at least 32 miles wide on each side of the Canal. The zone extended the entire length of the Canal with command centers at Ismailia and El Qantara, from which about 100 UN observers on the ground would assist in policing the cease-fire. The Soviet Union was reported to have given the U.S. a "categorical commitment" to abide by the requirement not to build up positions in the Egyptian sector of the zone during the truce.

UAR Accused of Missile Build-Up & Truce Breach

Israeli charges of an Egyptian missile build-up within the 32-mile truce zone along the Suez Canal a few hours before the cease-fire went into effect Aug. 7 were supported by photos released by the Israelis Aug. 19, 1970. The pictures of the missile sites were said to have been taken before and after the truce.

An Israeli army staff officer said that more than 12 SAM-2 missiles, all Egyptian-controlled, were positioned as close as 11 miles from the Canal, with a range extending, in some places, 12½ miles across the Canal over Israeli-held territory. He said Soviet-operated SAM-3 missiles had not been moved closer than 22 miles from the Canal. The Egyptian missiles, the staff officer contended, had been moved toward the Canal and made operational the weekend of Aug. 7–9. The Israeli officer displayed photos of 4 locations in Egypt. The first set was taken between 3:30 p.m. and 3:40 p.m. Aug. 7, before the midnight cease-fire. The 2nd set was taken of the same location Aug. 13 and 16, with the truce in force. The officer did not say how the photos were taken. The forward movement of the Egyptian missiles, the officer asserted, was "not catastrophic, but very serious" for Israel. This made it "difficult but not impossible" for Israeli aircraft to operate over the Canal, he said.

Prior to the release of the Israeli pictures, the U.S. Aug. 19 issued a statement acknowledging a "forward deployment of surface-to-air missiles into and within the zone west of the Suez Canal around the time the cease-fire went into effect." Although there "was some evidence that this was continued beyond the cease-fire deadline, our evidence of this is not conclusive," the statement said. The U.S. disclosed that it was examining further Israeli charges of a breach of the truce. The American assessment was handed to Egyptian and Soviet representatives. It was issued after an 11-day investigation into the Israeli allegations. Although the statement conceded that there was a violation of the truce, it did not openly accuse Cairo or request the withdrawal of its missiles. In releasing the statement, State Department spokesman Robert McCloskey did not concur with the Israeli claim that the shift of the Egyptian missile batteries into the prohibited truce zone had altered the military balance of power along the Canal. But he assured Jerusalem that the U.S. would not "permit [the military balance] to bend to the disadvantage of Israel."

Egypt Aug. 21 voiced objections to U.S. reconnaissance flights over the Suez Canal, which Washington contended was aimed at observing the truce. The semi-official newspaper *Al-Ahram* said such activity was "a very grave matter" that could provide Israel with intelligence information. Despite Cairo's complaints, the U.S. State Department indicated that the American U-2 surveillance flights along the Canal would continue. The department rejected the Egyptian charge that the object of the flights was to carry out espionage.

Continued Egyptian violation of the truce was charged by Israel Aug. 21 and 23. A military spokesman in Jerusalem said that the complaints, filed with the UN Truce Supervisory Organization (UNTSO), reported that the Egyptians were still building missile batteries and other projects 20 miles west of the Canal well within the 32-mile limit. Israel further charged Aug. 24 that Egypt had violated the cease-fire in regard to the treatment of prisoners of war. The complaint, filed with the UN, concerned a captured Israeli pilot whose death in prison had been announced by Cairo Aug. 10. The Israelis claimed that the pilot had appeared in good health on Egyptian TV the night of his capture. His body had not been returned.

Egyptian National Guidance Min. Muhammad Hassanein Heykal charged Aug. 24 that Israel was violating the cease-fire by "building fortifications, mending roads, [and] building new roads to new positions" along the Canal. Heykal said that he did not know the exact location of the alleged Israeli build-up but added, "I've been told by our military people" that the Israelis have been seen engaged in such activities "the last 3 days." Heykal asserted that Israeli charges of Egyptian truce violations were a coverup for U.S. deliveries of new electronic equipment for Israeli aircraft.

Israeli officials reflected Cairo's charges Aug. 24.

The Middle East peace talks were held in abeyance as Israel filed new complaints with UNTSO Aug. 30 and 31, accusing Egypt of continued violation of the cease-fire. The charges were the 7th and 8th submitted by Israel to the UN since the truce and military standstill began. The Israeli complaints told of aerial detection of evidence of further deployment of missiles and of the construction of new launching sites along the entire length of the Egyptian side of the Canal.

Egypt's first formal charge that Israel had violated the cease-fire had been presented to the U.S. and UNTSO. Cairo's semi-official newspaper *Al-Ahram* had reported Aug. 27 that, in its complaint, Cairo had accused Israel of moving a large number of soldiers into the 32-mile standstill zone on its side of the waterway and of building new fortifications and roads to improve its defenses since the start of the truce. A Foreign Ministry official was reported to have discussed the matter with U.S. envoy Donald C. Bergus in Cairo Aug. 26.

Nasser asserted Aug. 30 that Israeli allegations of Egyptian truce violations were designed to disrupt Gunnar Jarring's mediation efforts and to evade Israeli withdrawal from occupied Arab territories. Nasser added: "These [Egyptian] missiles had existed [in the Suez Canal zone] long before the cease-fire. It is clear that these missiles were the cause of Israeli Phantoms being shot down." (Nasser was referring to the reported downing of Phantoms from June 30 to Aug. 6 by SAM-2 missiles. *Al-Ahram* reported Aug. 31 that 14 Israeli planes, including 7 Phantoms, had been shot down during that period. 8 Israeli Phantom crewmen were captured, one was killed and one escaped, the newspaper said.)

Premier Golda Meir declared Aug. 31 that Israel was "now in the midst of a hard, difficult argument with the United States over Egyptian violations of the cease-fire. The U.S. government has guaranteed that neither side would improve its military position as a result of the cease-fire. But only a few hours had passed when the Egyptians began violating it. We cannot be weaker should the war along the Suez Canal resume."

U.S. government officials said Sept. 1 that Washington was now "satisfied" that Egypt had violated the cease-fire. The officials said the evidence, obtained largely by American U-2 observation planes and satellites, was presented Sept. 1 to Pres. Nixon as he met with his top political and military leaders for a full-scale review of the Middle East crisis. Among those attending were Vice Pres. Spiro Agnew and State Secy. Rogers.

Arab & Islamic Meetings

Egypt had intensified its diplomatic contacts with fellow Arab and Islamic-world countries in the first 8 months of

1970–until the Mideastern crisis was eased by the cease-fire.

An oil cooperation pact had been signed by Libya, Iraq and Egypt, and Algeria Jan. 7 following a 3-day meeting in Baghdad. A joint communiqué that said the agreement provided for "full cooperation and coordination . . . in the fields of developing oil and gas resources." It also provided for "concerted policies toward foreign monopolies exploiting the oil riches in the Arab world."

Representatives of the 5 Arab "confrontation countries" –Egypt, Syria, Jordan, Iraq and Sudan–had held a summit meeting in Cairo Feb. 7–9 in the wake of stepped-up fighting in the Middle East. (Iraq was maintaining troops in Jordan, and Sudan was keeping a battalion on the Suez Canal truce line.) A communiqué issued Feb. 9 vowed a continued struggle against Israel for the recovery of occupied Arab territories and was particularly scornful of the U.S. for its support of Israel. It charged the U.S. with "adopting a new hostile attitude against the Arab nation and unveiling its real links with the Israeli expansionist plan." "Israel would not have gone that far in her aggression . . . had it not been for her constant reliance on United States support and supplies of arms and aircraft and had it not been for the United States allowing its citizens to serve in the Israeli armed forces. . . ," the communiqué said. Alluding to U.S. oil interests in the Middle East the 5 states took the position that "the Arab nation refuses to see its resources and wealth being exploited and converted into assistance and weapons for Israel." The communiqué was signed by Egyptian Pres. Nasser, Jordanian King Hussein, Syrian Pres. Nureddin al-Attassi, Sudanese Premier Gaafar al-Nimeiry and Iraqi Deputy Premier Saleh Mahdi Amash.

The foreign ministers of Egypt and 23 other Islamic-world countries held their first conference in Jidda, Saudi Arabia Mar. 23–26 to promote political, cultural and economic cooperation. The conferees formed a secretariat to coordinate the work of the foreign ministers. Egypt, Libya, Algeria and Sudan had opposed a permanent association of Islamic countries.

The meeting rejected their demands that all Islamic states break off diplomatic and economic relations with Israel. (2 of those states—Iran and Turkey—traded with Israel.) The countries represented at the meeting were Afghanistan, Algeria, Cameroon, Egypt, Gambia, Guinea, Indonesia, Iran, Jordan, Kuwait, Lebanon, Libya, Malaysia, Mauritania, Morocco, Niger, Pakistan, Saudi Arabia, Senegal, Somalia, Sudan, Tunisia, Turkey and Yemen. The Palestine Liberation Organization and the Arab League were represented by observers.

A plan to integrate the economies of Egypt, Libya and Sudan was announced in Cairo Apr. 20. The economic alliance, concluded at the end of a 5-day meeting of the economy ministers of the 3 countries, would be open to other Arab countries, a statement said. The agreement provided for the 3 countries to end import fees, allow freedom of transport and transit and guarantee freedom of entry, work and residence for each other's citizens. The pact also called for the creation within 3 months of a joint development bank and cooperatives in trade, transportation, construction and other activities.

The leaders of Egypt, Libya and Sudan met in Khartoum May 26–29 to discuss the Middle East crisis and their tripartite alliance. A statement issued May 29 said that Egyptian Pres. Nasser, Sudanese Pres. Gaafar al-Nimeiry and Col. Mouammar el-Qaddafi, chairman of the Libyan Revolutionary Command Council, had "affirmed the fusion of the 3 countries' progressive revolutions in confronting the plots of world imperialism, Zionism and local reactionary forces." Nasser had declared at a mass rally in the Sudanese capital May 28 that the Arabs were fighting not Israel alone but "America represented by Israel."

Egypt, Libya and Sudan had agreed Dec. 28, 1969 to hold regular meetings every 4 months to coordinate military, economic and political action against Israel. This decision followed 3 days of talks among Nasser, Qaddafi and Nimeiry in Tripoli, Libya. At the end of a 3-day meeting in Cairo Jan. 13, 1970, Egyptian Foreign Min. Mahmoud Riad, Libyan Foreign

Min. Saleh Massaud Buysir and Sudanese Foreign Min. Farouk Abou Eissa agreed to have the 3 countries' military chiefs consider a coordinated strategy against Israel. The 3 foreign ministers also agreed to set up ministerial mixed commissions on communications, education, foreign policy, industry, land reclamation, agriculture and transportation. The commissions were to submit specific recommendations in these spheres to Nasser, Nimeiry and Qaddafi.

The foreign ministers and defense chiefs of Egypt, Syria, Jordan, Sudan and Libya met in Tripoli, Libya Aug. 5–6, 1970. The conferees were officially described as having agreed on improved military cooperation in their war against Israel and as having ignored current efforts to negotiate a peace settlement. The conference had been delayed for 2 days to permit Libyan Premier Moummar el-Qaddafi to persuade Iraq to reverse its announced boycott of the meeting. (Algeria, which had joined Iraq in opposing Egypt's and Jordan's acceptance of the U.S. peace plan, also stayed away from the conference.) Qaddafi returned from Baghdad Aug. 5 after failing to end the rift between Iraqi and Egyptian leaders. The Libyan Revolutionary Command then issued a statement denouncing what it termed "the slanderous campaign" against Nasser's leadership in the Arab world.

Iraq's opposition to Nasser's current stand on Middle East negotiations evoked a sharp attack from the Cairo newspaper *Al-Ahram* Aug. 6. The newspaper disclosed that at a meeting in Tripoli in June, Nasser had told Iraqi Pres. Ahmed Hassan al-Bakr that "We have no trust in you because you are always making political maneuvers." *Al-Ahram* quoted Jordanian King Hussein as having charged at the meeting that Iraq issued communiqués making false claims of attacks on Israel by Iraqi forces stationed in Jordan.

An Iraqi delegation visiting Moscow Aug. 5 stressed Iraq's policy differences with Cairo as well as with the USSR. Vice Pres. Hardan Takriti asserted that the problem of the Palestinians was the "cornerstone" of Baghdad's foreign policy and that Iraq fully supported their drive to recover all of their lands. Takriti's statement followed a pledge to the visiting Iraqis by Soviet First Deputy Premier Kirill T. Mazurov that Moscow would "do everything in its power to facilitate the attainment of a just political settlement of the Middle East conflict," to bring about the withdrawal of Israeli forces from all Arab territories and to satisfy the "just rights of the Arab people of Palestine."

The opposition of Iraq, Algeria and Syria to a political settlement of the 3-year-old Mideastern crisis was criticized in a Soviet statement Aug. 9. The statement, which hailed the cease-fire, accused Arab extremists of "artificially created obstacles" that were "irrational" and defeating to the Arab cause. The statement described the halt in the fighting as "an important first step" toward a lasting Middle East solution.

Nasser Spurs End of Jordanian Civil War

King Hussein of Jordan Sept. 15, 1970 began a major military drive against Jordanian-based Palestinian Arab guerrilla groups that had been attempting to show that they could sabotage the Egypto-Israeli-Jordanian 90-day cease-fire. Observers held that since the fighting jeopardized Nasser's plan for a Middle Eastern peace, it was to Nasser's interest to help end the civil war.

The event considered the immediate cause of the fighting began developing Sept. 6, when members of the Popular Front for the Liberation of Palestine (PFLP), described as an Arab guerrilla group of Maoist tinge, hijacked 3 commercial passenger jets over Europe and forced 2 of them to land in the Jordanian desert at Zerqa. The other was diverted to Cairo and blown up after the evacuation of passengers and crew. The PFLP then hijacked a British commercial passenger jet Sept. 9 to join the other 2 at Zerqa, Jordan. Those aboard the 3 planes were held hostage there for the release of 4 Arab suspected terrorists being held in western Europe. The guerrillas blew up the 3 planes Sept. 12 and kept 54 passengers and crew members prisoner. 20 of the hostages reportedly were American Jews.

Fierce fighting between Jordanian royal military forces and the guerrillas erupted Sept. 15 and continued until Sept. 25. The 2 sides had been engaged in an undeclared war since Sept. 1 after King Hussein escaped injury in an ambush as he was being driven to Amman's airport.

The level of fighting ebbed Sept. 25 as Yasir Arafat, leader of Al Fatah and chairman of the Arab guerrilla groups' collective central committee, announced shortly after midnight that he would meet with 4 envoys representing Arab chiefs of state who were meeting in Cairo to seek an end to the civil war. An appeal had been made Sept. 24 by the delegation's leader, Pres. & Premier Muhammad Gaafar al-Nimeiry of the Sudan, for such a meeting with the guerrilla chief. Arafat answered in a message over the Voice of Palestine, the commando radio suggested that they meet in the Egyptian embassy in Amman.

Several hours before Arafat's radio reply, the premier of the Jordanian military government, Brigadier Gen. Muhammad Daoud, had abruptly resigned. Daoud who had been named to the post Sept. 16 as head of the new military cabinet, said in a note to Hussein that he had left to make way for a government of "national unity." Daoud disappeared in Cairo, where he had gone to participate in the Arab summit talks. It was reported that he had gone into exile in Libya after having been snubbed by the Arab leaders meeting in Cairo.

Hussein and Arafat Sept. 27 signed at the Nile-Hilton Hotel in Cairo a 14-point agreement officially ending the civil war and naming Tunisian Premier Bahi Ladgham to head a plenipotentiary committee to supervise the agreement.

The 2 key provisions in the 14-point agreement provided that (a) Hussein would continue in control but under the supervision of other Arab nations until the situation in Jordan could be normalized, and (b) the guerrillas would have full support of the Arab world until "full liberation and victory over the aggressive Israeli enemy." The Arab leaders instructed the 3-man supervisory committee to prepare an agreement between the Jordanian government and the Palestinians "insuring the continuation of the Palestinian resistance and respect for the sovereignty of Jordan, with the exception of the needs of resistance activity."

In addition to Hussein and Arafat, the settlement was signed by King Faisal of Saudi Arabia, Sheik al-Sabah of Kuwait, Nasser, Premier Mouammar el-Qaddafi of Libya, Pres. Gaafar al-Nimeiry of the Sudan, Pres. Suleiman Franjieh of Lebanon, Ahmad al-Shami of Yemen, and Premier Ladgham of Tunisia.

The remaining airline hijack victims held hostage in Jordan by Arab commandos were freed in separate groups Sept. 25, 26 and 29 as part of a deal for the release of the Arab terrorists held in Europe.

The principal initiative toward ending the war appears to have come from Nasser, who sent Lt. Gen. Muhammad Sadek, the Egyptian army chief-of-staff, to Amman Sept. 17 to urge Hussein to order a cease-fire as soon as possible—"if only for 24 hours"—to halt the fighting, which Nasser called a "shame" to the entire Arab world.

Hussein replied that "the Jordanian army has today become the target for enemies even from a certain direction [i.e., the Syrians] that did not enter into the Palestine war [of June 1967], that drew you and us into battle and then surrendered its land without fighting. In response to your call I am going to order a cease-fire after the army has control over the situation. . . ." Hussein ordered a cease-fire at 6 p.m. Sept. 19.

The invasion of Jordan by a brigade of Syrian armor became generally known Sept. 20, when Jordanian forces engaged Syrian tanks on the Damascus-Amman highway at Ramtha. A heavy counterattack by the Jordanian 40th Armored Division, supported by the Jordanian air force, threw back the

Syrians with a heavy loss of tanks. Hussein said Sept. 23 that his troops had given the Syrians "a bloody nose."

Nasser also was instrumental, through a 2d appeal to Hussein Sept. 20, in bringing together in Cairo the leaders of 9 Arab countries (who subsequently ignored Hussein's emissary, Premier Daoud).

Egyptian Gen. Sadek, Tunisian Premier Ladgham, Sudanese Premier Nimeiry, Kuwaiti Foreign Min. Sheikh Sabah al-Ahmad al-Jaber and Kuwaiti Defense Min. Sheikh Saad al-Abdullah as-Salem flew to Amman from Cairo Sept. 23, met Hussein and 4 members of the Palestine Liberation Organization's (PLO) central committee and announced that both sides had agreed to a cease-fire based on 4 conditions: that (a) the guerrilla forces move to the Israeli-Jordanian cease-fire lines, (b) no guerrilla bases would be allowed in Amman or any other town in Jordan, (c) the guerrillas would be subject to Jordanian law and (d) the PLO would be recognized as the Palestinian Arabs' only valid representative.

Shortly afterward, however, Yasir Arafat repudiated the agreement as unauthorized, since the guerrillas who signed it were either Hussein's prisoners or had gone over to his side in the war. (One of the 4 PLO members who had signed the agreement was Abu Iyad, one of Arafat's leading lieutenants in Al Fatah.) Gen. Nimeiry returned to Amman Sept. 24 and arranged the rendezvous between Hussein and Arafat at the Egyptian embassy. The ensuing cease-fire lasted until mid-Oct. 1970.

Charges of cease-fire violations had been leveled at Hussein's soldiers as early as Sept. 26. Gen. Nimeiry in Cairo charged that Jordanian forces had fired on the Egyptian embassy in Amman, where his peace delegation was being housed during Hussein's discussions with Arafat. Nimeiry said that he held Hussein directly responsible for what he called the failure of the cease-fire and for what he termed a U.S.-Israeli plot to "liquidate the Palestinian people." Hussein replied that Nimeiry's charges were false and would worsen the "explosive situation in Jordan." (In Cairo, Nasser had wired Hussein early Sept. 26, also charging that Jordanian forces had violated the cease-fire terms.)

The resolution of the Jordanian civil war was considered by many observers to have been a major diplomatic triumph for Nasser. (After the late autumn clashes between guerrilla units and royal Jordanian forces, however, Hussein renewed his antiguerrilla drive. Government troops launched an inconclusive attack Jan. 8-14, 1971 in the Jarash area. Sporadic fighting occurred in March and April 1971, and a major battle took place near Jarash May 29. A final attempt to cripple the Palestinian commandos was mounted July 13 by Jordanian Premier Wasfi Tell. Tell told newsmen July 19 that the guerrillas had lost all their bases in Jordan. He also said that Jordanian troops had captured 2,300 *fedayin* and that no more than 200 others remained at large. Israeli officials confirmed the Palestinian defeat and said July 19 that 72 fleeing guerrillas were captured by Israeli forces.)

Aswan Power Project Completed

Soviet Amb.-to-Egypt Sergei Vinogradov, Egyptian Power Min. Muhammad Sidki Soliman and other Soviet and Egyptian officials attended a late morning ceremony in Aswan July 21, 1970. The 12th and final power-generating turbine—of 2.1 million-kilowatt capacity—was switched on, and work on the 12-year-old Aswan High Dam hydropower complex was in effect, completed. The Soviet Union had defrayed about ⅓ the cost of the $1 billion dam, had sent 5,000 workers and experts to Egypt to work on the project and had supplied a great deal of technical advice in its construction.

According to the Soviet news agency Tass July 21, "1970 marks the completion of the entire Aswan complex. The giant body of the dam, which is now the biggest stone-fill hydrotechnical structure, is now being clothed in granite. The importance of the Aswan complex for the UAR economy cannot be overestimated. Thus it was calculated by Egyptian specialists that the country's national income increased by E£90 million [$207 million] in 1967–8 thanks to the Aswan complex. . . . High voltage power transmission lines, strung from Aswan to Alexandria across the entire breadth of the country, will make it possible to begin an electrification program in the countryside, but particularly great prospects are being opened up before industry thanks to Aswan-produced power. The Aswan Power Dam will generate an average of up to 10 million kilowatt hours a year."

Pres. Nasser hailed the dam July 22 as "one of the biggest hydroelectric power stations in the world" and a "triumph . . . over the desert." He added: "With the High Dam, 10 billion kilowatt hours of electricity have been added to our capacity. Thus the annual Egyptian per capita share of available electricity rises to 500 kilowatt hours compared with less than 40 kilowatt hours the year before the [July 1952] revolution."

NASSER'S DEATH & AFTERMATH (Sept. 1970–Aug. 1972)

Nasser Succumbs to Heart Attack

Gamal Abdel Nasser died in Cairo Sept. 28, 1970, a day after the Arab summit meeting there at which Jordanian King Hussein and Yasir Arafat, the Arab commando leader, had signed a formal truce ending the Jordanian civil war. Nasser's death occurred just as the shaken Middle Eastern political balance seemed about to be restored. U.S. Pres. Nixon, in Italy on the first stop of a foreign tour, ordered a planned show of U.S. 6th Fleet strength in the Mediterranean to be muted and urged Egypt's new leaders to preserve the fragile Egypto-Israeli cease-fire along the Suez Canal.

Nasser had been stricken at Cairo's airport, where he was taking part in farewell ceremonies for Sheikh Sabah al-Salem al-Sabah, the emir of Kuwait, who was in Cairo for the negotiations ending the Jordanian civil war. Nasser, 52, was taken to his home in the suburb of Manshiet el-Bakri and he died at 6 p.m.

Nasser's death was announced by Vice Pres. Anwar el-Sadat later that evening on the Egyptian radio and TV network. Sadat, in tears as he spoke, said Nasser had died "while he was standing on the field of struggle, striving for the unity of the Arab nation and for the day of victory." "The only thing that can be commensurate with his righteousness and worth," Sadat declared, "is that the entire Arab nation should stand patient, steadfast—a steadfast, solid, heroic and able stand so that it can realize the victory for which the great son of Egypt and the hero of this nation . . . had lived and was martyred."

The news of Nasser's death plunged the Arab world into mourning and political uncertainty. Crowds surged through the streets of Cairo, Alexandria, Beirut (Lebanon) and other Middle East cities, including those of the Israeli-occupied

West Bank area of Jordan, chanting their grief and occasionally venting their hatred of Israel and the West with bursts of
gunfire. All Arab leaders and broadcasting and press facilities
voiced tributes to Nasser and his leadership of the Arab people. Arab governments—including the Syrian, Iraqi and other
regimes opposed to Nasser's relative political moderation—
expressed doubts about a future without him.

The question of Nasser's successor was not answered
permanently, but under Egypt's constitution, Sadat immediately became acting president. A committee was formed
Sept. 28 under Labib Shukair, speaker of the National Assembly, to organize the procedures for succession. According to
the constitution, a new president had to be chosen within
60 days. The new leader had to be nominated by a $^2/_3$ vote
of the assembly and elected by a simple majority of
Egypt's voters.

The semi-official Cairo newspaper *Al-Ahram* reported
Sept. 29 that Nasser had suffered from heart trouble but had
kept the knowledge from all but a few associates. *Al-Ahram*
reported that Nasser had suffered his first attack in Sept.
1969 and had been treated by Soviet cardiac experts in
Moscow in July 1970. Nasser had planned to rest for 2 weeks
at the Egyptian resort of Mersa Matruh but had been forced
to cancel the vacation to arrange the Cairo talks on the
Jordanian crisis.

Reports from Egypt said that hundreds of thousands of
mourners had converged on Cairo's Kubbeh Palace, site of
the government's executive offices, where Nasser's body lay
in state. All offices, shops and factories were closed Sept. 29
in Egypt and throughout most of the Arab world. Masses of
Egyptians were moving toward Cairo by rail and road and on
foot. UAR armed forces were placed on maximum alert
Sept. 28 to deal with any threat of disorders during the
period of public mourning.

In a statement issued from the aircraft carrier *Saratoga*
in the Mediterranean Sept. 29, U.S. Pres. Nixon offered his

condolences to Nasser's family—his wife, 3 sons and 2 daughters—and the Egyptian people and commented on the need for peace in the Middle East. He said: "This tragic loss requires that all nations, and particularly those in the Middle East, renew their efforts to calm passions, reach for mutual understanding and build lasting peace." Meeting newsmen following his arrival in Naples later that day, he expressed the hope that the new Egyptian government would "see its interest served" by maintaining the cease-fire with Israel and acting on the willingness expressed by Nasser to enter negotiations on a political settlement of Arab-Israeli differences. Nixon said that the U.S. hoped for good relations with all countries in the Middle East, including Egypt.

Nixon Sept. 29 named a delegation to represent the U.S. at the Cairo funeral rites for Nasser. The group headed by Health, Education & Welfare Secy. Elliot L. Richardson, included ex-Ambs. John J. McCloy and Robert D. Murphy, Donald C. Bergus, the senior U.S. envoy in Cairo, and Michael Sterner, head of the State Department's Egyptian desk. Presidential aides confirmed in Naples Sept. 29 that Nixon had discussed the possibility that he might go to Cairo for the funeral but that he had decided against it because the U.S. did not have diplomatic relations with Egypt. They conceded that the problem of assuring his safety and possible adverse reaction from Israel had entered into the decision.

Soviet Premier Aleksei N. Kosygin arrived in Cairo Sept. 29 to attend Nasser's funeral. Kosygin was accompanied by Vladimir M. Vinogradov, a deputy foreign minister specializing in Middle Eastern affairs, Marshal Matvei V. Zakharov, chief of the Soviet general staff, and 2 other military officials. The Soviet government and Communist Party Sept. 29 issued a statement of continued support for the Arab cause. It pledged that the "line aimed at a political settlement of the conflict in the Middle East and convincingly championed by the late Pres. Nasser will continue to enjoy our utmost support." The statement also said: "The best perpetuation of his memory will be the cohesion of the Arab states in their struggle against imperialism . . . . , the strengthening of their independence, economic and defense potential." (Soviet citizens were not informed of Nasser's death until 13 hours after radio broadcasts carried the news to most of the world.)

At least 5 million persons, including dignitaries from 60 countries, took part in Nasser's funeral in Cairo Oct. 1. Mourning rites were held in other parts of Egypt and throughout the Arab world. In Cairo, emotional crowds lined the route of the procession that carried the body of Egyptian leader to his burial place. The crowds broke through the ranks of troops to touch and kiss the coffin, borne on a gun carriage. Soldiers repeatedly beat back the mobs with whips and bamboo poles. 48 people were reported to have died in Cairo and other Egyptian cities in the mass demonstrations during Nasser's funeral.

Nasser's coffin was carried from the Kubbeh Palace, where his body had lain in state, to its burial place at a newly-built mosque in the Cairo suburb of Manshiet el-Bakri. The mosque, renamed for Nasser after his death, was located on the site where Nasser and his fellow revolutionaries had gathered with their troops July 23, 1952 to march against the government of King Farouk.

Among the foreign dignitaries who attended Nasser's funeral were Emperor Haile Selassie of Ethiopia, King Hussein of Jordan, Presidents Houari Boumedienne of Algeria and Nureddin al-Attassi of Syria, Premier Jacques Chaban-Delmas of France, Foreign Secy. Sir Alec Douglas-Home of Britain and Kuo Mojo, vice chairman of the Standing Committee of Communist China's National People's Congress.

The American magazine *Newsweek* carried an account of the funeral in which its correspondent observed that, "despite the significance of the occasion, the turnout was less notable than the roster of absentees." Yugoslav Pres. Tito, Indian Prime Min. Indira Gandhi, Tanzanian Pres. Julius Nyerere, Kenyan Pres. Jomo Kenyatta, King Faisal of Saudi Arabia and King Hassan II of Morocco were reported to be conspicuously absent.

Sadat Succeeds Nasser

The Arab Socialist Union (ASU), Egypt's only legal political party, recommended Oct. 3, 1970 that Acting Pres. Anwar el-Sadat succeed the late Gamal Abdel Nasser as president. The decision was announced in Cairo Oct. 5 by National Assembly Speaker Labib Shukair. The assembly formally nominated Sadat Oct. 7, and his name was submitted to public referendum Oct. 15.

In its first formal meeting to consider the presidential succession, the ASU's 8-member executive committee had unanimously agreed to Sadat's elevation, Oct. 3. The committee's decision was coupled with a report stressing the need for the continuation of Nasser's Middle East policy in the face of what it called threats to Egypt from Israel and "world imperialism." The committee's report was read by Shukair Oct. 5 at a meeting of the ASU's 150-member central committee. It said: "We must expect that Israel, which is occupying the Sinai Peninsula and other Arab territories, will try to exploit for its own interests the post-Nasser period in the hope of ultimatley annexing the Arab lands." To forestall this possibility, Egyptians must not permit a leadership vacuum that could "sow despair, panic and division in Egypt."

Sadat, 51, had been a close friend of Nasser since their early years in the army and was a fellow conspirator in the 1952 coup against King Farouk. Regarded as a strong enemy of Israel, Sadat had served as speaker of the National Assembly and as vice president 1964-6. He had been reappointed vice president Dec. 20, 1969 by Nasser, who had reestablished the office 2½ years after its abolition.

During Nasser's years in power, Sadat had edited the semiofficial Cairo daily *Al Goumhouria* (*Republic*) for awhile—including the period during the 1956 Suez crisis—and was Nasser's personal representative on many trips abroad, including visits to the U.S. He was born Dec. 25, 1918 in the Nile Delta village of Talah Monufiya. His mother was Sudanese. His father was a military hospital clerk. Anwar married a half-English girl. Sadat was admitted in 1936 to Abbassia Military Academy, where he met Nasser, who was 11 months older than he. After graduation, he, Nasser and 10 other officers garrisoned in the Upper Egyptian town of Mankabad in the winter of 1938 formed a "secret revolutionary society dedicated to the task of liberation." The Free Officers Committee that overthrew King Farouk was later formed around this secret society.

Sadat's hatred for the British occupiers of Egypt reportedly impelled him to collaborate secretly with the Germans during World War II. He was arrested in Oct. 1942, cashiered and imprisoned for 2 years. He escaped in Nov. 1944 but was again imprisoned in 1946 for nearly 3 years for alleged involvement in the assassination of ex-Finance Min. Sir Amin Osman Pasha (Sadat denied the charge). Sadat, released from prison in 1949, worked as a journalist until his commission was restored. He was stationed in the Sinai Desert as a captain in 1950 and kept up a liaison there between the Free Officers and civilian terrorists. In 1957 Sadat became general secretary of the National Union, the predecessor of the Arab Socialist Union, and left that post to become chairman of the National Assembly—which he remained until 1968. Sadat also served in the 1950s as secretary general of the short-lived Islamic Congress, set up by Nasser to promote Arab unity, and was one of Nasser's trouble-shooters in the 6-year Yemeni Civil War of the 1960s.

A Middle Eastern peace became the first focus of what would become Sadat's administration. Egypt and the USSR agreed in a communiqué made public Oct. 3 that they would continue to seek a peaceful settlement of the Middle East crisis. The U.S. State Department disclosed Oct. 3 that Egyptian officials had given Pres. Nixon similar assurances.

The joint Soviet-Egyptian statement was based on talks Premier Aleksei N. Kosygin and other Soviet leaders held with UAR officials in Cairo Sept. 29–Oct. 2 to assess the impact of Nasser's death. The Cairo newspaper *Al-Ahram* reported that Kosygin, in his talks with Sadat and other Egyptian leaders, had stressed these principal points: (a) Moscow would provide Egypt with "full and continuous support"; (b) the Soviet Union backed Cairo in its fight against imperialism "in all its forms"; (c) pressure must be applied against Israel to block its attempts "to obstruct the settlement of the Middle East crisis," but a political solution must not be rejected.

The Egyptian assurances to Pres. Nixon were communicated in private talks in Cairo Oct. 1–3 between Egyptian leaders and an American delegation headed by Health, Education & Welfare Secy. Elliot Richardson. The U.S. representatives in turn assured the Egyptians that Washington would continue to seek a peaceful settlement based on the UN Security Council's Middle East resolution of Nov. 22, 1967.

Richardson had disclosed at a news conference in Cairo Oct. 2 that he had urged the Egyptians to consider extending the 90-day cease-fire along the Suez Canal past Nov. 5 to gain more time to work out a peace arrangement. Washington officials disclosed Oct. 5 that Egypt and Israel had given "basically favorable" replies to this unofficial proposal. Israeli Foreign Min. Abba Eban had said Oct. 4 that Israel was "not going to start shooting just because it happened to be 90 days after the Aug. 7 cease-fire."

Charges of U.S. intentions to torpedo current peace efforts had been leveled at a meeting of the UN General Assembly and at one of the periodic Big 4 conferences on the Middle East Sept. 30. Muhammad H. el-Zayyat, Egyptian delegate to the UN, charged in the Assembly that the U.S. had repeated Israel's false charges of Egyptian truce violations. Zayyat's remarks were in reply to a plea by U.S. Amb. Charles Yost for the restoration of the integritiy of the Suez

Canal armistice to enable the 2 sides to start moving toward peace negotiations. Yost was reported to have said at the Big 4 meeting that day that the Gunnar Jarring mission could not operate in a vacuum and that it was vital that the military situation along the Canal be "rectified" to remove reported Egyptian truce violations. Soviet delegate Yakov Malik discounted Yost's appeal and accused the U.S. of attempting to block peace efforts.

Jarring's suspension of his peace mission was announced at the UN Oct. 2. The UN ambassador and Secy. Gen. U Thant had decided on the move because Jarring had "done all he can do" in the present circumstances, according to the announcement. Jarring was returning to his regular post as Swedish ambassador to Moscow.

The U.S. announced Oct. 6 that it wished to suspend the Big 4 talks pending "rectification" of the alleged truce violations. Israel's principal charge concerned the Egyptians' installation of SAM-3 missiles within the Canal cease-fire zone.

In an interview with associate editor James Reston of the *N.Y. Times*, printed Dec. 28, 1970, Sadat said that if Israel gave up "every inch" of occupied Egyptian territory, Egypt would recognize Israel's rights as an independent state and would be ready to negotiate Israel's "rights of passage" through the Strait of Tiran and Gulf of Aqaba. Israel's "rights of passage" through the Suez Canal, Sadat said, would depend on a satisfactory settlement of the Palestinian Arab "refugee problem."

Sadat Ousts Sabry, Consolidates Power

Aly Sabry, one of Egypt's 2 vice presidents, was dismissed from his post by Pres. Anwar Sadat. Sabry, whose ouster was announced in Cairo May 2, 1971, was arrested May 14 and charged with complicity in an attempted *coup d'état* against Sadat. He was convicted Dec. 9 and condemned to death, but Sadat commuted the sentence to life imprisonment.

No official explanation was given at first for the abrupt removal of Sabry, who was regarded as pro-Soviet. Sabry was reported to have been sharply critical of an Apr. 17 agreement to form a federation of Egypt, Syria and Libya. He had voiced his objections Apr. 25 at a meeting of the Central Committee of the Arab Socialist Union, Egypt's sole political party.

According to the U.S. newsweekly *Time* (May 17, 1971), the "real target" of Sabry's attack at the meeting was Sadat, to whom Sabry turned and said: " 'Where did you get the authority to agree to this federation?' " The magazine reported that Sadat, in a "May Day speech at Helwan, . . . pointedly ignored Sabry among 40 notables gathered on the dais. Then . . . he declared: 'I am responsible to the Almighty, the people, and myself.' Next day he stripped Sabry of the vice presidency."

The smashing of the attempted coup against the Sadat government was disclosed by Sadat in a country-wide broadcast May 14. Sadat declared that the alleged plot to oust him had stemmed from the resignations May 13 of 6 cabinet ministers and 3 top officials of the ruling Arab Socialist Union (ASU). He announced the formation of a new cabinet. Sadat's announcement was followed by the arrest of more than 100 suspected conspirators and a widespread shakeup of the government. Among those jailed were the 6 resigned cabinet ministers, including Lt. Gen. Muhammad Fawzi, ex-war minister, and the 3 ASU members.

In his broadcast, Sadat attributed the aborted coup to opposition to his agreement to join Egypt with Syria and Libya in a federation. He said the plot was discovered when he received tape-recordings May 12 of phone conversations by members of the ASU's Central Committee and a deputy of the National Assembly. The recordings, he said, revealed a plan to prevent him forcibly from addressing the country if he had sought to do so following the ASU's tumultuous Apr. 25 meeting on the proposed federation. Sadat said after accepting the resignation of one of the resigned cabinet men, Interior Min. Sharawi Gomaa, that an investigation revealed that a security police tape-recorder had been installed in the office of his home. Sadat charged that the resignation later of the 5 other ministers was designed to create the impression that his government was in a state of "collapse." Sadat said he had ordered the destruction of a collection of phone recordings. (The president May 13 had directed a ban on security police surveillance of citizens and recording of phone calls except as authorized by judicial authorities in national security and criminal cases.)

Sadat said that he was ordering free elections for a complete reorganization of the ASU. He added: "The people should elect whomever they want. We then shall be able to wage the battle [against Israel] because we then will be on solid ground." In addition to Fawzi and Gomaa, the cabinet officials who had resigned were Sami Sharaf, minister of state for presidential affairs; Muhammad Fayek, information minister; Helmy el-Said, electric power minister; and Saad Zayed, housing minister. The 3 members of the ASU's Higher Executive Committee who quit were Secy. Gen. Abdelmohsin Abu el-Nour, Labib Shukair and Diaddin Daoud.

A hint that a political crisis was brewing had appeared in a statement by Deputy Premier Aziz Sidky May 13 on the resignation of the 6 cabinet ministers. He said: "Finally the heads of conspiracy and rebellion have come into the open. The centers of power had wanted to impose their domination over the people, using means of suppression and deceit."

The new cabinet replacements announced May 13 were: Gen. Muhammad Ahmed Sadek (appointed war minister); Mamdouh Salem, governor of Alexandriz (interior); Abdel Kader Hatem (information); Muhammad Ahmed Muhammad (presidential affairs); Ahmed Sultan (electric power); and Aly el-Sayed (housing). Hussein el-Shafei was appointed to replace Sabry as vice president.

These other cabinet ministers also were dismissed (their

replacements in parentheses): Communications Min. Kamal Badir (Abdel Malek Saad); Youth Min. Muhammad Abul Ezz (Mustafa Kamal Tulbah); Scientific Research Min. Ahmed Mustafa Ahmed (Abdel Wahhab el-Burullusi); Culture Min. Badr el-DinAbu Ghazy (Ismail Ghanim); and Economy Min. Muhammad el-Khawaga (Muhammad Abdullah Marzaban). Sadat May 16 appointed Maj. Gen. Saad Hussein al-Shazli as chief of staff of the armed forces.

The National Assembly convened in special session May 14 and voted to expel 18 members suspected of being involved in the aborted coup. The ousted deputies included Labib Shukair, Deputy Speaker Kamal el-Hinnawi and Muhammad Fayek.

Thousands of persons thronged the streets of Cairo May 15 to express their support of Sadat and to denounce the accused conspirators. The armed forces pledged full support of Sadat May 15. The pledge was made by the new war minister, Gen. Sadek. The president received similar expressions of loyalty May 16 from a delegation representing the police and security agencies. Addressing the group, Sadat said: "The police are not the enemy of the people. They should be a shield. Your brothers in the trenches must be confident that there is a strong internal front protecting their families." Sadat warned of "bitter times" ahead as he continued to reorganize and consolidate his regime. But he expressed hope that "we will secure our internal front, preserve our national unity and build a new state in which every individual will feel free and secure in his home." At his meeting with police and security officers, Sadat agreed to their request that he be their commander-in-chief. Sadat also was supreme commander of the armed forces and chairman of the National Defense Council, as provided for by the constitution. He also was chairman of the ASU.

Maj. Gen. Gaafar el-Nimeiry, the Sudanese head of state, accused the USSR and all the Communist nations of East Europe except Yugoslavia Sept. 10 of having participated in an attempt to unseat him in July after unsuccessfully plotting against Egyptian Pres. Sadat in May. In an election speech near Khartoum, Nimeiry said: "The conspiracy began in the UAR 2 months earlier with Aly Sabry, who is now on trial there. When they failed, and were rounded up, they decided to try their luck with the Hashem Ata [Sudanese conspirators'] group." Nimeiry asserted that both plots had failed because "Moscow was as stupid as the conspirators were." The speech, believed to have gone unreported by any of the Arab news agencies, was said by the Western press Sept. 24 to have been made available through diplomatic sources.

Sabry and 3 other former Egyptian officials accused of conspiring to overthrow Sadat were sentenced to death by a 3-men Revolutionary Tribunal in Cairo Dec. 9. Sadat immediately commuted their sentences to life in prison. 87 other persons connected with the plot received sentences ranging from one year (suspended) to 15 years. 14 were acquitted. The 3 (aside from Sabry) whose death terms were commuted were Sharawi Gomaa, former deputy premier and interior minister; Sami Sharaf, former state minister for presidential affairs; and Farid Abdel Karim, former secretary of the Arab Socialist Union for the Greater Cairo District of Giza. Gen. Muhammad Fawzi, former war minister tried and convicted in a separate trial before a military court, drew a life sentence, which was later commuted by Sadat to 15 years at hard labor. Among those acquitted was former Transport Min. Ali Zein el-Abdin. The trial of all the accused had started Aug. 25.

The Arab Socialist Union had bestowed on Sadat July 26 "full powers" to take any steps deemed necessary against Israel to recover all Arab territories lost in 1967. The ASU's 1,700 delegates, ending a 4-day congress in Cairo, unanimously granted his request for such power.

Sadat reiterated a declaration which he had made at the party's opening session, that 1971 would be the decisive year of war or peace with Israel. Sadat said that "we must move, but politically as well as militarily. But we must escape from this stagnation of no war, no peace." In his July 23 statement to the ASU, the Egyptian leader had warned that he would not permit 1971 to pass without decisive action against Israel unless an agreement was reached on the withdrawal of Israeli forces from Arab areas.

Stressing the need for Egypt to be strong economically as well as militarily in confronting Israel, the ASU congress adopted a 10-year program to double national income and industrial output, rebuild the primitive villages of Egypt, and eliminate illiteracy. The party also indorsed Sadat's proposal for reopening the Suez Canal, backed the proposed federation of Egypt with Libya and Syria and criticized Jordan for its July drive against the Palestinian commandos.

Sadat Sept. 8, 1971 dissolved the People's Assembly, Egypt's 360-member legislature, and announced general elections for Oct. 27. The country's new constitution was overwhelmingly approved in a nationwide referendum Sept. 11. The Central Committee of the Arab Socialist Union was reorganized as the result of an election held July 1. All 3 actions constituted a further step toward Sadat's goal of completely overhauling Egypt's political structure.

In the Sept. 11 referendum, the new constitution was approved by 7,862,617 voters, or 99.98% of those who cast ballots. The constitution, which went into effect immediately, replaced an interim charter adopted in 1964. It strengthened guarantees against arbitrary arrest, seizure of property and other police-state abuses. Among other points of the constitution:

● The power of the People's Assembly was widened, although the president retained dominant authority, including the right of temporary rule by decree. The assembly was empowered to approve presidential decrees before they became valid. The legislature also could override a presidential veto by a $^2/_3$ vote.
● Councils of specialists, responsible to the president, were to be established to provide more efficient and responsive governmental machinery.
● A high constitutional court was established and could annul any legislation it judged to be unconstitutional.

Some officials hailed the new charter as the prelude to "a new stage of national action" to modernize Egyptian society and stimulate economic and social development.

A new cabinet was formed Sept. 19 as part of Sadat's administrative reforms program. The principal ministers were eliminated. One of 4 deputy premiers in the outgoing cabinet, Aziz Sidky, was promoted to first deputy premier. He remained minister of industry and petroleum. Foreign Min. Mahmoud Riad, Premier Mahmoud Fawzi and Gen. Muhammad Sadek, minister of war, were among those who remained. The ministries of Youth, Labor, Local Administration, National Assembly Affairs and Scientific Research were abolished. 2 new ministerial posts were formed—Military Production and Maritime Transport. Sadat ordered the creation of an Academy of Scientific Research & Technology.

The new cabinet: *Deputy Premier* and *Agriculture*—Sayed Marei; *Deputy Premier* and *Information & Culture*—Abdel Kader Hatem; *Economy & Foreign Trade, Acting Minister of Supply & Internal Trade*—Muhammad Abrullah Marzeban; *Planning*—Sayed Gaballah Sayed; *Treasury*—Abdel Aziz Kamel; *Presidential Affairs*—Muhammad Ahmed Muhammad; *Cabinet Affairs*—Ahmed Esmat Abdel Meguid; *Health* and *Acting Minister of Social Affairs*—Ahmed el-Sayed Darwish; *Manpower* (formerly Labor)—Adbel Latif Boltia; *Civil Aviation*—Ahmed Nouh; *Higher Education*—Muhammad Morsy Ahmed; *Electric Power*—Ahmed Sultan; *Housing & Construction*—Aly el-Sayed; *Transport & Communications*—Soleiman Abdel Hai; *Irrigation*—Muhammad Adbel Rakeeb; *Petroleum & Mineral Wealth*—Ali Wali; *Tourism*—Ibrahim Naguib; *Justice*—Muhammad Salamaa; *War Production*—Muhammad Ibrahim Hassan Selim; *Maritime Transport*—Vice Adm. Mahmoud Hamdi; *Deputy Planning Minister*—Ismail Sabri Abdullah.

Another new Egyptian cabinet was formed Jan. 17, 1972 in a move to shift the country's economy to a war footing. The new ministers were appointed by Aziz Sidky, who had been named premier Jan. 16 to succeed Mahmoud Fawzi. Sadat's appointment of Sidky was approved by the Central

Committee of the Arab Socialist Union. After the committee meeting, Sadat issued a decree naming Fawzi 2d vice president, a post that had been vacant since the ouster and arrest of Aly Sabry. The other vice president was Hussein el-Shafei. The cabinet appointed by Sidky also had 5 deputy premiers: Gen. Muhammad Sadek, minister of war and production; Muhammad Abdullah Marzeban, minister of economy; Mamdouh Salem, interior minister; Muhammad Abdul Salam el-Zayyat, first secretary of the ASU (former Deputy Premier Sayed Marei replaced Zayyat in the ASU post); and Abdel Kader Hatem, minister of information and culture. Muhammad H. el-Zayyat, chief delegate to the UN was recalled to become a minister of state for information. The cabinet reshuffle had been preceded Jan. 13 by a Sadat appeal urging the country to prepare for war with Israel. The cabinet was to follow guidelines that called for more production, less consumption and restrictions on middle-class privileges.

In a radio-TV address to the Egyptian people Jan. 13, 1972 Sadat asserted that Egypt's "year of decision" for war or peace against Israel, which he had specified would be 1971, had been delayed by the outbreak of war between India and Pakistan. The Egyptian high command, the president said, had formulated plans in Oct. 1971 for a military assault in December, but the eruption of fighting on the Indian subcontinent "upset our plans." The conflict there had disrupted the balance of power in the Middle East because of Soviet commitments to India and U.S. backing of Pakistan, Sadat explained. He added, "I gave orders to Gen. Muhammad Sadek, the minister of war, and told him to wait. We had to make our reassessment of the situation. Our battle cannot be separated from the balance between the big powers." Sadat said consultations with the USSR were continuing.

Egypt, Libya & Syria Federate

The Federation of Arab Republics formally took effect Sept. 1, 1971 as voters overwhelmingly indorsed the merger in a referendum in the 3 member states of Egypt, Libya and Syria. According to final results announced Sept. 2, 99.956% of the 7,776,837 Egyptian voters cast ballots in favor of the federation. Interior Min. Mamdouh Salem said 3,404 persons voted against the union and 2,471 ballots were defaced or otherwise disqualified. A total of 225,922 registered voters did not participate in the referendum, he said. In Libya, 98% of the voters expressed approval. The figure was 96.4% in Syria.

With the formal establishment of the federation, Egypt dropped the name United Arab Republic—adopted after the 1958 merger with Syria, which had failed—and assumed the name of Arab Republic of Egypt.

Pres. Sadat had asserted Aug. 30 that the federation was aimed primarily at Israel in a struggle that might continue for "20, 30 or even 50 years." He hailed the merger as an "Arab revival." Sadat deplored the "fragmentation" of Arab unity, which he said left only Egypt and Syria to confront Israel, with Libya and Sudan providing defense in depth. (Jordan, he declared, "is out of the battle"—an allusion to Jordan's campaign against Palestinian Arab guerrillas in Jordan and their Syrian supporters.)

After Egyptian consultations with Syrian and Libyan officials Apr. 28, the Arab Socialist Union's central committee, the Egyptian cabinet and the National Assembly Apr. 29 had unanimously approved a modified version of the original federation plan. The principal alteration in the proposed federation statutes was an amendment that required unanimity of the presidents of the 3 member countries in making federal executive decisions and selecting a president of the federation. The original plan had called for a simple presidential majority, raising Cairo's apprehensions that it could be outvoted by Syria and Libya.

2 other amendments had been adopted that would strengthen the individual sovereignty of the 3 countries in the federal government. An original draft that had provided

for a federal national assembly "to legislate for the federation" was changed to limit the assembly's function to legislate
"on the federation's competence." The other amendment
dealt with a federal court, whose powers were to be determined by a constitution yet to be written. The original draft
had said that the court, to be composed of 2 judges from
each member country, would be "concerned with deciding
on the constitutionality of laws and with settling disputes
between the institutions and the authorities of the federation
and the republics."

Libyan Pres. Mouammar el-Qaddafi disclosed July 23,
1972 that it was he who had proposed the merger of Libya
and Egypt into one country. Qaddafi said that he had made
the offer to Sadat in February and that Sadat had asked for
5 months to study the proposal. Qaddafi and Sadat agreed
Aug. 2 to establish by Sept. 1, 1973 a "unified political leadership" which would be the largest state in Africa.

The agreement emerged from 3 days of talks between the
2 men in Libya, at Tobruk and Benghazi, attended in the
later stages by Egyptian Premier Aziz Sidky. The declaration
emphasized that the process of unity would require a public
referendum in each state and could be vetoed by national
authorities, who would approve the "final version of the
unity plan." Before the declaration was read over Cairo
radio, the announcer revealed that Sadat and Qaddafi had
phoned Syrian Pres. Hafez al-Assad to tell him about the
agreement.

2 Syrian newspapers in Damascus—*Al Baath*, the Socialist
Party organ, and *Al Thawra*—said Aug. 3 that they favored
any development that would strengthen the Federation of
Arab Republics. Cairo newspapers described the accord as an
"historic event" Aug. 3.

Text of the Egyptian-Libyan statement:

The leaderships of the 2 revolutions have agreed to establish a complete unity between the Arab Republic of Egypt and the Arab Republic
of Libya as soon as possible and on the strongest possible basis.

Their discussions have resulted in the adoption of the following decisions:

(1) Formation of a unified political leadership from the 2 republics. A decision on its composition will be issued by the 2 Presidents.

(2) The unified political leadership will lay down as soon as possible the pioposed foundations for a complete unity of the 2 republics and will supervise the steps necessary for their implementation.

(3) The unified political leadership will form joint committees from the 2 republics to consider laying down the regulations on which the unity of the two republics will be based in the following fields: (A) Constitutional matters. (B) Political organization. (C) Defense and national security. (D) Economic systems. (E) Legislation and judiciary. (F) Administrative and financial systems. (G) Education, science, culture and information.

(4) These committees will submit reports on their work to the unified political leadership, which will adopt the necessary measures.

(5) The unified political leadership will approve and proclaim the final version of the unity plan for submission to the appropriate authorities in the 2 republics and for a public referendum.

(6) These measures will be completed on Sept. 1, 1973 at the latest.

The 2 Presidents, while announcing these steps to their peoples and the Arab nation, feel at the same time that the Arab nation is beginning with these steps a phase full of reasons for hope.

Sadat Expels Soviets

Pres. Sadat announced July 18, 1972 that he had ordered Soviet "military advisers and experts" to be removed from Egypt immediately. Sadat also directed that Soviet bases and equipment in Egypt be placed under exclusive control of the Egyptian forces. He indicated that his decision was based on difficulties Egypt had encountered in getting all the Soviet arms it wanted for its confrontation with Israel.

A Soviet government statement July 19 confirmed Sadat's surprise announcement but said that the Russian soldiers were being taken out of Egypt by mutual agreement with Cairo. The troop withdrawal was reported to be under way.

Neither the Egyptian nor Soviet statement made clear whether Sadat also was demanding the exit of an estimated

10,000 to 15,000 Soviet combat personnel who operated antiaircraft missiles and performed other air-defense duties or of the 200 airmen who piloted MiG-23 jets.

Sadat's announcement was made in a 90-minute speech to the Central Committee of the Arab Socialist Union. The Egyptian leader recalled Cairo's repeated failure to obtain the Soviet offensive weapons he had deemed necessary to implement his plans to invade Israel by the end of 1971. "These arms did not arrive on the agreed dates, and that is what made me say then we need to re-evaluate our position," Sadat said. He complained of conditions the Soviets had attempted to impose on the use of their equipment, presumably to prevent Egypt from attempting an attack. He said he had refused "to place any restrictions on the use of arms, whatever their kind, based on Egypt's principle that any political decision must be made in Egypt by its political leadership without having to seek permission from any quarters, whatsoever its status." Sadat said he had raised these objections in his meetings with Soviet leaders in Moscow in February and April.

Sadat suggested that Pres. Nixon's talks with Soviet leaders in May had influenced his decision to reduce the Soviet presence in Egypt. "After receiving Soviet explanations to the Moscow talks with Pres. Nixon I felt the need to review the situation . . . ," and "after reviewing the situation, . . . I found it necessary" to demand the withdrawal of the Soviet "advisers and military experts," Sadat said.

Despite Egyptian-Soviet differences, Sadat said he would not permit a total rupture with Moscow. But he said "we shall stand alone on the battlefield if need be." (Egypt's ambassador to the Soviet Union, Yenia Abdel Kader, had hailed the relations between the 2 countries in a TV broadcast in Moscow July 21. Without mentioning the rift, Kader said that "I want to take this opportunity to convey to the great Soviet people the assurances of feelings of love and friendship on the part of the people" of Egypt. Kader's address marked the 20th anniversary of the overthrow of the Egyptian monarchy.)

Sadat also proposed "a Soviet-Egyptian meeting, at a level to be agreed upon, to hold consultations to decide the next phase of operations." He insisted that his decision would not postpone "our battle against Israel, since it was never our intention to make our friendly Soviet experts fight with us."

Sadat's announcement had been preceded by reports from Cairo about a major development in Soviet-Egyptian relations. One report linked the diplomatic shift to Egyptian Premier Aziz Sidky's visit to Moscow July 13 to press Cairo's demands for offensive weapons. After receiving Moscow's rejection of Cairo's plea, Sidky reportedly informed the Russians of his government's decision to reduce the Soviet force in Egypt. Sidky, whose visit was to have lasted 3 days, returned to Cairo July 14.

In its statement on the troop withdrawal, as reported by Tass, Moscow said July 19 that since the Soviet military men had completed their training of Egyptian forces, both "sides deemed it expedient after an exchange of views to bring back to the Soviet Union the military personnel that had been sent to Egypt for a limited period." The Soviet forces, the statement emphasized, had been in Egypt on temporary "assignment in accordance with the requests of the leadership of Egypt for help in insuring its defense potential in the face of Israeli aggression. Both sides have many times expressed their satisfaction with the effectiveness of such measures." The statement quoted Sadat as saying that the move "in no way affects the foundations of Egypt-Soviet friendship." It was the first time that Moscow had publicly stated in such forthright manner the scope of its military assistance to Egypt. Like the Egyptian announcement, the Soviet statement made no mention of the number of soldiers involved in the withdrawal.

Many of the Soviet military advisers and technical experts were reported leaving Egypt July 19. The Russians, dressed in civilian clothes and accompanied by members of their families, were assembling at Cairo's airport and at Alexandria for the trip back to home. Soviet personnel reportedly had been making preparations to leave since July 17, one day before Sadat's public announcement. Egyptian military units were said to have taken over the installations and sites of the SAM-2 and SAM-3 missiles from Soviet personnel during that 24-hour period.

Sadat declared July 24 that the Soviet Union's "excessive caution" in providing Egypt with military support against Israel had prompted him to request the departure of Soviet military advisers. Sadat made this statement in a speech in which he further explained to the Central Committee of the Arab Socialist Union his decision July 18 to reduce the Soviet military presence in Egypt.

(Prior to Sadat's decision to expel the Russians, Egypt and the USSR had signed a new agreement under which Moscow was to provide Cairo with more arms. The newspaper *Al-Ahram* had reported this agreement May 18. The pact was signed in Alexandria by Soviet Defense Min. Andrei A. Grechko and Egyptian War Min. Muhammad Sadek. Grechko, who had been on a state visit to Cairo since May 14, returned to Moscow May 18.)

In his speech July 24, Sadat contrasted what he described as the Soviet Union's hesitant support of Egypt with the U.S.' allegedly wholehearted backing of Israel. The U.S., he said, was committed "to maintain Israel's military superiority in all circumstances" and was determined to prevent the start of peace negotiations except on conditions approved by Israel. The USSR, on the other hand, "is not engaged to do for us what the United States does for Israel," Sadat said. The Egyptian leader said his differences with the Soviet Union first emerged after his trip to Moscow Mar. 1, 1971. The Kremlin, he said, regarded the Middle East "as problem

3 or 4 in the world while we view it as Number one, as everything." After the signing of a 15-year friendship and cooperation pact in May 1971, Pres. Nikolai V. Podgorny had
assured him that Egyptian-Soviet differences "would be
solved 4 days after he returned to Moscow," Sadat said.
Sadat complained that in subsequent contacts with Soviet
officials through the remainder of 1971 and in meetings with
them in Moscow in February and April 1972, the Russians
had failed to give him assurances they would implement their
pledge "to help liquidate Israeli aggression."

Sadat said that the USSR's explanation of its talks with
Pres. Nixon in Moscow in May had ended all his doubts about
the Kremlin's promise to aid Egypt. He recalled that in antic-
ipation of those summit meetings he had warned the Russians
in April not to agree to a U.S.-Soviet arms embargo on the
Middle East as long as Israel occupied Arab territories and
not to be drawn into discussion of borders because the Arabs
would not surrender any of the occupied areas. The Soviet
response to his arguments, Sadat said, was "yes, yes, yes to
make things easy for us, but then we were caught in a
whirlwind."

U.S. intelligence sources in Washington said that there
were "strong indications" that the USSR was withdrawing
from Egypt most of its planes assigned with Soviet crews to
the Egyptian air defense, the *N.Y. Times* reported July 26. It
was said that the aircraft being pulled out included most of
the 18 TU-16 reconnaissance bombers, about 70 MiG-21 jet
fighter-bombers and about 6 advanced MiG-23s. Egypt,
according to the report, would keep more than 200 older
MiG-19s, MiG-21s and Sukhoi-7 bombers and surface-to-air
missiles, all operated and controlled by Egyptian personnel.
Other reported assessments of the U.S. intelligence: The
10,000 Soviet combat troops in Egypt would eventually be
pulled out. No more than 200 to 300 Soviet technicians
would remain to assist Egyptians in operating advanced

surface-to-air missiles in the Cairo-Alexandria area and around the Aswan Dam on the Upper Nile. The Russians would be permitted to retain their naval facilities in Alexandria, Mersa Matruh, Port Said and Sollum and also keep some navy personnel there.

The completion of Soviet military withdrawal from Egypt was announced by Egyptian and Soviet officials Aug. 6. Fewer than 3,000 Soviet missile Technicians and other instructors reportedly remained in Egypt. Egyptian War Min. Muhammad Sadek had given a farewell party for top-ranking Soviet military advisers in Cairo Aug. 2.

Al-Ahram reported Aug. 7 that Soviet Communist Party Gen. Secy. Leonid Brezhnev had sent a message to Sadat requesting a high-level meeting to improve their strained relations. The Egyptian government said the message did not amount to a "new breakthrough" in ties between the 2 countries but that the request for the talks was being considered. Egyptian Amb. Yehia Abdel Kader was recalled from Moscow for consultations. Soviet Pres. Podgorny had met with a visiting Egyptian parliamentary delegation Aug. 5 and had told them he was certain that "friendly Soviet-Egyptian relations would go on developing."

Fresh Israeli Peace Proposal

Israeli Premier Golda Meir July 26, 1972 took the departure of Soviet military personnel from Egypt as a fresh opportunity for Egypt and Israel to negotiate their differences. "It would seem that this hour in the history of Egypt can, indeed should, be the appropriate hour for change—and if it truly is the hour for change, let it not be missed," she said. In an address to the Israeli Knesset, Mrs. Meir reiterated her government's position on peace talks, that both sides must agree to negotiate without prior conditions. She said: "We have not declared permanent borders, we have not drawn up an ultimate map, we have not demanded prior commitments on matters which must be clarified by means of negotiations. We do not intend to perpetuate the cease-fire lines between us, or to freeze the existing situation."

The Israeli premier cautioned that although the withdrawal of the Soviet advisers constituted "a significant fact," there was no indication of "the cessation of the Soviet Union's role in Egypt." She then cited these figures: "The Soviet Union stationed in Egypt more than 7,000 advisers, experts and instructors in all the armed forces, and close to 10,000 additional military personnel to operate squadrons of MiG-21 and other aircraft, SAM-3 and SAM-6 battalion batteries and personnel in various command formations." Mrs. Meir stressed that Egypt's order for the removal of Soviet advisers did not apply to the instructors, who "will continue to function." She noted, however, that "the demand for the evacuation also affects the Soviet operational units which are integrated in the Egyptian air defense system."

A Reuters report from Cairo July 26 said that Egypt had rejected Mrs. Meir's proposal for direct talks. *Al-Ahram* was quoted as saying that her bid for talks to reopen the Suez Canal was "also rejected by Cairo because the reopening of the Canal is not an end in itself." In a speech at Alexandria, Sadat, making no direct mention of Mrs. Meir's peace bid, was quoted as saying: "Can anyone accept to negotiate while his land is occupied? Did the United States negotiate with Japan after Pearl Harbor?"

Sadat had denounced Mrs. Meir's statement as "propaganda" and had set down conditions for any negotiations with the Israelis, a member of the French Parliament said Aug. 1. Claude-Gerard Marcus, who had visited the Egyptian leader in Cairo the previous week with other French Parliament members, said Sadat had insisted that any Egyptian-Israeli discussions must be held in the presence of representatives of the U.S., Britain, France and the USSR, who were not to act as mere "observers." (The Israeli embassy in Paris said Aug. 1 that Sadat's proposal for Big 4 participation was "in the tradition of their [Egyptian] insistence on an imposed solution.")

Economic & Diplomatic Developments

A major oil field was found Apr. 1, 1971 in the desert 160 miles west of Cairo, Egypt reported Apr. 4. The discovery was made by Amoco-UAR. Egyptian Industry & Petroleum Min. Aziz Sidky said the gusher was "a big one" and of very high quality. (Yugoslav Pres. Tito had met Mar. 27 near Pisa with Egyptian Foreign Min. Mahmoud Riad for what was reported to be talks on Yugoslav aid for a proposed Suez-Alexandria oil pipeline.)

Pres. Sadat disclosed Aug. 27 that workers at an iron and steel plant in Helwan, 30 miles from Cairo, had staged a sit-in strike Aug. 19. He said the demonstrators had blocked exits, preventing thousands of other employes from leaving the factory for one night. Among those held hostage was the head of the Egyptian Federation of Trade Unions. An inquiry was ordered into the strike, the first since Sadat assumed office in Sept. 1970. Pending the probe, the plant's management, its labor committee and factory committee in the Arab Socialist Union had been suspended. The workers were believed protesting certain work rules, including sick pay.

Sadat's Mideastern foreign policy seemed caught in the first years of his administration in a conflict between peace's economic advantages and Egypt's commitment to a holy war against Israel on behalf of Palestinian Arabs and for territory lost to Israel in 1967. This conflict had international ramifications for Egypt beyond the Middle East.

Washington's decision to help Israel manufacture arms was assailed by Egypt Jan. 17, 1972. Tahsin Bashir, the Egyptian government's official spokesman, described the agreement as a "grave turn" in U.S.-Arab relations. He said it was part of an American attempt to assure Israel "weapons supremacy" and to impose a settlement of the Arab-Israeli conflict. Another U.S. decision to aid Israel—the resumption of the sale of Phantom jets—had been denounced by Sadat Jan. 13. He warned that Washington's support of Israel was endangering U.S. oil interests in the Arab world.

American diplomats in Cairo reported May 18 that Sadat had demanded that the U.S. reduce its diplomatic mission in the Egyptian capital from 20 to 10 staff members within a month. Egypt had also instructed that its mission in Washington be halved. The Egyptian newspaper *Al-Ahram* said Cairo's decision was in protest against a U.S. policy of "consolidating the continued Israeli aggression through the occupation of Arab territories." The U.S. had operated its mission in the Spanish embassy in Cairo since its break in diplomatic relations with Egypt in 1967. Cairo's action followed a speech in which Sadat May 14 had reiterated a Jan. 25 statement, that he had "ruptured all my relations with the United States because of deceit, delusions and lies."

On the other hand, Sadat saw fit to mend one of Egypt's burnt bridges. Diplomatic relations with the West German government were resumed June 8. Egypt was the 6th Arab nation to resume West German ties, broken following Bonn's recognition of Israel in 1965.

INDEX

285